THE PLAY
OF FAULKNER'S
LANGUAGE

John T. Matthews

THE PLAY OF FAULKNER'S LANGUAGE

Cornell University Press

ITHACA AND LONDON

Copyright © 1982 by Cornell University Press

First published 1982 by Cornell University Press.
Published in the United Kingdom by Cornell University Press Ltd.,
Ely House, 37 Dover Street, London W1X 4HQ.

International Standard Book Number 0-8014-1413-X
Library of Congress Catalog Card Number 81-12565
Printed in the United States of America
*Librarians: Library of Congress cataloging information
appears on the last page of the book.*

FOR SHARON

Contents

Man will keep on writing on pieces of paper, on scraps, on stones, as long as he lives.

—William Faulkner, interview
with Loïc Bouvard

[Southerners] need to talk, to tell, since oratory is our heritage. We seem to try in the simple furious breathing (or writing) span of the individual to draw a savage indictment of the contemporary scene or to escape from it into a makebelieve region of swords and magnolias and mockingbirds which perhaps never existed anywhere.

—William Faulkner, An Introduction
to "The Sound and the Fury"

Preface

Faulkner says that when he began to write *The Sound and the Fury*, he "had no plan at all. I wasn't even writing a book. . . . I did not realise then that I was trying to manufacture the sister. . . . I just began to write." In this book I attempt to show that Faulkner's fiction is propelled by a commitment to the freely inaugural motions of language. In his comments about his writing and in the narrative strategies, configurations of plot, and crises of his novels, Faulkner displays a preoccupation with the way in which language produces idea, sense, meaning, and personality. By insisting that to begin a novel he "just began to write," Faulkner reflects an initial forgetfulness of the world to be represented, a loss redeemed (and then incompletely) only in the text's created world. I hope to show that Faulkner's major fiction elevates fabrication over representation, confronts the loss of the original idea and subject, makes writing a kind of mourning (as it produces the very insufficiencies it seeks to overcome), and celebrates the playfulness of writing in the space (or play) between the written and the written about.

Absalom, Absalom!, of course, convinces us that Faulkner is interested in the customs of fabrication; I shall argue that the trials of invention inform the rest of Faulkner's fiction as well. *The Sound and the Fury* poses the Compson brothers' longing for Caddy as a synecdoche of the writer's desire for "manufactured" presence in the text. But *The Sound and the Fury* shows Faulkner that all novels frustrate and perpetuate desire; they are failures, unfinished and yet complete; they produce meaning through the play of limitless difference, of legitimately rival truths. In the fiction that precedes this "turning point" (as Faulkner called it) we may see Faulkner testing and rejecting more traditional aesthetic principles: the long conversations about art in *Mosquitoes* gradually move from exchanges of aesthetic platitudes to earnest discussions of the limits of referentiality in poetry, fiction, and sculpture; and *Flags in the Dust* discloses for Faulkner that the erotics of writing is rooted in the linguistic basis for the incest taboo, which separates culture from nature yet also connects them. The second and third chapters of my book trace these themes first in *The Sound and the Fury* and then in *Absalom, Absalom!*, which deepens the coincidence of desire, sorrow, and writing. *Absalom* suggests that every story fails to present a fully authoritative account, that every narrative allows its teller to embody (not simply to express) an identity, and that each telling is thereby true (as well as false) to the teller, the hearer, and the elusive subject. *The Hamlet* sets the pervasiveness of "textual" issues in an unexpected context by opposing alternative views of social convention and law: Flem Snopes apprehends that the hamlet's society rests on absolutely arbitrary codes of behavior, but Ratliff tries to oppose and contain Flem within an ethics of play, a sportive authority. *Go Down, Moses* epitomizes Faulkner's belief that writing is a kind of mourning. Each story of the cycle focuses on a character "dispossessed" of a past or origin, and considers how a kind of language—whether ritual, the rehearsal of myth, or a personal utterance—may seek to fill that loss.

My book has profited from the contributions of several colleagues, whose kindnesses it is a pleasure to acknowledge. Laurence B. Holland not only guided the early stages of my study of Faulkner but also gave me, and a generation of students, the highest ideals of scholarship and teaching to emulate, however imperfectly. His generosity was inexhaustible throughout this project, and I regret that he did not live to see the finished work. I am grateful as well to Avrom Fleishman for his reading of my dissertation and his continued interest in my work. I have learned much from my many conversations with colleagues and students at Boston University. With unfailing cheer and insight, William C. Carroll read the manuscript in its several versions and reminded me always of the reader's rights in the transactions of style. Stuart H. Johnson came to me first as a student but became all that one hopes for in the best students, a teacher; I have benefited greatly from our mutual exploration of recent critical theory. Preparing the manuscript was a task lightened by the expert typing of Mrs. E. P. Goodwin. Grants-in-aid from the Boston University Graduate School contributed to the costs of preparing the manuscript; I am also grateful to the English Department and The College of Liberal Arts for arranging release time from teaching duties so that I might complete the writing. My greatest debt is reflected in the dedication to my wife, Sharon. Surely this book is meager recompense for her years of encouraging the labor and having faith in its author; I am grateful that she knows that there are marriages beyond that of speaking and hearing.

Quotations from *Flags in the Dust* (ed. Douglas Day; published in England as *Sartoris*), *The Sound and the Fury*, *Absalom, Absalom!*, *The Hamlet,* and *Go Down, Moses* appear by permission of Random House, Inc., the literary estate of William Faulkner, Chatto & Windus, and Curtis Brown, Limited. A portion of Chapter 3 appeared as "The Marriage of Speaking and Hearing in *Absalom, Absalom!*," *ELH,* 47 (Fall 1980), 575–594, and appears here by permission of the journal.

JOHN T. MATTHEWS

Boston, Massachusetts

THE PLAY
OF FAULKNER'S
LANGUAGE

CHAPTER 1

"How to Approach Language"

i

Faulkner's style loves to perform. In the familiar description of Quentin Compson's and Shreve McCannon's storytelling in *Absalom, Absalom!* we encounter one of Faulkner's showy phrases—"nothing fault nor false." The roommates approach the mysterious topic of Charles Bon's fatal love for Judith Sutpen, and the narrator remarks that the tellers forgive each other for the

> faultings both in the creating of this shade whom they discussed (rather, existed in) and in the hearing and sifting and discarding the false and conserving what seemed true, or fit the preconceived—in order to overpass to love, where there might be paradox and inconsistency but nothing fault nor false.[1]

The stunt of this passage, which makes "fault" an adjective when it is usually a verb or noun, emphasizes sense through its contortion. Faulkner arrests us here at the site of a misusage or neologism—kindly violences performed by the writer on the common tongue—in order to accent the exercise of invention that the passage endorses. As Quentin and Shreve risk inconsistency and defy "all that had gone before" (*AA*, 316) in their labor of making meaning, so the narrator disfigures, discards, and pretends as he constructs the fiction. Language produces truth only as it faults.

---

1. William Faulkner, *Absalom, Absalom!* (New York, 1936), p. 316. All subsequent quotations will be from this edition (referred to as *AA*) and will be cited by page numbers in parentheses.

The Play of Faulkner's Language

The longer passage from which I have quoted briefly distills several of Faulkner's favorite ideas about language and fiction, and I shall draw the lines of my argument from it. Faulkner's coinage suggests a way to begin; "fault," as it appears with "faultings" elsewhere in the passage, evokes the vocabulary of the hunt: hounds are said to fault when they lose the trail.[2] When Quentin and Shreve passionately attend to "what seemed true, or fit the preconceived," they fashion a narrative that concedes the usual demand for fact, authority, and consistency. The roommates hunt explanations as hunters follow tracks, but once they have "overpassed to love," the quarry seems less compelling than the excitement of the pursuit. The narrative tracks down the Sutpen facts only to discover that they can never be brought to bay and that, instead, narratives are perpetual tracings and retracings. There is nothing "fault" because the trail is the destination. Storytelling for Faulkner is serious play, and its significance arises not in the capture of truth but in the rituals of pursuit, exchange, collaboration, and invention.

That language plays suggests there may be no actuality or truth behind the text's words that can be fully presented. At one point in *Absalom* the narrator assures us that the characters conjured up by Quentin and Shreve may never have existed and yet are "true enough" (335).[3] Correspondingly, the tellers of tales seem to have no life or consciousness—no selfhood—exterior to their speech; Quentin and Shreve do not merely "discuss" the shade of Sutpen, they "rather, exist" in it, as the passage above insists. Language—both as the characters manipulate it and as they are constituted by it in the novels—simultaneously erodes the autonomy and discreteness of selfhood even as it creates them. Characters exist in the words of their memories, imagination, and stories, in the "dark twin" of narration.[4] Faulkner's view of language overthrows traditional ideas about the expressive prerogatives of speech; language embodies consciousness, it does not reveal it.[5]

Just before the narrator describes Quentin's and Shreve's overpassing to love, he refers to their collaboration as "a happy mar-

2. Calvin Brown, *A Glossary of Faulkner's South* (New Haven, 1976), p. 79.
3. This narrator is not a final authority, but none of the narrators feels especially uncomfortable with the view that truth is fictional.
4. *Mosquitoes* (New York, 1927), p. 251. I quote from this edition throughout.
5. Stephen M. Ross makes this point about *As I Lay Dying* in "'Voice' in Narrative Texts: The Example of *As I Lay Dying*," PMLA, 94 (March 1979), 300–310.

riage of speaking and hearing." This complex image is an apt metaphor for the paradoxes of language that I have been charting. The correspondence in Faulkner's fiction between verbal discourse and sexual intercourse is pronounced and explicit; it suggests that teller and listener, or writer and reader, surrender themselves to engagement, exposure, embrace, intimacy, and creation. Narratives repeatedly issue from marriages in Faulkner, and I shall explore how the circumstances of a story's performance often remind us that "it takes two to make the book."[6] That individuals become themselves only in their words, that all representation is a kind of speaking and hearing, and that language plays in its failure to present what it represents are all components of Faulkner's figure of marriage.

I am also interested in one other suggestion made by the passage I have quoted from *Absalom*. In evoking the hunt to explain Quentin's and Shreve's tracking of truth, the narrator touches on a conviction that is central to Faulkner's understanding of language: any form of representation, any sequence of signifying gestures, behaves like a language. The ritual of the hunt, the customs of trade or commerce, various games—all constitute engravings of sense and share some of the properties of writing that I shall discuss. Unlike some modern novelists, Faulkner rarely troubles his books with plots about writing fiction; surely the grizzled backwoodsmen, entrepreneurial Indians, sewing machine salesmen, suicidal undergraduates, slobbering idiots, and Halloween Confederate colonels do not compose a community of writers in exile. But the novels regularly center their crises on the capacity or failure of characters to interpret, explain, master—in a word, to articulate—the common predicaments of loss, change, or desire. It is not only that storytelling is like hunting, but that hunting—like trade, or games, or rituals—is a kind of language.

Some of Faulkner's most provocative comments about language and fiction occur in the recently published typescripts of a preface for a printing of *The Sound and the Fury* contemplated for 1933.[7]

6. James B. Meriwether and Michael Millgate, eds., *Lion in the Garden: Interviews with William Faulkner, 1926–1962* (New York, 1968), p. 116.

7. William Faulkner, "An Introduction for *The Sound and the Fury*," ed. James B. Meriwether, *Southern Review*, 8 (October 1972), 705–710. I shall refer to this draft as Introduction (*SR*). The second draft appeared as "An Introduction to *The Sound and the Fury*," ed. James B. Meriwether, *Mississippi Quarterly*, 26 (Winter 1973), 410–415; I shall refer to it as Introduction (*MQ*).

Matched with some of Faulkner's less familiar public remarks about his writing, the preface elaborates the cluster of ideas I have been discussing and forecasts the major concerns of my readings in later chapters. In conversation Faulkner's statements about his craft are often cryptic, obvious, or cheerfully false. He always encouraged questioners to read him (rather than to talk to him), and the preface represents the deliberation of a written text: "'I have worked on it a good deal, like on a poem almost, and I think that it is all right now.'"[8] Looking at *The Sound and the Fury* after several years, Faulkner recalls that his fourth novel gave him new freedom as a writer; disappointed with *Sartoris'* repeated rejection, Faulkner "seemed to shut a door between me and all publishers' addresses and book lists. I said to myself, Now I can write."[9] *The Sound and the Fury* figures decisively in Faulkner's career for many reasons, one of which is its liberating recognition of the properties of fictional language. According to the preface, the apprenticeship for *The Sound and the Fury* suitably had concentrated on the nature of language: "I had learned a little about writing from Soldiers' Pay—how to approach language, words."[10] In their various approaches to language Faulkner's early works explore how the writer embodies himself in his art, how objects of representation acquire presence through the mediation of language, how writing implicates the writer in an economy of losses (the loss of the original idea or of completed meaning, for example), and how the truth of a story emerges from the play of its language.

One remark in the preface—perhaps its most famous—may misleadingly conduct us back into the presence of the author. Faulkner concludes the preface to the story of the Compson brothers' loss of their sister by wondering if he was not trying to "manufacture the sister which I did not have and the daughter which I was to lose,"[11] as if novels simply compensate their authors for frustrations or losses suffered in life. André Bleikasten, in his thorough reading of the novel, adduces this statement to confirm that *The Sound and the Fury* seeks to fill a "lack and a loss" and that the preface

8. William Faulkner, letter to Ben Wasson, quoted in headnote to Introduction (*SR*) by James Meriwether from the original in the Alderman Library, p. 707.

9. Introduction (*SR*), p. 710.

10. Ibid., p. 708.

11. Introduction (*MQ*), p. 413.

presents a theory of art as a "transnarcissistic" object of compensation.[12] Such a formulation assumes a prior state of grief in the author's life that may be soothed by an aesthetic substitution, and Bleikasten accordingly laments our insufficient knowledge about Faulkner's rumored personal disappointments at the time he was writing *The Sound and the Fury*. But Faulkner's account is more complicated: his writing *precedes* any sense of loss, and actually precedes the fact of loss in the case of his daughter. "When I began it I had no plan at all. I wasn't even writing a book."[13] "I did not realise then that I was trying to manufacture the sister. . . . I just began to write."[14] However fine a distinction this may seem to be, the consequences are considerable. To begin to write, to mark the page, *produces* the mood of bereavement, as if the use of language creates the atmosphere of mourning. Writing does not respond to loss, it initiates it; writing itself is as much a kind of loss as it is a kind of compensation. The double action—of making and losing— is figured in the preface's image of the writer as vase maker: "Now I can make myself a vase like that which the old Roman kept at his bedside and wore the rim slowly away with kissing it."[15]

In what respects does the activity of writing involve loss? How is "making" the novel like wearing it away? As he looks back on the composition of *The Sound and the Fury*, Faulkner realizes that the "ecstasy" of writing is produced by the very process that destroys it. Like the pleasure of sexual climax, the pleasure of writing is "release[d]" as it simultaneously fulfills and exhausts itself. Writing *The Sound and the Fury* gave Faulkner "that ecstasy, that eager and joyous faith and anticipation of surprise which the yet unmarred sheet beneath my hand held inviolate and unfailing, waiting for release."[16] The young writer senses the fullness of his self-presence, of his readiness to author; yet, paradoxically, the writer consummates himself only by losing that (perhaps illusory) fullness. The writer both takes the virginity of the page ("the yet unmarred sheet . . . inviolate") and surrenders his own to that "emotion defi-

---

12. André Bleikasten, *The Most Splendid Failure: Faulkner's "The Sound and the Fury"* (Bloomington, Ind., 1976), p. 46.
13. Introduction (*SR*), p. 710.
14. Introduction (*MQ*), p. 413.
15. Introduction (*SR*), p. 710.
16. Ibid., p. 709.

nite and physical," that ecstasy. In Faulkner's approach to *The Sound and the Fury,* conducted in earlier works, he "learned a little about . . . how to approach language . . . with joy, as you approach women: perhaps with the same secretly unscrupulous intentions."[17] Having seduced and been seduced by his words, the writer is surprised that the first ecstasy may never be repeated: "whatever novels I should write in the future would be written without reluctance, but also without anticipation or joy."[18] Thus the achievement of ecstasy is also its loss, and Faulkner foresees the remainder of his career to be barren of bliss, offering merely "cold satisfaction."

Faulkner's very way of putting this sense that the ecstasy of writing is not to return emphasizes that language can name only what is absent. The more mature author, already 'married' to his career, knows his earlier innocence only in having lost it in the ecstasy of writing. Even the adjectives Faulkner uses to describe the text's initial virginity already declare impending deflowerment— unmarred, inviolate, unfailing. And, in turn, the ecstasy of writing *The Sound and the Fury* is apprehended only when it is named in its absence; "I learned from the writing of Sanctuary [his next novel] that there was something missing; something which The Sound and the Fury gave me and Sanctuary did not."[19] The thing that is missing comes to be named ecstasy.

To become a writer was, for Faulkner, to negotiate an economy of losses: ecstasy replaces innocence, cold repetition deadens ecstasy. This economy also includes the way in which the writer transacts his 'original' idea into the written text, for such a conversion is also always a kind of loss. *The Sound and the Fury* began with the picture of "Caddy climbing the pear tree to look in the window at her grandmother's funeral" while her brothers watch below.[20] Having "put" that image into the book, Faulkner simultaneously realizes and loses "the only thing in literature which would ever move me very much." Subsequent novels may never bring him the ecstasy he felt in writing *The Sound and the Fury* because what that novel has made, it has also lost; what it has

17. Ibid., p. 708.
18. Ibid., p. 710.
19. Ibid., p. 709.
20. Ibid., p. 710.

represented, it has marred; the vase it has fashioned, it wears away. Surely Caddy—the "little girl" "manufactured" by the text—never achieves the presence or substance of a 'real' character; she is memorable precisely because she inhabits the memories of her brothers and the novel, and memory for Faulkner never transcends the sense of loss. Like the vase, the novel is a cold, bedside shape that at best parodies a living body. Faulkner confirms the idea of writing as a destruction or loss of original presence on several occasions. Earlier in the preface, of course, he says that the "approach to language" is like the approach to "dynamite" and "women"; language as readily triggers explosion as ecstasy. Or perhaps it triggers them simultaneously. When asked to describe his "ideal woman," Faulkner replies that "I couldn't describe her by color of hair, color of eyes, because once she is described, then somehow she vanishes."[21] Faulkner extends this idea of writing as loss in his comments about the relationship between the germ of a story and its embodiment. As if generalizing from the example of *The Sound and the Fury*'s seminal image, Faulkner remarks:

> There's always a moment in experience—a thought—an incident—
> that's there. Then all I do is work up to that moment. I figure what
> must have happened before to lead people to that particular moment,
> and I work away from it, finding out how people act after that mo-
> ment.[22]

If we compare this account even superficially with some of the famous incidents 'in' Faulkner's novels, we might argue that, like the ideal woman, the kernel of the story is precisely what vanishes into the words that describe it. Caddy's tree climbing, in fact, appears only fragmentedly in Benjy's section and hardly at all thereafter, as if the novel advances by losing the initial image in its own writing. Quentin's suicide, the murders of Charles Bon and Joanna Burden, Temple Drake's rape—all central moments in their narratives—function more as absences in the stories that surround them. As he outlines in the passage above, Faulkner does construct the narrative as leading up to and away from these incidents, but the events or thoughts themselves do not appear in the text. The mo-

21. Meriwether and Millgate, eds., *Lion in the Garden*, p. 127.
22. Ibid., p. 220.

ment of the story's origin is lost into the novel.[23] Perhaps Faulkner's remark that *The Sound and the Fury* is a novel about "the lost Caddy" carries a more ambiguous pathos than we have generally allowed.[24]

Faulkner refers to the paradox of fiction's loss-as-gain in his favorite description of *The Sound and the Fury* as his "best failure."[25] Each section tries to get the story "right," and each fails; the novel advances by admitting its own impossibility, accumulates authority by impugning it, succeeds by failing. *The Sound and the Fury* embodies this aspect of Faulkner's mature aesthetic; his paradoxical descriptions are not pointless riddles but rather terse formulae to describe the subversion of resolved meaning, closed form, and full representation by the language that aspires to those very achievements.

Just as the described objects of language "somehow vanish," so the writer must confront his own disappearance into his words. We are used to thinking of the kinds of presence that authors retain as they convert themselves into texts that survive them, but Faulkner also notices the distance and deathliness of written selfhood. A narrator's voice is one way for an author to *be* in a text, yet in *The Sound and the Fury* Faulkner is so far 'in' the opening three sections that he seems to disappear. By assuming the modes of perception—the visual rhetoric, we might call it—of each of the Compson brothers, Faulkner suppresses the distinctive qualities of the Faulknerian voice. When that more conventional voice finally appears in the last section of the novel, Faulkner surprisingly emphasizes its difference from the author's proper voice, which seems paradoxically to inhabit more fully the idiosyncrasies of the earlier sections. "I should have to get completely out of the book,"[26] Faulkner recalls about conceiving the last section. In such a view, the novel frames the absences of both its subject and its author: "It's fine to

23. I first noticed this idea in Faulkner's preface after a graduate student at Boston University, Stuart H. Johnson, made a similar argument about the relationship between the prefaces of Henry James and the plots of the novels in an essay written for me.

24. Frederick L. Gwynn and Joseph L. Blotner, eds., *Faulkner in the University: Class Conferences at the University of Virginia, 1957–1958* (New York, 1959), p. 31.

25. Ibid., p. 61.

26. Introduction (*MQ*), p. 415.

think that you will leave something behind you when you die, *but it's better to have made something you can die with.* Much better the muddy bottom of a little doomed girl climbing a blooming pear tree in April to look in the window at the funeral."[27] Caught in Faulkner's mind as she climbs out of the book, Caddy is the figure that the novel is written to *lose,* and to whom the writer may lose himself.

Readers familiar with Jacques Derrida's massive meditation on the nature of language may already have recognized his eye in the perspectives I have taken on Faulkner's statements about writing. I have begun by attending closely to Faulkner's own words not because I wish to conceal my methodology, which I shall discuss shortly, but because I have sought to accent neglected peculiarities in Faulkner without first attracting favorable or unfavorable biases. I hope to show that the marriage of Faulkner's homespun taletelling to French poststructuralism reveals new facets of both partners. Their conjunction is not so arbitrary as it may seem to some readers. Derrida's absorption by questions of language and representation he owes to an "event" of decentering, as he calls it,[28] which inaugurates a phase of self-consciousness in Western literature. Derrida makes available to us a radical terminology consonant with the particular sorts of linguistic, psychological, theological, and aesthetic doubts that burst in and worry the pages of many of Derrida's and Faulkner's main common precursors—Freud and Nietzsche, most importantly. I shall risk presenting abbreviations of some of Derrida's views because they have excited my readings of the six novels I shall discuss and because they enable us to appreciate more fully the subversive, profoundly modern tensions in Faulkner's fiction. I am not performing a Derridean deconstruction of the Faulknerian text, however; I do not seek the hidden principle, the knot of ambivalence, which characterizes the text for Derrida and which the reader must expose. Instead, I allow Derrida's insistence on the impossibilities of coherence, manifestation, and presence in philosophic texts to explain retrospectively developments in

27. Ibid.; emphasis added.
28. Jacques Derrida, *Writing and Difference,* trans. Alan Bass (Chicago, 1978), p. 278; first published as *L'écriture et la différence* (Paris: Editions du Seuil, 1967). Wherever possible I have relied on the familiar English translations of Derrida's works.

modern literature. The deconstruction of truth in the philosophic text is meant to problematize asserted meaning; but in literary texts proleptic of postmodern fiction—among which texts Faulkner's belong—the disestablishment of truth is welcomed by the impulse to play. The questions of the modern situations of Faulkner and Derrida, and of how my reading of Faulkner differs from more familiar ones, I shall take up at the conclusion of this chapter.

I would be pleased if a secondary consequence of my argument were to temper the common assumption (especially among critics of British and American literature) that Derrida's approach necessarily deadens the activity of reading. Surely the sportiveness of Derrida's own meticulous readings should combat such a suggestion, but I also hope to show that his import does not deprive us of our belief that literature is concerned with meaning, the conflict of values, character, or the many other human qualities that we cherish in our fiction. But Derrida does suggest that naive assumptions about such perquisites may conceal a disrespectful suspicion of writing: he can enliven us to the rich complexity with which literature casts its spells of meaning.

ii

One of Derrida's most fruitful observations is that much Western literature associates language with the separation of individuals. Rousseau, as the exemplary locus, shows that "language cannot be truly born except by the disruption and fracture of that happy plenitude" and that all "language will substitute itself for that living self-presence of the proper, which, as language, already supplanted things in themselves. Language *adds itself* to presence and supplants it, defers it within the indestructible desire to rejoin it."[29] Even the spoken word measures distance as it stretches between sender and receiver; but according to Rousseau, writing (*écriture*) constitutes the more severe lapse into deathliness for language: "it is at the moment that the social *distance,* which had led gesture to speech, increases to the point of becoming *absence,* that writing becomes necessary."[30] I shall have more to say about a hierarchy of

29. Jacques Derrida, *Of Grammatology,* trans. Gayatri Chakravorty Spivak (Baltimore, 1976), p. 280; first published as *De la grammatologie* (Paris: Editions de Minuit, 1967).
30. Ibid., p. 281.

language that is based on proximity to the presence of the thing itself, but first I want to elaborate on the absences that writing implies.

Even to name oneself is to risk losing self-presence: "When I say *I*, even in solitary speech, can I give my statement meaning without implying, there as always, the possible absence of the object of speech—in this case, myself?"[31] The word, as sign, stands for the thing itself; and therefore it seems to declare the unavailability of what it names and also of the namer. "And the original absence of the subject of writing is also the absence of the thing or the referent."[32] In this perfectly obvious sense—but as one that our reflection on language regularly tries to forget—writing (or speech) depends on the absences of both the subject and the object of the text. The important consequences of this situation (which Derrida finds widely in his panoply of texts) is the double, contradictory movement of writing.

In Rousseau the project of language is to restore presence and immediacy; speech stands closer to the original plenitude, and we might expect Rousseau to rely on it to reconstruct presence. But Rousseau recognizes that even in "the spoken address, presence is at once promised and refused."[33] "We are dispossessed of the longed-for presence in the gesture of language by which we attempt to seize it."[34] Writing, rather than speech, becomes the method by which the speaker's and referent's self-presence may be reappropriated in the 'voice' of the text, in its ideas and images—through its representative power. Writing is embraced because speech "denies itself as it gives itself"; but writing is paradoxically depreciated at the same time. "Rousseau condemns writing as destruction of presence and as disease of speech. He rehabilitates it to the extent that it promises the reappropriation of that of which speech allowed itself to be dispossessed."[35] This contradictory valuation of writing is suggested in Rousseau's use of "supplement" to describe writing's function.

31. Jacques Derrida, *Speech and Phenomena, and Other Essays on Husserl's Theory of Signs*, trans. David B. Allison (Evanston, Ill., 1973), p. 95; first published as *La Voix et le Phénomène* (Paris: Presses Universitaires de France, 1967).
32. Derrida, *Of Grammatology*, p. 69.
33. Ibid., p. 141.
34. Ibid.
35. Ibid., p. 142.

Supplement has become one of Derrida's master conceptions;[36] describing it fastidiously as a movement rather than as a property or feature of language, he locates two impulses in the performance of language. As Rousseau displays the problem, thought should be fully self-present in speech, and yet speech, as we have seen, also carries deathliness and absences. Thus writing is added to speech so as to represent it; but in adding itself it comes to take the place of speech, just as speech has arisen in the absences of speaker and referent:

> Writing is dangerous from the moment that representation there claims to be presence and the sign of the thing itself. And there is a fatal necessity, inscribed in the very functioning of the sign, that the substitute make one forget the vicariousness of its own function and make itself pass for the plenitude of a speech whose deficiency and infirmity it nevertheless only *supplements*. For the concept of the supplement—which here determines that of the representative image—harbors within itself two significations whose cohabitation is as strange as it is necessary. The supplement adds itself, it is a surplus, a plenitude enriching another plenitude, the *fullest measure* of presence. It cumulates and accumulates presence. . . .
>
> But the supplement supplements. It adds only to replace. It intervenes or insinuates itself *in-the-place-of;* if it fills, it is as if one fills a void. If it represents and makes an image, it is by the anterior default of a presence.[37]

Derrida nicknames the double movement of the supplement *différance;* the word plays on the ideas of difference and deferment (denoted by the double meaning of the French *différer*) as it gathers up the motions of adding on and also replacing. The supplement adds itself as different from the original plenitude, and then defers the reappropriation of the thing itself, which can be constituted only as "the anterior default of a presence." Of course, the movement of differing and deferring establishes a perpetual series of surpluses, detours, and fillings: a chain of supplements. "Difference is what makes the movement of signification possible only if each element that is said to be 'present,' appearing on the stage of pres-

36. Derrida would put the terms "conception" and "theme" under erasure since they naturally suggest forms of presence.
37. Derrida, *Of Grammatology*, pp. 144–45.

ence, is related to something other than itself but retains the mark of a past element and already lets itself be hollowed out by the mark of its relation to a future element."[38]

Before moving on, I wish to secure one point about the movement of deferment. As language seeks to reconstruct the broken presence, it yearns for total reappropriation of the thing itself in its representation. Yet were the supplementary writing to succeed in reappropriating presence, it would sacrifice itself entirely: instead *différance* defers the reappropriation of what it can never represent. "Without the possibility of differance, the desire of presence as such would not find its breathing-space. That means by the same token that this desire carries in itself the destiny of its nonsatisfaction."[39] For Rousseau, the supplement comes to *protect* the writer from the very reappropriation he desires: the supplement is an economy of *différance* which prolongs desire and resists the annihilation caused by total self-presence:

> The supplement has not only the power of *procuring* an absent presence through its image; procuring it for us through the proxy [*procuration*] of the sign, it holds it at a distance and masters it. For this presence is at the same time desired and feared. The supplement transgresses and at the same time respects the interdict.[40]

Although I have already risked a long excursion from Faulkner's fiction, I wish to return through a detour. Derrida's positions have rarely been summarized well, and one common misunderstanding of his project is that he simply wishes to elevate writing (in the ordinary sense) over speaking. Jonathan Culler, whose elegant lucidity is usually convincing, argues that Derrida executes a merely "logical point" when he strives to see speech as a species of writing:

> Derrida wants to take his argument a step further and, having maintained that writing cannot be treated on the model of speech, show that the features which he has first isolated in writing are also present in speech, which must, therefore, be conceived according to the new model of writing. . . . But this further move is a purely logical point,

38. Derrida, *Speech and Phenomena*, p. 142.
39. Derrida, *Of Grammatology*, p. 143.
40. Ibid., p. 155.

which someone concerned with the social facts can afford to neglect: even if Derrida shows that we ought to think of speech as a kind of writing, we may arrest the play of his concepts by saying, simply, that within Western culture there are crucial differences between the conventions of oral communication and those of literature which deserve study whatever their ideological basis.[41]

Derrida, of course, might question Culler's confidence that "social facts" are external to the social discourse (or writing) which articulates them. But Culler's explicit point about the conventions of oral and written communication demands even closer attention, for Derrida's methodology does not eradicate such difference, it elucidates it. The common properties of all forms of representation—called the general structure of writing by Derrida—provide one crucial and long-neglected basis for the kind of distinctions Culler quite rightly wishes us to protect. Surely Derrida repeatedly opens that distinction as he moves between the conventions of speaking and writing in Rousseau, for example.

Derrida prompts us to measure the common ground of all forms of articulation, and it is this force in his thought that I think may open up Faulkner's novels in a new way. Faulkner clearly honors the speaking voice; many novels celebrate the customs of taletelling, and several studies have noticed the techniques of oral rhetoric in his style.[42] Yet Faulkner does not subordinate writing in his mature fiction: speech and writing similarly depend on the particular kinds of absences, differ from their desired objects, and defer the expectation of full reappropriation. They share the structure of what Derrida calls writing in the general sense. Moreover, characters in Faulkner's fiction manipulate a wide variety of languages that share these properties. What permits the common analysis of these languages is Derrida's critique of the sign. All forms of representation, all systems of significance deal in signs. Derrida summarizes the usual view of the sign:

> We ordinarily say that a sign is put in place of the thing itself, the present thing—"thing" holding here for the sense as well as the referent. Signs represent the present in its absence; they take the place of

41. Jonathan Culler, *Structuralist Poetics: Structuralism, Linguistics, and the Study of Literature* (Ithaca, 1975), p. 133.
42. See, for example, Helen Swink, "William Faulkner: The Novelist as Oral Narrator," *Georgia Review,* 26 (Summer 1972), 183–209.

the present. When we cannot take hold of or show the thing, let us say the present, the being-present, when the present does not present itself, then we signify, we go through the detour of signs. We take up or give signs; we make signs. The sign would thus be a deferred presence. Whether it is a question of verbal or written signs, monetary signs, electoral delegates, or political representatives, the movement of signs defers the moment of encountering the thing itself, the moment at which we could lay hold of it, consume or expend it, touch it, see it, have a present intuition of it.[43]

Derrida seeks to question this classical formulation by undermining presence as the basis for the sign, by proclaiming the indivisibility of signifier and signified. There is no signified, no presence, no thing itself apart from the signifying system: Saussure already implies that "the signified concept is never present in itself, in an adequate presence that would refer only to itself."[44] Derrida attempts to persuade us that "from the moment that there is meaning there are nothing but signs. We *think only in signs.*"[45] I am not interested in defending these statements as psychology, but they lead to Derrida's notion that there is never anything but a kind of writing at the 'origin' or in the representation of the signified. To follow the career of language in Rousseau's texts, for example, is to realize that despite himself Rousseau presents a condition in which "the absolute present, Nature, that which words like 'real mother' name, have always already escaped, have never existed; that what opens meaning and language is writing as the disappearance of natural presence."[46] Thus, disappearance, absence, articulation all obtain within presence or speech:

But Rousseau could not think this writing, that takes place *before* and *within* speech. To the extent that he belonged to the metaphysics of presence, he *dreamed* of the simple exteriority of death to life, evil to good, representation to presence, signifier to signified, representer to represented, mask to face, writing to speech. . . . The supplement is none of these terms. It is especially not more a signifier than a signified, a representer than a presence, a writing than a speech.[47]

43. Derrida, *Speech and Phenomena*, p. 138.
44. Ibid., p. 140.
45. Derrida, *Of Grammatology*, p. 50.
46. Ibid., p. 159.
47. Ibid., p. 315.

Faulkner is sufficiently modern to grasp the interiority of writing. I hope to emphasize the regularity with which moments of insight, perception, or understanding occur in characters strictly as language. Everywhere in Faulkner it is the act of playing with signs that generates meaning. Ideas, conceptions, the facts of the past, and so on are never fully recovered by language in Faulkner; *The Sound and the Fury* recognizes that the life of the mind is always a life of writing, of language as the indistinguishable unions of signifier and signified, representation and presence.

All modes of representation, whether 'internal' to consciousness or 'external' as expression, are structured like language. Normally we assume a plenitude that *is* the mind of a character or author behind the words, gestures, or behavior that embody some portion of that original presence. But Faulkner's fiction, like other modern literature, challenges the consequences of the "metaphysics of presence." The usual provinces of full self-presence—imagination, memory, perception—are raided by the deathliness of signs. Derrida remarks that "imagination is the power that allows life to affect itself with its own representation" and so "like death" it "is *representative* and *supplementary*."[48] According to Derrida, such absences and deathliness do not reduce discourse to meaningless word games; rather, the possibility of meaning arises in the text's liberation from the tyranny of presence:

> The absence of intuition—and therefore of the subject of intuition—is not only *tolerated* by speech; it is *required* by the general structure of signification, when considered *in itself*. It is radically requisite: the total absence of the subject and object of a statement—the death of the writer and/or the disappearance of the objects he was able to describe—does not prevent a text from "meaning" something. On the contrary, this possibility gives birth to meaning as such, gives it out to be heard and read.[49]

If all representation bodes absence, loss, separation, and the disappearance of the thing itself, then there can be no hierarchy of representations. According to the usual metaphysics, that which is closer to original self-presence is the more natural, less dangerous

48. Ibid., p. 184.
49. Derrida, *Speech and Phenomena*, p. 93.

supplement. One might see "the exteriority of writing to speech, of speech to thought, of the signifier to the signified in general."[50] But all systems of articulated significance—games, economies, rituals, writing, speaking—depend on the play of *différance.* There is nothing behind or beyond these representations; the play of the discourses produces the meaning rather than establishes a route to the transcendental signified. Even "imitation, principle of art, has always already interrupted natural plenitude; . . . having to be a *discourse,* it has always already broached presence in differance."[51] I plan to concentrate in the following essays on the rich array of languages in Faulkner's fiction, all of which make their meaning through the play of difference, the deferring of conclusive truth, the pure pleasure of making marks. Characters constitute their consciousnesses as they invent suitable forms of language. Whether Lucas Beauchamp articulates indignity, genealogical chance, and dispossession in the signs of the hunt or Isaac McCaslin does so in his ledger entries or the statement of his renunciation, both characters create identities that cohere in the texts of their lives. Conversely, characters who are silent, such as Rider, Joe Christmas, Bayard Sartoris, and finally Quentin Compson, do not transcend circumstance through the fullness of their refraining minds, but vanish into voids of wordlessness. For Faulkner's characters not to speak—in whatever language—is for them not to be, and hence the urge to speak, to write on scraps and stones. Quentin and Shreve do not just discuss the shades of the past, they "exist" in them.

As far as the play of language produces meaning from *différance,* meaning arises from the lack of authoritative, unique, absolute, or central significance. In both their plots and their themes, Faulkner's novels often appear bereft of conclusive sense. The author whose literary ambition is to "leave a scratch on that wall—Kilroy was here"[52] discovers the meaning of his works *as* he writes them. In the moment before starting *Light in August,* for example, Faulkner trembles with the hope of repeating the ecstasy stimulated by *The Sound and the Fury:* ". . . then I began Light in August, knowing no more about it than a young woman, pregnant, walking along a strange country road. I thought, I will recapture it now, since I

50. Derrida, *Of Grammatology,* p. 82.
51. Ibid., p. 215.
52. Gwynn and Blotner, eds., *Faulkner in the University,* p. 61.

know no more about this book than I did about The Sound and the Fury."[53] Pregnant with undelivered meaning, the writer simply begins scratching his pen on the blank page. "Meaning must await being said or written in order to inhabit itself, and in order to become, by differing from itself, what it is: meaning. . . . It is because writing is *inaugural,* in the fresh sense of the word, that it is dangerous and anguishing. It does not know where it is going. . . ," Derrida remarks.[54]

Like Sutpen's architect from Martinique, Derrida may seem a fancy interloper among the denizens of Yoknapatawpha, but I have tried to suggest how Faulkner's views of fiction reflect the sophisticated equivocations and inquiries that force the eventual "decentering" of structure, as Derrida has described it. Certainly Faulkner would feel comfortable with Derrida's temperamental fondness for paradox, and it should prove significant that their reading included such shapers of modern paradox as Nietzsche and Freud. I shall appeal in one respect to simple history to ease our doubts about the alignment of modern fiction and recent theory; one of the best current books on Faulkner[55] situates his work in the context of Freud and Nietzsche, and I shall discuss shortly its relevance to my study. Without diluting the growing interest in confronting the consequences of our methodological assumptions, however, I want to admit that I would be disappointed if my study were not tested by its aspiration to offer fresh, persuasive, coherent accounts of some of Faulkner's most familiar novels. It was my estimate of the resources of Faulkner's fiction—its rich contradictions and tensions—that encouraged my attention to aspects of his craft unturned by earlier studies.

Though uneasy with all of the word's ramifications, Derrida refers to the "event" in Western thinking that shakes the conception of centered structures. Before this movement, the structurality of structure was always referred to "a point of presence, a fixed origin";[56] after it, "the center could not be thought in the form of a

---

53. Introduction (*SR*), p. 709.

54. Derrida, *Writing and Difference,* p. 11.

55. John T. Irwin, *Doubling & Incest/Repetition & Revenge: A Speculative Reading of Faulkner* (Baltimore, 1975).

56. Derrida, *Writing and Difference,* p. 278. The many quotations from this text in the following paragraphs will be cited by page numbers in parentheses.

present-being..." (280). "This was the moment when, in the absence of a center or origin, everything became discourse—provided we can agree on this word—that is to say, a system in which the central signified, the original or trancendental signified, is never absolutely present outside a system of differences. The absence of the transcendental signified extends the domain and the play of signification infinitely" (280). Derrida attributes this episode in modern thought chiefly to three writers:

> ... We doubtless would have to cite the Nietzschean critique of metaphysics, the critique of the concepts of Being and truth, for which were substituted the concepts of play, interpretation, and sign (sign without present truth): the Freudian critique of self-presence, that is, the critique of consciousness, of the subject, of self-identity and of self-proximity or self-possession; and, more radically, the Heideggerean destruction of metaphysics, of onto-theology, of the determination of Being as presence. [280]

In her dense, unnaturally arduous, but rewarding preface to her translation of Derrida's *Of Grammatology,* Gayatri Spivak helpfully elaborates some of these affinities. One of her central ambitions is to emphasize Derrida's gesture of erasure, his attempt to use words while denying their metaphysical assumptions. ("Event," above, is an example.) Derrida's reading of Nietzsche notices that his paradoxes are forms of erasure: Derrida finds Nietzsche to have contributed to the liberation of the signifier from its dependence on the signified;[57] he relishes Nietzsche's awareness that truth is an illusion now forgotten to be illusion ("a process of figuration and a process of forgetfulness," Spivak comments [xxii]); he is inspired by Nietzsche's efforts to undo the will to power by dissolving opposites and reversing perspectives repeatedly in order to unsettle the (impossible) distinction between truth and error (xxviii); and he extends Nietzsche's destruction of usual oppositions such as good and evil, truth and error, theory and practice, purpose and accident, death and life (to cite Spivak's list [xxviii–xxix]). Nietzsche anticipates the gesture of erasure, then, in attempting to speak the destruction of metaphysics within the language of metaphysics.

Freud is a heroic modern for Derrida because, even though he is

---

57. Derrida, *Of Grammatology,* p. xxii.

within the logocentric metaphysics, Freud contributes to the "moment when language invaded the universal problematic... when... everything became discourse." Freud postulates that the unconscious may be understood only as the trace of a conscious that is itself already written. Thus the "unconscious text is already a weave of pure traces, differences in which meaning and force are united—a text nowhere present."[58] Second, even the conscious present (perception, intuition, experience) is also already a representation: "the present in general is not primal but, rather, reconstituted, ... it is not the absolute, wholly living form which constitutes experience, ... there is no purity of the living present."[59] And when Freud discovers the mystic writing pad as the appropriate analogy for the operation of memory, he discovers that "writing supplements perception before perception even appears to itself [is conscious of itself]. 'Memory' or writing is the opening of that process of appearance itself. The 'perceived' may be read only in the past, beneath perception and after it."[60] That the private realms of the conscious mind are themselves already structured like language is a recognition that Faulkner's deepest experiment with narrative consciousness, *The Sound and the Fury,* struggles to achieve. The earlier fiction wonders whether memory and imagination may embody the full self-presence of an idea, or render a moment of perception, or recover lost objects of love. But the grieving protagonists of Faulkner's first four novels discover that every memory is already the inscription of loss, that imagination can represent only what is not present, that to speak is to lose.

In his enormously persuasive psychoanalytical reading of Faulkner, John T. Irwin has yoked Faulkner, Freud, and Nietzsche in a triangle of denied influence.[61] Though each in turn disputed the influence of his predecessor, Irwin reverses the denials to read as suppressed acknowledgments of debt. The three "addressed themselves to many of the same questions," and Irwin focuses particularly on their association of narration and repetition (in which narration seeks to repeat the past and so gain revenge on time) and on the mechanism of deferment (which makes modern tragedy a

58. Derrida, *Writing and Difference,* p. 211.
59. Ibid., p. 212.
60. Ibid., p. 224.
61. Irwin, *Doubling & Incest,* p. 5.

"sense of the tragic absurd, . . . not the sense of the meaningless but of the almost meaningful—the sense of the meaningful as the always deferred").[62] That Nietzsche, Freud, and Faulkner share such interests stimulates Irwin to "evoke" two structures: one "structure that exists in the interstices between [Faulkner's] novels" and another "beyond Faulkner's work as well—in the interstices between his writings and the work of writers like Freud and Nietzsche who shared his preoccupations, for the structure that is created by Faulkner's writing simultaneously creates that writing, at once in and beyond, contained and container."[63] Irwin's conception of structure seems indebted to Lévi-Strauss (he cites *The Raw and the Cooked* to explain the form of his own study), and though he does not mention him, his view of Freud resembles Jacques Lacan's. These resemblances reinforce Irwin's confidence that the interstitial structure may be made present in his text; in Lacan's psychoanalysis, the text of the unconscious is pursued with the expectation that the patient can fully articulate it, can make the real story appear through the lapses and distortions.[64] Derrida would want to make the idea of structure more problematic: structure is a part of the metaphysics of presence, and Derrida more readily notices the unavailability of the truth itself (the unconscious, the transcendent signified, etc.). Spivak comments epigrammatically: "Whereas Derrida sees 'truth' . . . as being constituted by 'fiction,' Lacan seems to use fiction as a clue to truth."[65] When Irwin refers to the process by which the structure "exists" between the novels, or by which Quentin expresses his "own life story" (p. 28) in the Sutpen tale, he suggests that the proper truth of Faulkner or Quentin resides outside a series of partial constitutions. Irwin is interested in discovering and presenting this reserved, exterior plenitude. On the other hand, I wish to examine the suspicion in Faulkner's writing that the unconscious is never available except as a "weave of traces," a linguistic fabric that always stands in the place of the unconscious and of truth 'themselves,' and which is always aware that it does so. Faulkner's language plays with the

62. Ibid., pp. 8–9.
63. Ibid., p. 3.
64. See Jacques Lacan, *The Language of the Self,* trans. Anthony Wilden (Baltimore, 1968).
65. Derrida, *Of Grammatology,* p. lxiv.

loss of authoritative truth, the center, the signified realm, the place of origin, innocence. Faulkner's novels display a nostalgia for such losses, but also a spirit of lively play about the possibilities of infinite interpretation. Derrida has noticed that the opposing attitudes toward "the lost or impossible presence of the absent origin" are "the saddened, *negative,* nostalgic, guilty Rousseauistic side of the thinking of play" and "the Nietzschean *affirmation,* that is the joyous affirmation of the play of the world and of the innocence of becoming, the affirmation of a world of signs without fault, without truth."[66]

iii

Surely criticism of Faulkner has suffered from neither dearth nor unanimity. But in studying Faulkner's language from an approach abrasive to most traditional criticism of English literature, I have been struck by the extensive biases that define the subjects of our study and shape our judgments. Biases are unavoidable and finally fruitful, but we also need strife for the sake of critical vitality. Assumptions about writing and speech, for example, preside powerfully over our views of Faulkner's morality, theology, sexuality, psychology, aesthetics, and even the achievement and contour of his career.

One commonplace in traditional thought about language is that it follows perception and is subordinate to it. Our metaphysics uniformly insists that the present perception of experience is the only reliable measure of reality 'itself.' Henri Bergson offers an index to this position useful not only because his work reflects the beginning of decentering in philosophy, but also because Faulkner pointed to him as a significant influence.[67] Bergson challenges any naive confidence in the processes of intellection. Whatever the mind knows about experience is imperiled by the falsification of symbols, words, or conceptions: "Thus the different concepts that we form of the properties of a thing inscribe round it so many circles, each much too large and none of them fitting exactly."[68] As much as he

66. Derrida, *Writing and Difference,* p. 292.
67. Loïc Bouvard, "Conversation with William Faulkner," trans. Henry Dan Piper, *Modern Fiction Studies,* 5 (Winter 1959–60), 364.
68. Henri Bergson, *An Introduction to Metaphysics,* trans. T. E. Hulme (New York, 1949), p. 29.

is able, then, the philosopher must rely on intuition, which sinks into "the absolute, which is the object and not its representation, the original and not its translation."[69] Language cannot render all that is present in perception or experience: "we fail to translate completely what our soul experiences: there is no common measure between mind and language."[70]

It is neither surprising nor misleading that critics should discuss Faulkner's attitudes toward language within this tradition of subordination to perception, action, or experience. I shall be exploring these biases not in order to discard them, but to oppose them with positions that can amplify Faulkner's dissonances. Still the most provocative book on Faulkner in many respects, Olga Vickery's *Novels of William Faulkner* discusses the place of language in the fiction. For the moment I want to focus on a central assumption of her study: "Non-verbal experience must always provide the ground or basis for truth, for in the last analysis truth for Faulkner is the inseparability of the word and the act."[71] According to Vickery, action, experience, objects themselves, and the perceiving subject compose the primary reality in Faulkner's fiction; it is "the experiential foundation of language" that is celebrated, since Faulkner is aware "of the perils and deceits inherent in language" (267, 275). Vickery is a gifted reader of Faulkner's complexities, and so she does not overstate her argument; she notices, for example, that Faulkner loosens the "direct relationship between the word and its referent" (267) and that he never suggests that "truth cannot exist in a verbal formulation" (275). But the grain of her reading displays a familiar mistrust of language and a corresponding one in Faulkner. When language hardens into moral code or precept, it no longer functions as communication (its only apparent good), but "orders experience and hence all reactions to it" (272–273). This is a dangerous kind of "linguistic determinism" (273). Faulkner's moral and aesthetic values, on the contrary, are rooted in "the preconscious and therefore preverbal state of 'just being'." The novelist's words follow along after his thought: "Language, when used creatively, is a pictorial representation of the mental world just as graphs and diagrams are of the physical world" (280). And

69. Ibid., p. 23.
70. Henri Bergson, *Time and Free Will*, trans. F. L. Pogson (New York, 1910), pp. 164–165.
71. Olga Vickery, *The Novels of William Faulkner* (Baton Rouge, 1959), p. 275.

although it is only through language that the past is preserved and that the individual becomes "aware of his [preverbal] knowledge," language still serves the higher claims of presence and "experience": "By the very nature of language the writer cannot invent but only invoke that which is already present in the memory of all men. . . . The task of the man dedicated to language is to reveal to man his endless potentialities and to make him more cognizant of the quality of his experience" (281). Vickery repeats these views, of course, in her interpretations of the novels. Thus *Mosquitoes* embodies a "linguistic scepticism" because "truth is dependent not on words but on a moment of comprehension which usually occurs when the individual is least concerned with intellectual activity" (8). *As I Lay Dying* endorses Addie Bundren's distinction between "intensely felt reality . . . [and] a mere conventional form of speech and behavior" (53). Addie considers words empty unless they "are grounded in non-verbal experience" (53), a theory of language that Faulkner endorses, too, according to Vickery. Even more tersely, Vickery argues that *Absalom, Absalom!* is troubled fundamentally by the unreliability of words, "which by their very nature falsify the things they are meant to represent" (86). We are, as critics of Western literature, far better attuned to the voices that abuse language in our literature. We might also see, however, that Faulkner abides by paradoxes more complicated than Vickery's formulations: silence, preconsciousness, perception, memory, and action are all structured by writing. They are systems of difference and deferment, devoid of any "ground" of authority, shaken from the centers of presence or referential significance. I have presented Vickery's positions in detail both because she draws exemplary criticism from them and because I shall allow hers to typify the many subsequent studies of Faulkner's language that display similar assumptions.[72]

72. Floyd C. Watkins' discussion of Faulkner in *The Flesh and the Word: Eliot, Hemingway, Faulkner* (Nashville, 1971) is explicitly indebted to Vickery. Watkins believes that Addie Bundren's "denial of the efficacy of a moral vocabulary and her reliance on concrete image, fact, and action are reflections of the best aesthetic principles of Eliot, Faulkner, and Hemingway early in their careers" (p. 182). The best language is that which suppresses itself, for "experience lies outside language" (p. 207). Donald M. Kartiganer also depends on this assumption as he analyzes the "difference between contemplation and action, telling and doing" in *The Sound and the Fury* ("*The Sound and the Fury* and Faulkner's Quest for Form," *ELH*, 37 [December 1970], 626). I regret that Kartiganer's *Fragile Thread* (Amherst, 1979)

One charge against language in Faulkner criticism, then, is that it is exterior to the reality of experience or perception, just as the signifier is considered exterior to and distinct from the signified. A second and consonant charge accuses language of failing to restore the presence of the object or idea for which it stands. According to this view, Faulkner's language searches tirelessly but vainly for a full expression of truth, for a complete rendering of experience. Failing, the novelist despairs of purpose and meaning altogether. A most morose version of this conviction is the basis for Walter Slatoff's *Quest for Failure*.[73] Slatoff reads Faulkner patiently and closely but uncovers pattern after pattern of paradoxical (even desperately oxymoronic, he suggests) irresolution. Because he expects the ultimate appearance of a truth, insight, or point of view, Slatoff inevitably concludes that

> many of [Faulkner's] leaps and shifts of ground are as much a way of escaping having to resolve his thoughts or feelings as they are a way of reaching for something farther. It is as though he is determined to avoid clarifying or finishing his ideas, almost as though he feared to take hold of them, to give them full shape or realization.   [260]

Slatoff assumes that language might achieve such a "full shape," a "realization" of the ideas it signifies. Faulkner's inability to accomplish this realization Slatoff finally attributes to his "temperament," a gesture that emphatically underlines our common assumptions about texts. The text looks not only toward manifest meaning, but also toward its manifested author; presences always should appear

---

appeared too late for me to take note of it throughout my argument; his reading of *The Sound and the Fury*, however, coincides with that of his earlier published essays. Eric Larsen argues that Faulkner's language attempts to become experience by leaving truth unresolved; the reader may sink into authentic knowledge—the truth of perception—only by leaving language behind ("The Barrier of Language: The Irony of Language in Faulkner," *Modern Fiction Studies*, 12 [Spring 1971], 19–31). Walter Brylowski suggests that Faulkner's "mythic mode" aspires to break down the aesthetic barriers between meaning and experience by rendering reality more directly (*Faulkner's Olympian Laugh: Myth in the Novels* [Detroit, 1968], p. 152). Terrence Doody insists that Quentin must know Sutpen most intimately because he is beyond the need for words ("Shreve McCannon and the Confessions of *Absalom, Absalom!*," *Studies in the Novel*, 6 [Winter 1974]. 454–469).

73. Walter J. Slatoff, *Quest for Failure: A Study of William Faulkner* (Ithaca, 1960).

behind their denotations.[74] But Faulkner apprehends that the meaning of the story may inhere in its play around voided centers of authority, being, and signified ideas. Stories may mean without signifying, constitute selfhood without expressing it. Faulkner offers a view not of his extreme temperament, but of the extreme nature of language.

If language originates in exile from reality and is blocked from returning to it, one might wonder if the best language is not that which denies itself perfectly: silence. Such a strain of thought runs through the earlier Faulkner fiction, but it has been discussed in ways with which I disagree. Paul R. Lilly[75] offers a recent account of the position that for Faulkner the highest language is silence. Concentrating on the examples of Caddy and Addie as speakers of an "impeccable" language, Lilly argues that Faulkner's ideal "was to render in words the illusion of a language purer than words" (171). Language, as it constrains, limits, and distorts thought, is seen as a contaminant; and even though Faulkner recognizes that the dream of an impeccable speech is only an "imaginary hypothesis," he seeks to create moments that embody the "illusion that language is most alive when it can thrust itself beyond words"

74. Warren Beck, in an early, influential, and often wise essay, succinctly summarizes Faulkner's extralinguistic intention: "In his most characteristic writing Faulkner is trying to render the transcendent life of the mind, the crowded composite of associative and analytical consciousness. . . . To this end the sentence as a rhetorical unit (however strained) is made to hold diverse yet related elements in a sort of saturated solution, which is perhaps the nearest that language as the instrument of fiction can come to the instantaneous complexities of consciousness itself" ("William Faulkner's Style," *American Prefaces,* 6 [Spring 1941], 195–211, as reprinted in *Faulkner: A Collection of Critical Essays,* ed. Robert Penn Warren [Englewood Cliffs, N.J., 1966], pp. 62–63). Whether language *is* outside consciousness "itself" is a question that shapes much of Faulkner's fiction; *The Sound and the Fury,* moreover, settles the question in a way antipathetic to Beck's formulation, for the novel shows that even consciousness has the structure of writing. Building on assumptions similar to Beck's, James Guetti argues that *Absalom, Absalom!* embodies Faulkner's view that "human experience cannot be understood" (*The Limits of Metaphor* [Ithaca, 1967], p. 108). Guetti reaches this conclusion by superposing the narrators' failures to tell Sutpen's story comprehensively on Sutpen's own failure to find a metaphor to explain circumstance and master the arbitrary. Both Sutpen and his narrators exhaust the potential of explanation, and thus *Absalom* "is the most thoroughgoing of those works of fiction that call into question the possibilities of language and meaning" (108). Like Slatoff, Guetti demands that meaning be something achieved, present, univocal, and permanent.

75. Paul R. Lilly, Jr., "Caddy and Addie: Speakers of Faulkner's Impeccable Language," *Journal of Narrative Technique,* 3 (September 1973), 170–182.

(173). In her pure silence, Caddy constitutes the perfect narrator, released, as Faulkner suggested, from the dirtying obligation to talk. Addie, though she has a monologue, Lilly sees as speaking in a voice that is "outside process itself"; she "has already achieved the voicelessness" that makes her "free at last of words" (175). Both characters occupy "a real zone of consciousness" that entertains the impossible but "imaginary hypothesis of complete expression" (177). To speak is to befoul, and thus the only pure word in *As I Lay Dying,* and the synecdoche for Faulkner's impeccable language, is the blank space at the center of Addie's section. This space speaks purely, but the novel recognizes that art must resign itself to losing its innocence to its words; it must accept the chasm between "the plenum of silence and the poverty of vocabulary" (180).

Any reading of the passages that Lilly cites is imperiled by their flood of cryptic paradoxes, but I want to offer some alternatives to this version of animosity toward the word. Although Lilly quotes Faulkner on the ideals of silent poetic language ("pure and esoteric"),[76] it is Lilly's inference that such silence is wordless. Faulkner's brand of silence, on the contrary, is a worded silence—a silence that corresponds most nearly to the space of writing. Faulkner mentions to Loïc Bouvard that " 'I find it impossible to communicate with the outside world. Maybe I will end up in some kind of self-communion—a silence—faced with the certainty that I can no longer be understood. The artist must create his own language. This is not only his right but his duty. Sometimes I think of doing what Rimbaud did—yet, I will certainly keep on writing as long as I live.' "[77] Lilly quotes these words to suggest that Faulkner's prose idolizes Rimbaud's absolute silence by internalizing it in the style; but we might wonder if Faulkner is not describing the region of writing, that place beyond the spoken in which language and communication nevertheless continue. (Addie listens not to a wordless silence but rather to the land's voicelessness.) Faulkner's silence would not be Rimbaud's, no "plenum" beyond words, but rather a private scene of writing. (We think of Faulkner shutting the door on the reader in order to write *The Sound and the Fury.*) Like Caddy's and Addie's virginity, the plenum of silence is always already lost

76. Meriwether and Millgate, eds., *Lion in the Garden*, p. 96.
77. Ibid., p. 71.

("The shape of my body where I used to be a virgin is in the shape of a   ," Addie reflects [165]). The dream of impeccability becomes in my reading a specter of death and meaninglessness, the site at which the demand for innocent and perfect referentiality extinguishes the play of fallen language. Faulkner's metaphors for his writing always involve making a mark, never leaving the body of the page blank. While the ideal of full expression exercises a powerful attraction to the Compson brothers and to the Bundren family (not to mention the other silent protagonists of the early fiction), such a dream is soon seen to be impossible (since even silence bears the structure of writing) and finally pernicious (because it is the very image of deathliness and meaninglessness). But the blank space is also, as the sense of Lilly's argument implies, a silence that refers to the state of the body's virginity only through the function of the words around it. The 'pure' space of silence is in fact already a syntactical unit, part of the system of articulated differences that constitutes writing. In this more complicated way Addie's virginity (like Caddy's) is not the "hypothetically pure" language that Lilly suggests, but a voiceless yet already written language.

The desire that language transcend its deficiencies has yielded a distinctive psychology of the reader in Faulkner criticism. If the truth of experience or consciousness must be some sort of presence, and if language cannot render that object fully, perhaps, the argument runs, the reader must assemble the full expression in his own creative imagination. In this view the incompleteness of any linguistic performance is finished by the reader, in whose mind perception or sense becomes fully present. Arnold L. Weinstein argues that Faulkner presents "fragments of 'raw' feeling, enigmatic emotional exchanges, and the burden of interpretation and response lies heavily on the reader."[78] Faulkner's art, according to Weinstein, "hallows the intuitive, the imaginative, and the affective" (114) by compelling the reader to function like Quentin and Shreve in *Absalom:* ". . . the Past, the world of Others, can come alive for us, yield its secrets to us, only by an act of love" (151). For André Bleikasten, too, the reader's consciousness is the site on which the full story becomes present; Bleikasten's reading of *The Sound and*

78. Arnold Weinstein, *Vision and Response in Modern Fiction* (Ithaca, 1974), p. 113.

the Fury urges that the speaking voice is the epitome of writing's aspiration and that Dilsey apprehends the entire Compson story in the same way the reader should—through faith in the self-consuming voice:

> ... Shegog's sermon reads indeed like the transcript of an oral performance.
> ... This is what makes the sermon a unique moment in the novel: it marks the intrusion of the mythic into the fictional, the non-literary into the literary, and by the same token it also signals the writer's willing renunciation of his authorial pride and of his prerogatives as a fiction-maker. It becomes very tempting, then, to see the preacher-figure as a double of the novelist himself: do not both surrender their identity as speakers/writers to become the vehicles of a mythic voice?[79]

Faulkner's search for the moment at which "language moves paradoxically toward its own extinction" (197) and his quest for the "mirage" of the "absolute presence of language to itself" reflect what Bleikasten calls Faulkner's "dream of presence and plenitude as well as the priority granted to the spoken word over the written" (242, n. 47). Bleikasten explicitly places Faulkner within the metaphysical tradition questioned by Derrida, but I shall argue that Faulkner's fiction is more radical and unsettled than Bleikasten allows. According to him, the "active participation" of the reader yields a novel in which the "writing process manages to create an order of its own" (205); Faulkner seems less confident of that possibility when he emphasizes the incompleteness and repeatability of the text.[80]

Our fundamental assumptions about language have also deeply affected our estimation of Faulkner's career. For all the innovations we have witnessed, some critics of modern literature still remain suspicious of language that is too patently itself. Joseph Gold's

---

79. Bleikasten, *Most Splendid Failure,* pp. 200, 201.

80. Like Weinstein and Bleikasten, Arthur Kinney (*Faulkner's Narrative Poetics* [Amherst, 1978]) has also probed the implied reader of Faulkner, concluding that the novelist perfects his effects in the "constitutive consciousness" of the reader. Kinney argues that Faulkner's stylistic and formal devices are calculated to enlist the reader's active construction and vision of an aesthetic totality available only to the mind of a spectator.

following description of Faulkner's career, for example, depends on the conviction that talking is to be mistrusted in a novel, and that the "myths" of fiction are exempt from the discourse that presents them:

> "The Bear" is in many ways the turning point in the work of Faulkner, the signpost which indicates his change of direction from the creation of myth to the construction of discourse, from the play of imagination to the exercise of ratiocination.
>
> The increasing desire to speak about his faith in mankind led Faulkner to take a more conscious and a more desperate hand in planting that "talking" in his later work.[81]

This representative view of Faulkner's later work illustrates how underlying biases against language encourage us to esteem fiction that denigrates or suppresses its own medium.

The next section concentrates on the emergence of some of Faulkner's more subversive practices in his early fiction, practices not always noticed by traditional readings of Faulkner. The works that precede *The Sound and the Fury* in Faulkner's career possess a seminal ambivalence toward language: how does one learn to approach language with both "alert respect" and "joy" (as the 1933 preface puts it)? How are the explosively destructive and ecstatically creative impulses of language arbitrated? The novels through *Sartoris* not only pursue the obvious tasks of apprenticeship—finding a narrative voice, inventing a fictional world, and sorting out the claims of the author's traditions—but also probe the economy of losses entered by the writer. Both *Mosquitoes* and *Flags in the Dust* (as *Sartoris* was called before it was cut severely for publication) test the supplemental, uncentered nature of representation. When Quentin has lost Caddy, he notices that all his past actions have gone "shadowy paradoxical . . . with the denial of the significance they should have affirmed,"[82] as if to represent the natural presence of Caddy would be the only way to restore natural significance. If the word never achieves such a condition of transparent

---

81. Joseph Gold, *William Faulkner: A Study in Humanism from Metaphor to Discourse* (Norman, Okla., 1966), p. 49.

82. William Faulkner, *The Sound and the Fury* (New York, 1929; Vintage ed.). I shall quote throughout from this edition.

representation, but instead defers, loses, and encodes the thing itself, then writing (like other forms of representation) becomes play that has meaning but not significance. Perhaps tales full of sound and fury, signifying nothing. *Mosquitoes* frames its widely ranging discussions of representation with the extreme positions of two characters, one of whom comprehends it as nothing but a substitution for the ideal, the other of whom recognizes no difference at all between the object and its representation. *Flags in the Dust,* which anticipates *The Sound and the Fury* in many respects, questions the power of language to reappropriate lost presence, explores the bonds among language, desire, and incest, and exposes the structure of writing in the deepest and most private realms of the consciousness.

iv

It is not surprising that early in his career Faulkner should use his single novel of ideas to explore the possibilities of his calling. Faulkner's second novel, *Mosquitoes* (1927), arranges nearly interminable conversations about the arts, the lives of artists, theories of representation, and the nature of language. Through its partial portraits of the artist as grotesque, *Mosquitoes* eventually anticipates Faulkner's mature aesthetic: art cannot simply represent either its subject or its creator's mind. But the novel advances by letting more traditional notions of artistic creation talk themselves out. The characters in *Mosquitoes* travesty conventional opinion, the two principal positions on representation taken implicitly by Ernest Talliaferro, who emblematizes the commonplace assumption that signs simply "defer the moment of encountering the thing itself" (as Derrida puts it), and Gordon, whose sculpting pretends to an ideal of perfect representation and self-expression.

Talliaferro is an attendant, a hanger-on, in the court of artists, though he admires their private lives more than their works. Talliaferro's comic misfortunes ostensibly derive from erotic anguish; he lusts mightily after a variety of female acquaintances but despairs of ever possessing the knowledge or courage to consummate his longings. He envies his artist friends, Gordon and Dawson Fairchild (a novelist), for example, because their devotions seem to have opened to them erotic as well as aesthetic secrets. Yet when Fairchild does consent to recommend a suitable "plot" and dialogue for a seduction scene that Talliaferro is contemplating, Talliaferro himself retreats from its execution. This seller of ladies' undergarments embodies a popular incomprehension of the importance to the artist of craft and vocation for their own sakes. To his mind, language is useful only as it balances desire and a fear of satisfaction through flirtation and insinuation. Talliaferro heaps the detritus of language—gossip, innuendo, pretentious conversation—into a stay against the animal passions that he believes they merely pacify or screen.

Talliaferro repeatedly sustains and suspends his desire by representing it. Talk makes intimacy out of intimation: "Mr. Talliaferro believed that Conversation . . . with an intellectual equal consisted of admitting as many so-called unpublishable facts as possible about oneself" (9–10). Talliaferro regrets that he never "acquired the habit of masturbation in his youth" because self-stimulation might be the most excitingly naughty secret to admit; but Talliaferro's use of words as solitary, substitutionary sex is itself a kind of masturbation. For not only does he allow words to insinuate erotic satisfaction, he also depends on them to protect him from it. In love with desire and afraid of consummation, he assiduously substitutes words for women: "Jenny danced on placidly, untroubled by Mr. Talliaferro's endless flow of soft words against her neck, hardly conscious of his hand sliding a small concentric circle at the small of her back" (130). But when Jenny threatens to engulf him in "the sweet cloudy fire of her thighs" (189), Talliaferro desperately listens for "the dry interminable incoherence of his own voice"; when that fails to protect him, he simply flees (189–190).

Worded desire both is and is not desire for Talliaferro; his behavior rests on a popular, simplistic assumption about language—that the name is at once external to the thing and also intimately related to it. Fairchild indirectly comments on Talliaferro's situation when he complains about language:

> "Well, it is a kind of sterility—Words," Fairchild admitted. "You begin to substitute words for things and deeds, like the withered cuckold husband that took the Decameron to bed with him every night, and pretty soon the thing or the deed becomes just a kind of

shadow of a certain sound you make by shaping your mouth a certain way." [210]

Talliaferro represents the word's subjugation not because he has been completely seduced by language but because he has not fully surrendered to it; that is, like the withered cuckold, he wants to take the book to bed only to remind him of the woman he cannot. The word, the image, all representation is never more sterile, never more subordinate, than when it is used as if to signify a presence that is merely unavailable. Talliaferro is a comic prefiguration of those characters in Faulkner's subsequent fiction (the more tragic Bayard Sartoris, Quentin Compson, Addie Bundren, and Joe Christmas) who insist that the thing itself is always beyond its representation. Fairchild sneers that Talliaferro's worship of the artist derives from "the illusion that art is just a valid camouflage for rutting" (71). Talliaferro's ear takes refuge in the minute difference between writing and rutting.

Talliaferro is a burlesque magnification of the common conviction that language defers, disguises, and deadens the presence of thought or emotion. The narrator, with callow sophistication, concurs about the sterility of language: "Talk, talk, talk: the utter and heartbreaking stupidity of words," and elaborates by noticing that "ideas, thoughts, become mere sounds to be bandied about until they were dead" (186). Even Fairchild, whose vocation encourages some confidence that "words brought into a happy conjunction produce something that lives" (210), nevertheless worries about "cold print. Your stuff looks so different in cold print" (211).

In the presumed gap between the object itself and the colder, extrinsic denotation for it lives Talliaferro. *Mosquitoes* derides this naiveté as fully as it modifies a companion innocence, Gordon's haughty confidence that there is no gap at all between his art and the idea it signifies. Gordon's sculpture, at least early in the novel, pretends to a full embodiment of his intention, to a transparent representation of the artist's consciousness. The sculpture that most satisfies Gordon illustrates his faith: it is "the virginal breastless torso of a girl, headless, armless, legless, in marble temporarily caught and hushed yet passionate still for escape, passionate and simple and eternal in the equivocal derisive darkness of the world"

(11). Although a few acquaintances conclude that the piece has no "objective significance," Gordon insists that it does: "'This is my feminine ideal: a virgin with no legs to leave me, no arms to hold me, no head to talk to me'" (26). Gordon's explication insists that the artifact is a self-evident representation of his conception. It also suggests that the work is the completion of its creator. Gordon is cast by the novel as a masculine ideal of sorts, quiet, passionate, erotically self-confident; perhaps his sculpture completes the person of the creator by complementing his creative masculinity. (Fairchild once refers to the "emotional bisexuality" of artists [251].) Gordon also innocently assumes that the production remains the property of the producer. The piece can neither talk to Gordon (since it has no head) nor leave him (since it has no legs), and Gordon steadfastly refuses to sell or trade it.

Gordon's sculpture invokes one other aesthetic ideal that *Mosquitoes* eventually tempers: the artifact seeks to conceal the articulation that has made it. Gordon's embodied ideal seems virginal because it shrinks from differentiating itself in the actual. It is sexless, memberless, breastless; its body has scarcely been articulated, thus it seems to deny the estrangement that representation implies. Fairchild emphasizes this in joking that the statue's virginity "will remain inviolate without your having to shut your eyes to its goings-on" (318). And Julius marks the inhuman unnaturalness of the ideal when he wonders who would buy such a statue: who "would pay out good money for a virginity he couldn't later violate, if only to assure himself it was the genuine thing"? (318). Gordon's bust seeks to be an unarticulated representation, a work of art that the artist will not lose or part from, which completes his proper self and remains fully his property.

Yet Gordon's sculpture cannot eradicate the marks of articulation, and his later mask of Mrs. Maurier reflects this condition of art, as I shall argue shortly. When Julius jokes that it is not too late to add "udders and a fig leaf" (318) to the torso, he indirectly calls attention to the articulated state of the work. To make the virgin mature is simply to *deepen* the carving already begun. Moreover, Julius's suggested touch—the fig leaf—evokes the iconography of the fallen Eve, who, with Adam, is suddenly shamed by the knowledge of sexual difference. Fairchild once describes women as "articulated genital organs" (241), reminding us that sexual difference makes our very bodies analogues for linguistic difference. (Often in Faulkner's early fiction the protagonists who suddenly recognize the state of sexual difference and separation also lament the alienation of language, and seek to evade it.) Gordon recognizes that his fully rendered "feminine ideal" has already begun to imply his absence, possesses an "objective significance" that is strictly subjective, and implicates the artist in an economy of loss.

Other characters in *Mosquitoes* suggest alternative views of artistic creation, and the two works of art devoted to Mrs. Maurier near the novel's conclusion anticipate more confidently Faulkner's subsequent experiments. Fairchild, even if he is a less than flattering portrait of Faulkner's onetime mentor, Sherwood Anderson, seems never to be gainsaid when he remarks that literature is "just words." Fairchild even suggests that life is validated by literature, rather than the reverse: "'love, youth, sorrow and hope and despair—they were nothing at all to me until I found later some need of a particular reaction to put in the mouth of some character of whom I wasn't at that time certain'" (320). Fairchild concurs with Eva Wiseman and Julius that "'subject, substance, doesn't signify in verse, that the best poetry is just words'" (248). Patricia likewise explains to her aunt that Gordon's statue need not signify anything: "'What do you want it to signify? Suppose it signified a—dog, or an ice cream soda, what difference would it make?'" (26). Julius summarizes laconically that "'the Thing is merely the symbol for the Word'" (130).

Faulkner may not fully trust the reversed grounds of language and experience, but it is crucial that such a possibility finds its voice early in the play of his ideas. These ideas do gather some legitimacy as they stimulate the closing performances of *Mosquitoes;* in doing so, they forecast a central feature of Faulkner's aesthetic. Gordon contributes one of these artifacts, a mask of Mrs. Maurier. Unlike his earlier pieces, however, the caricature of his would-be patroness possesses at once a striking "verisimilitude" and also a frustrating irrelevance. For Gordon cannot represent Mrs. Maurier's central essence in his sculpture; he can neither embody her identity nor tell her history. Rather, his art reveals only an exterior: "there was something else—something that exposed her face for the mask it was, and still more, a mask unaware" (322). His sculpture—like her identity itself—remains the trace of the unknowable. Julius attempts to supply this lack by telling a story about Mrs. Maurier's past, but his narrative falls equally short of locating a center or origin for her. Its greatest allegiance is to "the sake of the story," as Fairchild puts it when Julius demurs over a crucial point. Julius's story, though it makes an extravagantly romantic and spellbinding tale, cannot represent Mrs. Maurier coherently as even a forebear of her present self. Instead, it is a violet story of decaying Southern aristocracy, parvenu ambition, and frustrated imperial designs in a cadence and palette quite remarkably Faulknerian. Julius may discover in his tale that world of the past that "perhaps never existed anywhere" which Southerners are doomed to write about, the world that Faulkner presents in his next novel.

We have known *Sartoris* since its appearance in 1929 as the novel that first surveys Faulkner's "little postage stamp of native soil," the book that opens the Yoknapatawpha cycle and inaugurates Faulkner's mature imaginative realm. However, the publication in 1973 of the original manuscript of *Sartoris,* titled *Flags in the Dust,* has enabled us to see that his third novel not only augments Faulkner's subjects, but also continues the uneasy approach to language. In the sections restored in *Flags,* the novel broods on the coincidence of representation and loss; it tests the capacity of the word or image to reappropriate former plenitude; and it suggests how a variety of languages—memory, legend, local ritual, rites of marriage—inscribe meaning. The rites of mourning inhabit every recess of this novel, as it balances Bayard's inconsolable grief over the death of John with the dim nostalgia of Horace and Narcissa Benbow for the paradisal affection of childhood. Both sets of siblings suffer the loss of complementary wholeness, and the survivors struggle to express sorrow and to reach out for what has been lost. The space between these characters is filled with kinds of writing—Horace and Narcissa use words both to present and to prevent their incestuous urges, and Bayard Sartoris inescapably represents John's loss despite his rejection of voiced sorrow.

Like many of Faulkner's pairs of siblings, Horace and Narcissa Benbow share a passion that is loudly narcissistic and not too faintly incestuous. Their powerful affection lasts with uncommon ardor into their maturity, but World War I and their enforced separation have harried them toward adulthood:

A road along which he and Narcissa walked like two children drawn apart one from the other to opposite sides of it; strangers, yet not daring to separate and go in opposite ways . . . behind and before and about them pervading, the dark warm cave of Belle's rich discontent and the tiger-reek of it.[83]

Both of them recognize that they ought to transfer their passions to others, and it is understandable that Belle Mitchell's intrusion into their pure passion carries the ferocious "tiger-reek" of adult sexuality; Belle's sultry imminence is like "a presence, like the odor of death" (228).

Both Horace and Narcissa are attracted to mates who travesty and disfigure their true, but renounced, partners. Belle is a coarser, experienced, already married substitution for Narcissa, whose red hair and mournful piano music are unseated by Belle's flaming hair and vampish playing. Narcissa seems drawn to the silent, sullen, also once married Bayard Sartoris because he likewise contorts the image of Horace, who must be relinquished. Such exchanges are explicable in psychological terms, yet Faulkner suggests that the taboo against incest—the sanction that compels their separation and grief—functions as a *written* proscription. Virtually all of the many enforcements of the taboo in *Flags* occur while characters contemplate the authority of language. One wonders why Horace considers his running off with Belle an insult to Narcissa that resembles "an adolescent scribbling on the walls of a temple" (406).[84]

Horace and Narcissa agree to separate in a house founded on the Books of the Law. In Freud's family romance the father must enforce the taboo against incest between brother and sister, and the Benbow household is ruled by a father whose name is Will and who practices the law. Lawyer Benbow's efforts to uphold the order of culture are signaled by his destruction of an unruly flower bed on

83. William Faulkner, *Flags in the Dust* (New York, 1973; Vintage ed.). I shall quote throughout from this edition.

84. Derrida discusses how for Rousseau the sanction against possessing the mother is related to language: "Society, language, history, articulation, in a word supplementarity, are born at the same time as the prohibition of incest. That last is the hinge [*brisure*] between nature and culture" (*Of Grammatology*, p. 265). Moreover, "language is neither prohibition nor transgression, it couples the two endlessly" (p. 266).

the house's grounds—a flower bed "broken by random clumps of jonquil and narcissus" (178). Will wants to "obliterate" the narcissistic, incestuous desire that would naturally flourish between his children, and he successfully instills a reverence for the law in his son, who returns from the war to reopen his father's office. The Benbow legal practice is modest, comprised of cases that, almost too predictably, "wended their endless courses without threat of consummation" (194). All law is embodied in the law against incest, since it is the condition for culture, and that law is a pure language.

Horace becomes a lawyer "principally through a sense of duty to the family tradition, and . . . he had no particular affinity to it other than a love for printed words, for the dwelling-places of books" (184). The printed (and even the spoken) word marks the passage from nature to culture. Horace appreciates this function of the words he so esteems: Nature watches man try to "wean himself away from the rank and richly foul old mire that spawned him," away from the "petty, ignoble impulses which man has tried so vainly to conjure with words out of himself" (338). Language cannot obliterate such impulses; it only combats them.

Horace's epistles to Narcissa reflect this function of language. His initial telegram to Narcissa announcing his return proves to be a "mixed-up sort of message," "incoherent" (32), and Aunt Jenny immediately assumes that Horace has gotten himself entangled with "some war-orphan's mamma." Horace's letter reinitiates an intimacy with Narcissa that it also threatens to end. Later, when he writes to Narcissa about his continued frustration and loneliness despite his marriage to Belle, he would endanger the prohibition of incest by exposing the fact that Belle has merely been a substitute for his sister—*would* endanger it, except that his letter is "practically illegible." Horace's language necessarily dissembles: "I daresay you cannot read this as usual, or reading it, it will not mean anything to you. But you will have served your purpose anyway . . ." (398). All of Horace's writings seem to couple the prohibition and transgression of incest; he thinks about "the quiet, the intimacy the writing and the touching of it [the letter], had brought him" (403).

Horace and Narcissa contrive other, similar networks to encode their incestuous desire. They occupy the shelter of language not only as they write but also as they read, for example. Narcissa repeatedly buries her unconfronted longing for Horace in the pages of her book:

> I will be glad when Horry gets home, she thought going on.
>   She turned on her light and undressed and took her book to bed, where she again held her consciousness deliberately submerged as you hold a puppy under water until its body ceases to resist. And after a time her mind surrendered wholly to the book. [162]

Books protect the brother and sister from any but a safe "surrender." When Horace returns after an evening with Belle, Narcissa, like a betrayed wife, greets him coldly as she reads:

> [Horace] picked up another book. "I never knew you to read so much."
>   "I have more time for reading, now," she answered. [283]

As it prohibits incest, the word also advocates the sanction of marriage. Narcissa carries her reading to Bayard, as if at first to repel the threat of consummation. She deflects his sexual innuendo by reading "swiftly, as though she were crouching behind the screen of words her voice raised between them" (272). At first, the goal of such reading is always to put Bayard's passion to sleep. Gradually, however, her deadly performances are replaced by his violently alive stories; the shift prepares for their sexual intimacy and for Narcissa's forfeiture of Horace. Narcissa glosses her theory of reading in her comments to Horace about Shakespeare. As one who uses words as a screen, Narcissa criticizes Shakespeare for a lack of "reticence": "'Shakespeare doesn't have any secrets. He tells everything'" (185). Narcissa identifies the seductiveness of language with its power to conceal, never quite realizing that language has been made erotic because it presents the incest it prohibits.

Horace's garbled messages and innuendo declare his passion as they defer the satisfaction of his desire. I have argued that Horace's devotion to language is indistinguishable from his respect for the prohibition of incest and that the double dealing of his words reflects central properties of the word in general. We are in a better position to see how the approach to language is like the approach to women, as the 1933 preface puts it. Byron Snopes's epistolary courtship of Narcissa provides an appropriate summary of the complexities of writing considered by *Flags in the Dust*.

Byron is the main Snopes in the novel that introduced the Snopeses in Faulkner's fiction. Like all Snopeses, Byron is a grotesque, a parodic exaggeration.[85] In *Flags in the Dust* Byron Snopes exploits the dilemmas of language and in doing so magnifies and defines them more clearly. Byron thirsts hopelessly for Narcissa Benbow, whose beauty and standing make her unattainable. Discovering that writing obscene letters to her approximates intimacy, Bryon hires an amanuensis, young Virgil Beard, to transcribe his dictated cycle of love letters. Byron's writing declares that it is a substitute for physical intimacy, that the written word both traverses and protects the distance between sender and receiver: " 'I could touch you you would not know it Every day. But I can not I must pore out on paper must talk . . .' " (286). In their separation, writing reconstitutes forms of the correspondents' presence; Byron's remarks about Narcissa's unavailability suggest that she is present as a trace or memory in his text. Each letter produces a remembered Narcissa, and each glimpse of his letters in Narcissa's purse convinces Byron that she remembers their writer: " 'I thought once I would try to forget you. But I cannot forget you because you cannot forget me. I saw my letter in your hand satchel today' " (117). As we have seen, writing arises to supplement separation by producing representations of the writer and the receiver, who are also the objects of these letters. Inscriptions of loss and acts of memory, Byron's letters also serve to defer his desire. Byron wants Narcissa herself, but his writing, like all writing, performs as if to postpone that gratification which is impossible. Byron threatens the inconceivable: " 'Some day we will both know together when you got used to it' " (117).

Though it represents both the writer and his beloved, Byron's writing obsesses him precisely because representation cannot make absence a presence. The trace of the writer is the self both represented and departed. The letter has no natural connection to its author or sender; it is dead to its origin. When Byron tries to disguise the letters' purpose from Virgil, he puts them into a

85. Warren Beck, *Man in Motion: Faulkner's Trilogy* (Madison, Wis., 1963), p. 139.

"code." Part of the code requires a false superscription and a false signature, which Byron later eliminates before mailing. However, the marks on the page could never reveal the full presence of the sender anyhow: Narcissa judges that the letter "bore writing in a frank, open script that at first glance divulged no individuality whatever; a hand youthful yet at the same time so blandly and neatly unsecretive that presently you speculated a little" (69). She is right about the hand, but cannot learn anything about Byron's person by analyzing Virgil's handwriting. The dilemma reminds us that writing always screens and secrets its writer; Virgil is the equivalent of this function. As Byron writes, he absents himself; fevered with "thwarted desire and furious impotent rage" (292), Byron "pores" himself into his bookkeeping. The pure lines of figures on the page somehow quench him: "It was a sort of stupor, and he wrote on and on" (293). And finally the hands that write obscene letters appear even to the writer as alien, "his idle hands on the desk before him as though they were not his hands" (256–257). This is a moment in which Byron approaches the writer's realization that he has encoded himself in the text to the point of losing self-presence.

Virgil's role in Byron's writing is to personify the dangers of mediation. According to simpler views of writing, the letter establishes a genuine intimacy between reader and writer, and, on another level, the discourse transparently presents its signified meaning. Virgil troubles both of these assumptions. Byron's attempt to disguise personal messages with an impersonal frame does not fully fool his secretary; Virgil wants the airgun promised to him as payment, and he threatens Byron with the power of recall: " 'I remember ever' one of them letters. I bet I could sit down and write 'em all again' " (118). Like Freud's mystic writing pad,[86] Virgil's memory retains the texts of earlier impressions. The sheer permanence of language is a danger, and later, when Narcissa's letters are stolen, she worries that she has become liable to "a stranger casually

86. Derrida discusses Freud's search for a metaphor for the structure of the psychical apparatus; the "magic" writing pad, a child's toy, suggests to Freud an appropriate embodiment of the psyche's paradoxical abilities both to accept new impressions and also to retain the traces of former impressions. (See "Freud and the Scene of Writing," in *Writing and Difference,* trans. Alan Bass [Chicago, 1978].) Virgil objectifies the mechanism by which Byron both remembers and erases his passion.

raising a stray bit of paper from the ground" and learning of her 'dishonor.'[87] Virgil also represents language's forfeited privacy. Letters may always be misdirected, or lost (as Byron claims about the order for Virgil's airgun), or stolen.

For a while Byron's one-way messages satisfy him, but Narcissa's failure to write back constitutes a breakdown of the economy. Were letters to be exchanged, the sexual travesty would be complete; each could view the other anonymously and indistinctly through the veil of words (as Byron peeps at Narcissa undressing). Narcissa seems to keep the letters for the same reason Byron sends them, moreover, since she pleasures in the erotic secrets of language. But Byron's fever demands treatment, and he exposes the supplemental nature of his language even when he violates its economy. Having warned Narcissa to write—"You better answer soon I am a desprate man" (286)—Byron finally breaks into her bedroom in her absence. His trespass inaugurates a significant sequence in Byron's career because his 'explosion' marks his despair at a life of writing. Byron launches himself onto Narcissa's bed, "his head buried in the pillows, writhing and making smothered, animal-like moanings" (300). He steals the packet of letters, leaves another, but stands for a moment with "his face crushed against one of Narcissa's undergarments"; the image suggests the exteriority of letters—intimate apparel, but apparel nonetheless. Immediately on fleeing, Byron rouses his girlfriend, Minnie Sue. She becomes, as Byron assaults her, a body substituted for Narcissa's: "soon she held him helpless while he sprawled with his face against her throat, babbling a name not hers" (305). Minnie Sue resists Byron's efforts to turn her into another word for Narcissa, and his limping exit from the novel steps off the frustration that language can never present the thing itself.

87. Byron's mad 'courtship' of Narcissa is consummated when the letters he steals and later discards are found by a federal agent on his tracks ("There Was a Queen," in *Collected Stories of William Faulkner* [New York, 1934, 1950]). The agent negotiates their return to Narcissa in exchange for her sexual favors. Narcissa recalls the fragmentation of herself as a written subject, her lost sense of property and propriety:

"'So they were out in the world. They were somewhere. I was crazy for a while. I thought of people, men, reading them, seeing not only my name on them but the marks of my eyes where I had read them again and again. I was wild. When Bayard and I were on our honeymoon, I was wild. I couldn't even think about him alone. It was like I was having to sleep with all the men in the world at the same time.'" [739–740]

Language represents what it cannot present; this condition is what draws together incest and mourning in *Flags,* for the novel's other major plot traces Bayard Sartoris' efforts to arbitrate loss and replacement. Bayard's desperate gambits illustrate two preoccupations that survive into Faulkner's subsequent fiction: his refusal to mourn John's death by enemy fire in the war reflects his intuition that any expression of grief or memory only augments loss; and Bayard's renunciations of mourning themselves become inscriptions of John's ineradicable absence.

The younger Bayard suffers his brother John's death as a sensible diminishment of his own self-presence. Their twinship appears as an original unity that is presented in the novel only as already lost. Returned from the war that has taken his brother's life, Bayard "was thinking of his dead brother; the spirit of their violent complementing days lay like a dust everywhere in the room" (49). John's death exaggerates the inevitable separation of siblings; the innocence of childhood is defined by their having been scarcely differentiated—sharing a single bed as complements. When John plunges from his burning airplane, he reenacts the primal fall into difference and death. Bayard will not talk about his loss, however, because he knows that the word can represent his brother only as past. His grief issues in inarticulate "groaning" (49), and he desperately destroys mementos of John—a "coat and the Bible and the trophy and the photograph" (240)—because such traces represent loss rather than retrieve presence. To preserve such memorabilia would be to accept loss and to choose condolence.

When Bayard does break his silence it is to show that the processes of displacement and forgetfulness have already invaded the shrine of his memory. He uses the story of John's death curiously as a kind of seduction narrative in his overtures to Narcissa. This second wife, like the first, occupies the place of John in a bed once shared fraternally. Returning to his room, he notices that his first wife's memory is only a passage to John's, "the spirit of their violent complementing days ... obliterating the scent of that other presence" (49). And the martial imagery that describes Bayard's assaults on Narcissa testifies to his search for the dead twin soldier: "And yet, despite her armed sentinels, he still crashed with that hot violence of his through the bastions and thundered at the very inmost citadel of her being" (158–159). Such behavior coincides with Bayard's efforts to replicate the very circumstances of his brother's fatal crash; as he pilots his sedan, "the car slid on with a steady leashed muttering like waking thunderous wings" (156). His death in an aerial test crash only culminates a career composed of stunts designed to undo the past by repeating it. Bayard's silent concentration on his brother's absence betrays itself as a kind of psychical writing despite itself; his gestures coarsely but graphically inscribe his grief.

In his remarks about *Flags in the Dust,* Faulkner, too, points to the writer's acceptance, even inauguration, of loss when he begins to write. He remembers the work as an effort of commemoration, but in the following passage we may notice that the preparation to write makes the writer think about the world that he is "already preparing to lose and regret," and that writing does not reappropriate, recover, re-present, or even preserve that already lost world—it merely produces its trace. The "kernel" defers to the "skeleton":

> . . . nothing served but that I try by main strength to recreate between the covers of a book the world as I was already preparing to lose and regret, feeling, with the morbidity of the young, that I was not only on the verge of decrepitude, but that growing old was to be an experience peculiar to myself alone out of all the teeming world, and desiring, if not the capture of that world and the feeling of it as you'd preserve a kernel or a leaf to indicate the lost forest, at least to keep the evocative skeleton of the dessicated [sic] leaf.[88]

Bayard's dream that enshrining the departed in one's memory may restore its presence and arrest the fading of grief lingers in Faulkner's imagination. Bayard anticipates roughly the elegant, terrible, unvoiced lamentation of Quentin Compson; like his predecessor, Quentin refuses to yield his loss to the repetition and estrangement of the word, yet his memory, too, is dismantled as already a writing of loss, a sequence of images that encode Caddy as ever vanishing. For all the agonies of its economy of losses, language nevertheless graces its user; silence, on the other hand, imprisons and suffocates.

Light in August nearly allegorizes this dilemma as it presents Joe Christmas' irremediable separation from his origin, a separation

88. Joseph Blotner, *Faulkner: A Biography* (New York, 1974), pp. 531–532.

that many of Faulkner's characters suffer but which some overcome in the strength of self-composition. Christmas, however, can scarcely speak; the dietician's accusation silences him, and he is soon tyrannized by McEachern's goliath of a Bible. McEachern wishes to teach Joe to speak in words not his own, but the child prefers defiant dumbness. Though he cannot provide words for himself—we think of him pawing through cheap magazines, foraging through someone else's plots—Christmas nevertheless is destined to receive a mark of articulation. He is caught throughout the novel between blackness and whiteness; his "parchment colored face" invites a stroke of definition. The conclusion of *Light in August* presents Christmas' fatal failure to mark, to author himself. It is left to his community to blacken his face as it executes him.

Representation compromises the presence of its object, and Faulkner repeatedly figures this condition in the gesture of loss that initiates his subsequent novels. The openings of Faulkner's novels frequently demarcate sites of loss. The narratives often need to register an absence in order to get under way; it is striking to consider the number of Faulkner's works that center on funerals or recent deaths. *Soldiers' Pay* attends to Margaret Powers' grief over her dead soldier husband and to the Reverend Mahon's pathetic receipt of his blinded, dumb son, Donald. A similar disturbance sets off *Flags in the Dust,* since we learn that Bayard Sartoris has come home to Jefferson after the war only to discover that he cannot control his grief over his dead brother and wife. Obviously, *The Sound and the Fury* meditates on many kinds of loss ("the grief of bereavement"),[89] and Faulkner referred to it as a novel about the funeral of the grandmother.[90] *Sanctuary,* which may have been composed before *The Sound and the Fury* but rewritten and published after it, also begins with steps of recovery: Horace seeks his stepdaughter Belle and in doing so prefigures Temple Drake's later lamentation for her (nearly) lost innocence. From the sawing for Addie's coffin in *As I Lay Dying,* through Lena Grove's setting out after her perfidious lover in *Light in August,* in Rosa's first words of bereavement for Sutpen, and on into *Go Down, Moses,* which was, Faulkner explained, about a black man's "funeral,"[91] the first

89. Introduction (*MQ*), p. 413.
90. Meriwether and Millgate, eds., *Lion in the Garden,* p. 146.
91. Ibid., p. 48.

gesture of Faulkner's narrative is commonly to measure a loss, to inscribe absence. This is an important term in Faulkner's "grammar of narrative." Tzvetan Todorov, in using that phrase, suggests that the "minimal complete plot consists in the passage from one equilibrium to another. An 'ideal' narrative begins with a stable situation which is disturbed by some power or force."[92] The disequilibrium is then rectified by a force in the opposite direction, establishing the resting point for the conclusion. But Faulkner's novels, in contrast, start with a disequilibrium already established, as if they are already slanting away from the original moment of self-present rest. The syntax of Faulkner's narrative doubles the condition of language, since whatever is articulated is already lost, because already written.

To speak is to long. Derrida associates all imagination with desire: "If we desire beyond our power of satisfaction, the origin of that surplus and of that difference is named imagination."[93] Thus desire for what is withheld is scarcely distinguishable from sorrow over what has been lost: imagination is the gap between satisfaction and the sought object. Faulkner also suggests this equivalence of sorrow and desire, making Ernest Talliaferro in *Mosquitoes,* for example, prey to "a troubling unhappy desire like an old sorrow," and having Narcissa Benbow in *Flags in the Dust* muse about her love for Bayard: "Lost, lost; yet never to have had it at all."[94] Surely the most moving example of the twinship of desire and sorrow is Quentin Compson's longing to recover Caddy in all her innocence, to reappropriate, if only in the hell of memory, their lost intimacy. A profound aspect of language's destructiveness is that it flourishes amid the absences we have been identifying. Many of Faulkner's early protagonists seek to evade the explosiveness of language; they are inconsolable in grief because they demand the restitution of presence. Margaret Powers wants a substitute to replace her lost husband; Bayard helplessly auditions versions of his brother John—his wife, then Narcissa—until he is reduced simply to repeating John's crash; Quentin will not believe that his recollection of

92. Tzvetan Todorov, *The Poetics of Prose,* trans. Richard Howard (Ithaca, 1977), p. 111; first published as *La Poétique de la prose* (Paris: Editions du Seuil, 1971).
93. Derrida, *Of Grammatology,* p. 185.
94. *Mosquitoes,* p. 31, and *Flags in the Dust,* p. 279.

Caddy and childhood are already and always condemned by the deathliness of images, that memory produces traces that defer recovery and hence substitute difference. Faulkner's early meditation on language discovers that its supplementariness governs all modes of representation—the memory, 'living consciousness' and perception, as well as speaking and writing. Quentin's agony comes to recognize that even memory re-presents, that memory is "again," which is sadder than "was"; and he submits to the horror that memory is already voiced. Even "the voice that breathed o'er Eden" measures distance: "*Only she was running already when I heard it*" (*The Sound and the Fury,* p. 100).

The subsequent chapters pursue these topics through detailed readings of four major novels. *The Sound and the Fury* persistently undermines distinctions among silence, speech, perception, and memory; each of the first three sections reveals a consciousness that is structured by writing (I use that term in Derrida's widest sense). The dream of reappropriating the past or of incarnating the author's ideal—synonymous desires figured by Caddy at two levels of the book—becomes a deathly dream, one that would cost the very life of writing. Benjy's topographic memory, the poetry of Quentin's commemorative perception, and Jason's elaborate financial edifice all may be seen as kinds of inscription. That language always escapes the simple dichotomy of presence and absence is a principle that also governs *Absalom, Absalom!* Each narrator embodies (invents, discovers) an identity in the words of the story he or she tells, and each telling is both true and false to the absent center—Sutpen's 'real' story. Sutpen is analogous to Derrida's trace, a product of language whose absence is encased in the movement of narrative's difference, and whose presence is endlessly deferred by it as well. *Absalom* is governed by a paradox central to writers who have apprehended the decentering of structure: the nostalgia for presence, authority, the transcendental signified defines itself in opposition to the exhilaration of infinite interpretation. We may account both for the shades of sorrow and despair among the narrators of Sutpen's story (and for Sutpen's own furious puzzlement) and for the moments of gleeful, intoxicating invention. A different formulation of this paradox contributes to the dramatic conflict of Flem Snopes and Ratliff in *The Hamlet,* and I hope to show that the novel contemplates Flem as a figure of the deathliness of writing.

Deathliness is locked in perpetual struggle with the economies of play in the community, but such play—and its allegedly natural morality—is actually predicated on the very lack of authority that permits Flem's brutal assertion. In *Go Down, Moses,* where the mood and rites of nostalgia are given their most stunning pageant in Faulkner's fiction, we may also notice impulses to mark, to inscribe meaning. The various tellings of the better past, like the endless rounds of hunting, attain power because they are structured as writing: they represent what can appear in nothing but words, recognizing their difference from any origin, and acknowledging the perpetuity only of deferment.

Though the necessity for focus risks the implication, my argument is not that Faulkner's fiction is exclusively about writing, or that writing can be used simply as a metaphor to describe any imaginative structure, or that the novels have no subjects. But the aspects of language pursued in Derrida's critique of metaphysical assumption do appear regularly in Faulkner, and to appreciate his modernity is to give those aspects their play. So many convincing studies of Faulkner's morality, theology, sexuality, sociology, and philosophy have appeared that we are in no danger of depersonalizing the author. We might also, however, attend to Faulkner's consuming devotion to matters of technique, language, and pure craft, and we ought to heed his own view that idea is just another unit in the syntax of narrative play: "A message is one of [the author's] tools, just like the rhetoric, just like the punctuation."[95] Of course, the artist does not create simply "to show your versatility with your tools" but to "tell about people"; I want to suggest that one thing Faulkner's novels tell us is that our life is our language, and that language means more than it can say.

95. Gwynn and Blotner, eds., *Faulkner in the University,* p. 239.

CHAPTER 2

The Discovery of Loss in
The Sound and the Fury

i

Though Faulkner told several versions of the genesis of *The Sound and the Fury,* in nearly all of them he explained Benjy as less a character than a way of seeing grief. Faulkner remarked to Jean Stein:

> You can't feel anything for Benjy because he doesn't feel anything. He was a prologue. . . . He serves his purpose and is gone. . . . He recognizes tenderness and love though he could not have named them, and it was the threat to tenderness and love that caused him to bellow when he felt the change in Caddy. He no longer had Caddy; being an idiot he was not even aware that Caddy was missing. He knew only that something was wrong, which left a vacuum in which he grieved. He tried to fill that vacuum.[1]

In Nagano, Faulkner identified Benjy with "the idea of the blind, self-centeredness of innocence, typified by children, if one of those children had been truly innocent, that is, an idiot."[2] The predicament of loss and articulation also governs Faulkner's reading of the dilemmas of the other Compson brothers and the narrator in section 4.[3] Beginning with Benjy's, each section broods on how to "fill that vacuum." Can memory or speech successfully reappropriate

1. Jean Stein, "William Faulkner," *Paris Review,* 4 (Spring 1956), as reprinted in *Writers at Work,* ed. Malcolm Cowley (New York: Viking, 1958), p. 131.
2. James B. Meriwether and Michael Millgate, eds., *Lion in the Garden: Interviews with William Faulkner, 1926–1962* (New York, 1968), p. 146.
3. Ibid., pp. 146–147.

the natural presence of Caddy, whose absence initiates the discourse? To recover Caddy would be to restore full natural significance to the world. Each brother denies, at the same time that his section reveals, that memory is supplementary, like a kind of writing. Benjy and Quentin are doomed to reappropriate nothing except Caddy as already disappearing; she is, in their sections, already the trace that is an origin, and her absolute plenitude can never be evoked in their minds. A permutation of this pattern carries us into Jason's section, for he has apparently satisfied himself with an elaborate financial compensation for the inaccessibility of Caddy. Yet his incessant frustration feeds on the necessary failure of the supplement to recover the thing itself. The unresolvable contradictions of each brother's vision ripen in the last section into the rich paradoxes of Faulkner's mature fiction. The novel, as it approaches its cessation, wins the recognition that articulation can never "fill the vacuum," but only create within it; that it can never successfully convert the original image of Caddy's muddy drawers suspended in the tree into a finished story; and that it may luxuriate precisely in the endlessness of the task.

Benjy is the necessary prologue because his agony is literally the dumbshow of the novel's crises. If his idiocy is the formal arresting of childhood, it is because the infant-man registers loss purely, manipulates the simplest expressions of that loss grotesquely, can never know the more consoling, more dangerous powers of speech, and is locked in a section that mirrors rhetorically—in its simple style and narrative voicelessness—his impotence to grieve well.

The Sound and the Fury opens to a disequilibrium already accomplished.[4] The double movement of the opening passages is Luster's "hunting" for his lost quarter and Benjy's incomprehending search for something that the word "caddie" reminds him of.[5] As we subsequently learn, of course, his sister's disappearance eighteen

---

4. Tzvetan Todorov, "The Grammar of Narrative," in *The Poetics of Prose,* trans. Richard Howard (Ithaca: Cornell University Press, 1977). Todorov argues that an " 'ideal' narrative begins with a stable situation which is disturbed by some power or force" (p. 111). *The Sound and the Fury*, like many of Faulkner's novels, does not begin with such repose.

5. For a contrary view, see Olga Vickery, *The Novels of William Faulkner* (Baton Rouge, 1959). Vickery argues that Benjy makes himself immune to loss by creating a changeless order that transcends time: ". . . Benjy is saved by being outside time" (p. 36).

years earlier has tipped the child into the fallen world of loss, memory, time, and grief. In the interval, Benjy remains perfectly arrested on this threshold, surrounded by signs of Caddy's absence. According to Bergson, the primary activity of the mind as it encounters pure duration (which "might well be nothing but a succession of qualitative changes . . . pure heterogeneity)[6] is to spatialize. The mind converts time into space as it conceptualizes, imposes images, and finally "solidif[ies] our impressions in order to express them in language."[7] Benjy's pertinence to Faulkner's deep exploration of the nature of articulation in *The Sound and the Fury* begins with this impulse to translate raw change into a kind of topo[s]graphic stability.

One consequence of this activity is that the Compson grounds become a simple analogue for the memory. Every site of Benjy's domain opens immediate access to all of the moments that have ever occurred there: to duck through the "broken place" in the fence with Luster in 1928 is to emerge with Caddy two decades earlier (2–3). The garden gate, the fence along the pasture, the "graveyard" on the lawn, and so on, all have their special associations. Physical location must serve in the mind of this truly innocent child for the topos of an idea, image, or word. Once Caddy has vanished, Benjy's constrained memory cannot sufficiently recall her (the Appendix affirms that he "could not remember his sister but only the loss of her" [423]); the formal equivalent of his bondage to tangible reminders of his sister is his physical confinement (" 'Yes sir.' Versh said. 'We dont never let him get off the place' "[4]).

Discussion of *The Sound and the Fury* has well established that Benjy primitively stabilizes his world by hoarding relics of Caddy after she leaves.[8] Olga Vickery refers to the process of "mechanical identification" that designates the slipper, the spot where the mirror once hung, the smell of trees, the jimson weed in the bottle, and so on as things whose presence partially fills the void left by Caddy.[9]

6. Henri Bergson, *Time and Free Will,* trans. F. L. Pogson (New York, 1960; first published 1910), p. 104.

7. Ibid., p. 130. I also distinguish my position from that of Donald M. Kartiganer ("*The Sound and the Fury* and Faulkner's Quest for Form," *ELH,* 37 [December 1970], 613–639), who views Benjy as being preintellectual.

8. Richard Chase, *The American Novel and Its Tradition* (Garden City, N.Y., 1957), p. 226.

9. Vickery, *Novels of William Faulkner,* p. 34.

The Play of Faulkner's Language

Benjy's spatialization of loss succeeds in his strictly sensual realm; he needs objects to see and to fondle, objects that above all must be *there*. Luster can always torment him by duplicating the process of dispossession: when he hides Benjy's flowers "they went away. I began to cry.... The flowers came back.... 'Hush.' Luster said. 'Here they is. Look. It's fixed back just like it was at first. Hush, now'" (66–67). Of course, Benjy's collection of sacred relics has evident symbolic logic for the reader; for example, the mirror, which Benjy also senses is some kind of door, may suggest the narcissistic essence of sibling love and incest;[10] or the jimson weed may be appropriate because of its phallic associations.[11] But Benjy's selection of certain objects also has an internal logic that deserves attention because it enriches the crisis of articulation that Benjy himself experiences and initiates for the novel.

One of the more moving portions of Derrida's *Of Grammatology* rehearses a moment in Rousseau's *Essay* that imagines the intrusion of gesture into the immediacy of love. Rousseau believes that love invents the gesture of drawing: "How she could say things to her beloved, who traced his shadow with such pleasure! What sounds might she use to render this movement of the magic wand"?[12] The drawing and speaking constitute primal articulation—an effort to signify *within* the moment of full pleasure and presence. Derrida systematically uncovers Rousseau's own confession of the impossibility of such simultaneity, and yet, for the moment, he recapitulates Rousseau with tenderness:

> The movement of the magic wand that traces with so much pleasure does not fall outside of the body. Unlike the spoken or written sign, it does not cut itself off from the desiring body of the person who traces or from the immediately perceived image of the other. It is of course still an image which is traced at the tip of the wand, but an image that is not completely separated from the person it represents; what the drawing draws is almost present in person in his *shadow*. The dis-

10. John T. Irwin, *Doubling & Incest/Repetition & Revenge: A Speculative Reading of Faulkner* (Baltimore, 1975), p. 42.

11. André Bleikasten, *The Most Splendid Failure: Faulkner's "The Sound and the Fury"* (Bloomington: Indiana University Press, 1976), p. 85.

12. Jacques Derrida, *Of Grammatology*, trans. Gayatri C. Spivak (Baltimore, 1974, p. 234; first published as *De la grammatologie* (Paris: Editions de Minuit, 1967).

tance from the shadow or from the wand is almost nothing. She who traces, holding, handling, now the wand, is very close to touching what is very close to being the other *itself,* close by a minute difference; that small difference—visibility, spacing, death—is undoubtedly the origin of the sign and the breaking of immediacy.[13]

Benjy's heart fixes on some of the objects in his collection precisely because they are just barely separated from the body of the beloved. The "minute difference," the tiniest of gaps, separates Caddy from her slipper. What she has worn has been quite nearly her body itself, and now Benjy seizes the article that encased an extremity, as if detaching the garment from the foot constitutes the very passage from the other itself to that which "is very close to being the other itself." A similar impulse accounts for Benjy's infatuation with firelight. From the standpoint of the novel's thematics, of course, Caddy's association with fire in Benjy's naive memory connotes her passion and affection; but Benjy himself notes that when Caddy sat before the hearth, her "hair was like fire, and little points of fire were in her eyes" (88). Benjy unthinkingly preserves the substance that has helped him to describe (or draw) her body for him. In her absence, Caddy also 'becomes' the fragrance of trees; such an association extends the principle of selection at work here, for an odor is both part of and already minutely different from the body itself. It seems to linger and hover between absolute presence and absence. Benjy remembers the mirror (which by 1928 has faded into a dark spot on the wall) for similar reasons. The figures of childhood pass into a not quite present, not quite absent state when they appear in the mirror: "we could see Caddy fighting in the mirror and Father put me down and went into the mirror and fought too. . . . Father brought Caddy to the fire. They were all out of the mirror" (79). The mirror is the spot where "visibility, spacing, death" signify the "breaking of immediacy."

Benjy, who has barely emerged into time, responds to loss with the barest of articulations. And yet the time "which shadows every mans brow even Benjy's" (as Mr. Compson later puts it) presents dead spaces in the very core of Benjy's relics. The objects can neither substitute fully for Caddy nor reappropriate her presence;

13. Ibid., p. 234.

they derive meaning only as they embody Caddy as already dying from the plenitude of full presence. The firelight 'contains' Caddy, but when Benjy reaches into it to regain her, he burns his hand in its alien, destructive difference. Similarly, Benjy associates the fragrance of trees contradictorily—both with Caddy's virginal innocence and with the onset of her sexual betrayal. That she always "smelled like trees" makes the paradox of natural innocence and natural maturation sensible to Benjy's nostrils; at the heart of his memory of her full presence is already the trace of her disappearance. And when Caddy steps into the mirror she does so to fight—to flee the mirror herself or to drive another out of it. Derrida's discussion of the trace at the origin and of the inescapable deathliness of the supplement refreshes our conception of how Benjy's fumbling attempts to neutralize grief initiate the crisis of articulation that informs the novel.

Once Benjy commits himself to filling the vacuum, in fact, he has fully ceded Caddy to the difference of signs. Accordingly, some of his mementoes become much more arbitrary designates of loss: the jimson weed, its bottle, and the narcissus are—for all the symbolic properties apparent to us—unmotivated signs for Benjy. They have no intrinsic meaning. Curiously, this arbitrary substitution of one presence for a first, more natural presence stands at the implicit center of *The Sound and the Fury*. It is a commonplace in psychological discussions of the novel to identify Mrs. Compson's coldness and inaccessibility as the root of the brothers' diseased obsession with their sister, who accepts the mantle of surrogate maternity. But we might also consider Mrs. Compson herself as a shadow of whatever the absolute plenitude would have been. For Derrida, such a site cannot exist, for as soon as it has been signified it is no longer: at the absolute origin one finds only the architrace. To the extent that *The Sound and the Fury* is about the relationship between the felt loss of plenitude and the necessity to substitute, we might describe Caddy's role in the novel as the architrace. She is herself, that is, a supplement. For Derrida's Rousseau, "presence, always natural, which for Rousseau more than for others means maternal, *ought to be* self-sufficient."[14] Therefore, Rousseau can recognize supplementarity only as dangerous. Likewise, Caddy re-

14. Ibid., p. 145.

places her mother (who fails to embody maternal fullness) and becomes the dangerous supplement, the necessary addition to what should have been self-sufficient. Benjy, like his brothers, sought his mother but found his sister. After Mrs. Compson pities her "poor baby" idiot son, Caddy objects: " 'You're not a poor baby. Are you. You've got your Caddy' " (8). The supplement's wealth enriches the dispossessed child.[15]

The articulated shapes of loss, those sites and objects that embody the "visibility, spacing, death" that Derrida finds at the 'origin' of the sign, provide tenuous peace for Benjy. They are variations of the "smooth, bright shapes" (92) that lull Benjy into the relative calm of having forgotten Caddy and remembering only her loss, as the passage I quoted earlier from the Appendix puts it. The configuration of loss, indeed, governs virtually every detail of Benjy's picturing of the past. The scenes that populate his memory emerge only because they present a Caddy who is already dying to Benjy. André Bleikasten correctly notices that "most scenes in which [Benjy] is directly implicated are scenes of dispossession" and that death permeates the episodes that he remembers.[16] But Benjy also blindly struggles with a paradox of memory: the Caddy he wishes to remember can be recalled only when her absence is absolute. Memory, speech, and desire depend on the unavailability of their object. Remarkably, Benjy's memories of Caddy embody the paradox since they cannot represent her except as beginning to disappear. Her first appearance in his section occurs at the point of a breach: crawling through the fence's broken place, Caddy guides their exit from the grounds. Moreover, she has been sent by Uncle Maury to deliver instructions for his assignation with a neighbor; thus even in childhood she is the agent of sexual license and treachery, and ultimately she will suffer exile from the garden. (And, in bearing a written message, she signals the burden she accepts throughout the novel as a word-laden escapee.) The conflation of Damuddy's funeral, Caddy's muddying, the wedding, and Mr. Compson's funeral confirms the fact that Caddy can be remembered only as already contaminated by the process of change

15. Caddy announces her role as a substitute for her mother: " 'Mother's not coming in tonight,' [Caddy] said. 'So we still have to mind me' " (*The Sound and the Fury*, p. 91).
16. Bleikasten, *Most Splendid Failure*, pp. 75, 84.

and impending absence. So far as I can tell, Benjy never remembers a moment of untroubled, blissful intimacy with Caddy. When he hugs her it is mutely to protest her infidelities; when she cradles him in bed, he can register only that first she has stayed away or that she keeps her bathrobe on for the first time. The discourse of Benjy's memory conforms to Derrida's definition of the supplement as that which both recognizes its difference and defers the (impossible) reappropriation of presence. Benjy's rudimentary version of these difficulties opens the way to Faulkner's deepest commitment to renouncing the illusion of natural presence and accepting the ecstasy of writing.

Benjy is a grotesque born of an experiment. The true innocence of this child resides—as Faulkner suggested in the comments I quoted at the beginning of the chapter—in his inability to name his grief. Benjy can produce sound but cannot mark it; moaning and bellowing place him eternally on the threshold of speech. The vision of loss without the power of utterance is the opening cut of the novel.[17] Caddy summarizes succinctly as the hands of dispossession encircle her:

> "No, no," Caddy said. "No. No."
> "He can't talk." Charlie said. "Caddy."
> "Are you crazy." Caddy said. She began to breathe fast. "He can see. Dont." [57]

The pulse of Benjy's section is disturbance and placation. Every loss that he suffers—whether it is Caddy disappearing into marriage or merely his flower being snatched away by Luster—must be met with some effort to "fix [it] back again just like it was at first." Benjy's mute arrangement of relics and his dumbshow of protest whenever Caddy threatened to leave in childhood suggest the nature of his innocent articulation. That he cannot actually "talk" does not exclude him from primitive efforts of speech, however. When Caddy applies her perfume, Benjy moans at her betrayal ("So that was it. And you were trying to tell Caddy and you couldn't tell her" [51]). When he passes the gate and assaults the Burgess girl, he is reaching out to repossess Caddy. Long after Caddy's schooldays, three years after her marriage, Benjy faithfully awaits his sister's

17. Kartiganer (see note 7 above) discusses the private visions of the 'narrators.'

return from absence. The little girl who comes into view is momentarily given significance in Benjy's silent speech:

> They came on. I opened the gate and they stopped, turning. I was trying to say, and I caught her, trying to say, and she screamed and I was trying to say and trying and the bright shapes began to stop and I tried to get out.   [64]

The conflation of Benjy's "trying to say" and his sexual assault on the Burgess girl leads us back to the connection between desire and speech.[18] Benjy's verbal and sexual impotences keep him from intercourses that would more nearly figure reunion with Caddy. Benjy's assault and punitive castration epitomize his imprisonment in the infancy of the imagination. His clutching at the little girl and his howls of dispossession are both clumsy burlesques of the other brothers' (and the whole novel's) attempts to recover and relate, to touch and to tell. Quentin likewise finds himself powerless to engage either some other female or the remembered past so as to transform and replace Caddy. Faulkner, as I shall discuss shortly, thoroughly grasps both the accomplishments and dangers of the word as the novel unfolds the crisis of articulation. As for Benjy, the time that captures Caddy and creates his sense of loss cannot be mastered by his brute voice: "I could still hear the clock between my voice" (72).

To the extent that criticism of *The Sound and the Fury* has been willing to recognize 'authorial' interests in each of the sections, it has suggested that the Compson brothers' and Dilsey's difficulties in dealing with loss reflect the novelist's familiar frustrations with language. Bleikasten, for example, is surely right in reading Benjy's "trying to say" as a motto for the troubled efforts of the novel to articulate its own meaning.[19] I wish to argue, however, that a conflicting urgency fills out what is for Faulkner a paradox of the word: the inability of language fully to embody the absolute, the lost origin, becomes the happy resource of the prolonged life of speech. I think that this argument might expose areas of contact

18. Bleikasten suggests that writing is associated with sex and death: Benjy's "trying to say" through the act of attempted rape becomes a motto for the novel's status as a "transnarcissistic" object (*Most Splendid Failure,* pp. 83–84).

19. Bleikasten (ibid.) applies the phrase to the troubled efforts of all four narrators to tell their stories.

between Faulkner and the protagonists of *The Sound and the Fury* that have not been sufficiently thought about. For example, Benjy's inescapable muteness confers a kind of tranquillity and order that a novelist might dream about and then forswear in order to write.

Despite the prevailing mood of barely eased agony in the first section, Benjy has managed to stabilize his world. His terrible muteness—although it prevents a nameable knowledge of his loss—paradoxically blesses Benjy with serenity. Precisely because he has forgotten Caddy and can remember only her loss, the pitiful collection of relics can placate him. As an individual, Caddy has disappeared into the signs that Benjy substitutes for her. By clutching to himself these things that are just barely different from Caddy herself, Benjy arrests processive dispossession: Caddy is never closer to returning in our eyes, but she is never any farther away in Benjy's. There are two aspects to Benjy's 'successful' silence, then: Caddy has been frozen by the objects associated with her and can never be any 'more absent' than she is, and Benjy's grief can grow neither greater nor smaller. Unlike Quentin, who relies entirely on his memories of his sister, Benjy need not worry that someday his grief will be less painful. He cannot give his agony away fully to the deadening, distancing properties of language.

That Benjy intuits the deadly properties of the word may be seen in his reaction to the utterance of his sister's name. Unlike his handful of tangible mementoes, the word "Caddy" is a terrifying representative of the absent one. From the opening lines of the novel we learn the unique word that will set Benjy howling. So violent a reflex may suggest the powerfully threatening magic of the uttered word. To begin with, the word flirts with intimate knowledge. Benjy's howls never incarnate a version of Caddy, and so he never enjoys the illusion of reappropriation that language allows. Since he cannot formulate Caddy as word, he forgets her and remembers only her loss. To name is to know; later in the novel, when hunger arouses Ben's whimpering, it is "hunger itself inarticulate, not knowing it is hunger" (345). In addition, the spoken word seems to mediate presence and absence more profoundly than other signs: the name magically seems part of presence itself. A name may summon (when she was a child, to call Caddy was to have her); the name is the owner's most intimate possession (Caddy uses her name consistently when she talks to Benjy about herself in the third person); the uttered name is a tactile presence (evoking the absent one) which is also an absence (it disappears into the hearer). And the spoken word even reproduces the rhythm of possession and dispossession as it is spoken and then fades from audibility: speech itself becomes a kind of dispossession. One's words fall from the mouth and are 'stolen' as others receive them. Benjy, like Quentin and Jason, guards against such a second theft. Moreover, the acoustic sign for Caddy only intensifies the general dilemma; that which is most proper to Caddy, her name, is also least the property of her person. The name outrages Benjy by speaking an absence.

From this point of view I hope to see how the novel takes quite seriously the prohibitions against language in the opening sections. The novel fears the realizations of two opposing and equally impossible dreams: on the one hand, pure silence beckons as the realm of unarticulated representation, a place where immediacy has never been broken. Benjy's and Quentin's memories strive, unavailingly, to exorcise the curse of mediacy from their imaginations of the past. But what they remember is already clouded by deathliness and forgetfulness, as we have begun to see. On the other hand, the novel as a whole makes acrobatic efforts to tell its whole story fully—to "get it right." The nature of language, Faulkner comes to suggest, forbids the illusion that any original idea, image, or sense can be embodied in words. Instead, *The Sound and the Fury* discovers, the fun of writing is in the play of failures, in the incompleteness, deferment, and repeatability of texts. The fiction veers away from resolution and completion in order to prolong its life. Accordingly, the novel makes two sorts of gesture toward silence, one toward the refusal to speak, the other toward deliberate mutations of the narrative's self-satisfaction.

A most arresting consequence of the paradox of silent speech in *The Sound and the Fury* is the mode of the novel. The stream-of-consciousness 'monologues' accomplish more than the simple trick of simulating the immediacy of mental processes.[20] They succeed, as well, in effacing any presumed narrator. In effect, they formally respond to the aspiration of writing a novel that is beyond the usual constraints of language. Gerard Genette's *Discours du récit* (in *Figures III*) may provide a vocabulary for our discussion.[21] The *mode*

20. For a more traditional view of the stream-of-consciousness technique, see Shiv K. Kumar, *Bergson and the Stream of Consciousness Novel* (New York, 1963).
21. Gerard Genette, "Discours du récit," in *Figures III* (Paris: Editions de Seuil, 1972), especially chaps. 4 and 5.

of a work of fiction may be determined by attention to two aspects: distance and perspective. Distance governs the proximity of the 'actual' events to the occasion or scene of their recounting. Perspective is the point of view from which these events are seen. The question of "Qui voit?," however, is separate from the question of "Qui parle?" The latter opens a consideration of the *voice* of the novel, as opposed to its mode. If we apply Genette's further discriminations within these categories, we may arrive at a deeper understanding of *The Sound and the Fury's* rhetoric of silence. For we can easily decide that the monologues of *The Sound and the Fury* are examples of what Genette calls *discours immediat* (p. 193), with no apparent distance between the events of April 7, 1928, and their recitation. Moreover, Benjy's perspective rules his section (as each protagonist's does in the subsequent two sections). Yet we cannot successfully address the problem of a speaking voice in the opening sections because they deliberately both imply and deny the presence of a narrator's voice. Despite the first-person voice, Benjy surely cannot be speaking his section as an interior monologue (the situation is multiplied in *As I Lay Dying*); but neither can we posit even an impersonal narrator recounting Benjy's impressions on some timeless occasion of the novel's telling. Rather, the section emerges as a text intent on masquerading as a state of mind. The act of narration effaces itself in the mode and voice of the early stream-of-consciousness sections of the novel. The monologues simply appear as written discourse, issuing from no voice or hand. Such a strategy marks Faulkner's discovery of the space of writing—outside the boundaries of personal presence or presumed consciousness.

Some familiar aspects of the style of Benjy's section endorse the impression that this first telling of the story is an artificially circumscribed, or partially silenced, performance. We recognize, for example, the preponderance of simple sentence structure and the actual repetition of many sentences.[22] Benjy's sensations, like the sentences that render them, produce only the bluntest discriminations: when he registers Caddy's presence it is because "Caddy smelled like trees," a sentence that recurs frequently (5, 50, 51, 54, 58). The fondness of the style in this section for particular phrases

22. Cf. Bleikasten's discussion of syntax in Benjy's section (*Most Splendid Failure*, p. 69).

and images sympathetically imitates Benjy's fondness for familiar objects and sites. Once the discourse has surveyed Benjy's world, it does not compel the narrative to advance. Style elaborates and expands Benjy's world, but it does not increasingly deepen or unfold it.

A related inertness in the style records Benjy's dependence on the senses, particularly his sight. His section is crowded with prepositions that perpetually strive to locate experience in a static visual array. ("Through the fence, between the curling flower spaces, I could see them hitting," the novel begins.) Moreover, the language of his mind is inhospitable to anything except the simplest pictures: "They were hitting little, across the pasture. I went back along the fence to where the flag was. It flapped on the bright grass and the trees" (2). In the preceding sentence we may notice that an adjective ("little") usurps an adverb's place, draining the verb of its energy and slowing it into a picture; and the flag flapping "on" the grass and trees suggests the superimposition of foreground on background.

As Benjy reckons with his loss through primitive forms of articulation, so his section reflects the difficulties with which a novel begins to fashion its meaning. The imagery and allusive symbolism that eventually accrete significance as they recur through the novel are presented 'innocently' in Benjy's discourse. The true innocence of the infant's mind permits us a glimpse into the processes by which the structures of a work grow into a kind of authority from arbitrary origins. The opening section serves as a primer for the novel's education in articulation.

The gesture of defining and naming permeates Benjy's eternal childhood. Caddy, for example, recognizes that one of her responsibilities is to teach Benjy the words for things. Stopping at the branch on the way to the Pattersons', Caddy scoops a piece of ice to show Benjy: " 'Ice. That means how cold it is' " (14). Death, Caddy explains to her brothers, is " 'when Nancy fell in the ditch and Roskus shot her and the buzzards came and undressed her' " (40). Frony, likewise, offers the definition of a funeral:

"What's a funeral." Jason said.

. . .

"Where they moans." Frony said. [39]

At one point Caddy herself needs information, which her older brother supplies: "'When is the Lawd's own time, Dilsey.' Caddy said. 'It's Sunday.' Quentin said" (29). Occasions of definition in the first section make a figure of the act of naming, and that figure may be noticed in other levels of the discourse. In addition, these definitions happen to share the theme of death: Caddy's running out of childhood into adulthood epitomizes the processes of cooling, disrobing, and mourning which contribute to the thematic and symbolic essence of *The Sound and the Fury*.

Throughout Benjy's section images and episodes struggle to present themselves as potentially significant. The process resembles the literal acts of naming by equipping the reader with a lexicon that promises eventual fluency in the novel's terms of discourse. For example, we notice Benjy's infatuation with Caddy's veil at her wedding: "*Then I saw Caddy, with flowers in her hair, and a long veil like shining wind. Caddy Caddy*" (47). Only Quentin's poetic associations convert the veil from image to symbol, however. To him the veil screens him from his mirrored image (the narcissism that is his incest); it muffles the voice of childhood's Eden; it signifies the shadow of time and death:

> ... running out of the mirror the smell roses roses the voice that breathed o'er Eden. Then she was across the porch I couldn't hear her heels then in the moonlight like a cloud, the floating shadow of the veil running across the grass, into the bellowing. She ran out of her dress, clutching the bridal. . . . Shreve said, "Well. . . . Is it a wedding or a wake"? [100]

In Quentin's section the veil becomes the marriage adornment and the funeral shroud—the barrier to repossession. Benjy's innocent eyes can see none of this. Similarly, the section naively introduces the tree-climbing episode and the imagery of the muddy drawers. To Benjy they mean nothing:

> He went and pushed Caddy up into the tree to the first limb. We watched the muddy bottom of her drawers. Then we couldn't see her.
> "Just look at you." Dilsey said. She wadded the drawers and scrubbed Caddy behind with them. "It done soaked clean through onto you." she said. "But you wont get no bath this night." [91]

But Quentin's preoccupation with sexuality, filth, and mortality subsequently give these lines impressive prophetic implications, since Caddy's literal undressing becomes (as Caddy's description of Nancy's death hints) the prefiguration of her death to her brothers. And Dilsey's "It done soaked clean through onto you" must finally be read as marking the end of a childhood. What we find throughout Benjy's section—in the mode, voice, style, imagery—is only the rudimentary articulation.

For the novel as a whole we might want to think of these common processes of initial definition as prefiguration, the naming of gestures and images that will be repeated as governing structures. It is prefiguration only in a limited sense, however, for the novel steadfastly avoids developing any fully coherent system of meaning. No single telling can ever get its part of the story "right" or final; instead, the novel increasingly incites the play of meaning. The supplement can never eradicate its "difference." While veils, shadows, and so on may be important to Benjy's and Quentin's sections, wholly different symbolic economies govern Jason's mind. There are certainly points of contact among the sections, but the prevailing impression among readers is probably represented by Donald Kartiganer's sensible discussion of the separately clarified visions of each section.[23] Perhaps the status of the allusions to Christianity best exemplifies the novel's manner. As is well known, Benjy's section introduces the comparison of Caddy to Eve; Caddy climbs the pear tree (later confused with an apple tree in Faulkner's memory), consorts with snakes, disobeys her "paw's" command to stay out of the tree, and is once called "Satan" by Dilsey. And yet, like the Passion Week structure with which it harmonizes, the Fall paradigm coheres fully neither within Benjy's section nor within the novel as a whole. The pattern satisfies momentary discursive needs as it evokes the fall into sexual differentiation for Benjy and Quentin, or reminds us, perhaps, of the deceit of the devil's tongue, but Faulkner forestalls the emergence of any fully intelligible analogues in *The Sound and the Fury*. (Contrast the meticulous model of *A Fable*.) I have been suggesting that such a forestalling reflects both the impossibility of the supplement (Benjy's memory and the written novel) to reappropriate presence and the recognition that such a limitation opens the possibility of the endless pleasures of writing. Benjy's mind constitutes the most natural, primitive activity of articulation. His serenity is predicated on a kind of speech. As the

23. See note 7.

novel's closing words intone, "his eyes were empty and blue and serene again as cornice and facade flowed smoothly once more from left to right; post and tree, window and doorway, and signboard, each in its ordered place" (401). The signboards replace the absent Caddy even as they differ from the original plenitude. Similarly, the deep resources of narrative as supplement are barely tapped in the first section. The novel must accustom itself to its own activity: submerged in an idiot's mind, the narrative voice effaces itself; confronted by tumultuous change, the style repeats itself; deprived of assertion, the symbolism can only insinuate and forecast.

ii

The Sound and the Fury leaves Benjy on the threshold of expression, groping innocently to "fill that vacuum" of Caddy's loss with mute speech. Unlike his brother, Quentin has perfect license to engage his formidable memory, imagination, and eloquence in the task of articulating a response to loss. And yet his suicide expresses a refusal to accept the conditions and consequences of filling the vacuum. Since Sartre's fine early essay, criticism has fruitfully discussed the disappearance of Caddy as the precipitating crisis of Quentin's warfare with time.[24] The indulged tyranny of his obsession with the past, his notorious clock phobia, his preoccupation with virginity and imaginary incest, and his eventual suicide may all, of course, be read as desperate gambits to deny Caddy's loss and to reappropriate her presence. In Derrida's terms, Quentin wants to reappropriate a lost plenitude. What has not been studied carefully about Quentin's mind is his horror at having to regain Caddy through a mere simulacrum of her 'original' presence. Although he is equipped to invent substitutions for the absent Caddy, Quentin

24. The first discussion of Quentin's warfare with time appeared in Jean-Paul Sartre, "On *The Sound and the Fury:* Time in the Work of Faulkner," in *Literary Essays,* trans. Annette Michelson (New York, 1957). The original essay appeared in 1939 and is reprinted in *Situations I* (Paris: Gallimard, 1947). An important early study in English criticism of the novel was Peter Swiggart, "Moral and Temporal Order in *The Sound and the Fury,*" *Sewanee Review,* 61 (Spring 1953), 221–237. A recent survey of the critical treatment of time in *The Sound and the Fury* appears in Douglas Messerli, "The Problem of Time in *The Sound and the Fury:* A Critical Reassessment and Reinterpretation," *Southern Literary Journal,* 6 (Spring 1974), 19–41.

recoils from the intuition that even memory is a kind of supplement that arises out of the breakage of immediacy, that necessarily acknowledges "visibility, spacing, death."

As it does for Benjy, Caddy's loss seems to constitute time's destruction of childhood's absolute and innocent love for Quentin. We are familiar with Quentin's capacity to explain the disturbance of his world abstractly; Caddy's sexual maturation—her lost virginity—becomes the apparent synecdoche of the universal processes of time: "When the shadow of the sash appeared on the curtains it was between seven and eight oclock and then I was in time again, hearing the watch," Quentin's section begins (91). Time is indisputably Quentin's antagonist because it has stolen Caddy, but it is equally responsible in Quentin's mind for a second threat, one that has not always been attended to. Quentin seeks desperately to devote his memory to the rites of commemoration, to neutralize Caddy's loss by occupying himself solely with memories of her. But time weakens memory itself, as Mr. Compson's voice insists:

> and i temporary and he you cannot bear to think that someday it will
> no longer hurt you like this now were getting at it   [220]

The danger that so paralyzes Quentin is not that the past will overcome the present, as Sartre and others have argued, but that the present will extinguish the possibility of remembering the past. Faulkner's own conviction that "was" cannot exist because if it did there would be no grief helps to point up Quentin's crisis.[25] His private vision of half-imagined, half-remembered incest aspires "to isolate [Caddy] out of the loud world so that it would have to flee us of necessity" (220); it is a vision consecrated to recovering the fullness of love and meaning that Caddy's absolute presence now seems to have constituted. If his memory fails to hold on to Caddy, Quentin risks the annihilation of sense, identity, continuity. In moments of despairing anguish Quentin glimpses a past denuded of Caddy's focal power:

> ... until after the honeysuckle got all mixed up in it the whole thing
> came to symbolise night and unrest I seemed to be lying neither asleep
> nor awake looking down a long corridor of grey half-light where all

25. Cowley, ed., *Writers at Work*, p. 141.

> stable things had become shadowy paradoxical all I had done
> shadows all I had felt suffered taking visible form antic and perverse
> mocking without relevance inherent themselves with the denial of the
> significance they should have affirmed thinking I was I was not who
> was not was not who.   [211]

By inciting his memories of Caddy from childhood to invade the present, Quentin temporarily fights off this world of meaninglessness. Caddy is Quentin's decreed center of inherent or natural significance, the base of stability, the core of original identity. Quentin's memory seeks to retain this center (or to reappropriate its presence).

The underlying irony—and it is paradigmatic of Quentin's dilemma—is that Caddy could never have been an original source of significance or plenitude. As we have noted in Benjy's section, Caddy's importance to her brothers springs from Mrs. Compson's premature retirement. Withholding herself from her sons, the mother forces them to find nurture and affection in their sister. Methods of psychoanalysis offer the readiest explanations of what such a substitution might mean,[26] but we may also consider Caddy's status in the context of the problems of loss and articulation. Once Quentin has reached his last day and Caddy is dead to him, the oldest Compson son confesses a prior absence: "if I'd just had a mother so I could say Mother Mother" (213). Quentin has no one to call mother and so his first act of articulation is to designate Caddy as substitute. I do not think it is overstating the case to say that Quentin "supplements" Caroline Compson's insufficiency with Caddy. Dramatically, Caddy herself plays the role of the supplement of the maternal presence; she appears as the trace at the origin, the opening of expressible sense.

Because she is his sister, Caddy is a most 'natural' supplement for Quentin's mother. Both incestuous desire and its sanction have been transferred across the tiniest of gaps; the ambivalences of the son toward the mother may remain suspended in Quentin's attitudes toward Caddy. To this extent Caddy indirectly reappropriates the forces of maternal presence. Yet she also behaves according to her difference. Quentin cherishes Caddy's virginity partially because it marks her pure maternity to him. Caddy is the 'mother'

26. Irwin, *Doubling & Incest,* passim.

who has never been possessed by the son's father. Her lost virginity signals to Quentin the loss of his substitute mother; he shrinks from her pregnancy because it signals her literal (rather than functional) motherhood. (Her daughter's name, Quentin, surely underscores the irony of Caddy's treachery.) Caddy's virginity represents that impossible condition of absolute, original intactness that cannot be known until lost. Mr. Compson instructs: "Women are never virgins. Purity is a negative state..." (143). And in *Absalom* he amplifies: virginity "must depend upon its loss, absence, to have existed at all" (96).

That Quentin uses Caddy as a supplement may also be seen in the tension of their preadolescent attraction. What protects Caddy's virginity is, oddly enough, Quentin's incestuous love. Incest constitutes a limit of desire; it represents the necessary frustration of passion. Quentin never seeks possession of Caddy, for to do so would be to accept the supplement as a full presence in its own right, thereby destroying it. Instead, Quentin enjoys the deferring of passion enforced by the taboo against incest. He asks whether Caddy has not seen his face in those of her lovers, but he knows enough about the source of the supplement's life to reject the idea of actual sexual possession of his sister: "and he did you try to make her do it and i i was afraid to i was afraid she might and then it wouldnt have done any good..." (220). Caddy's value inheres in her unavailability, in the necessity of deferment. Herbert Head's caution to Caddy about her brother—"dont let Quentin do anything he cant finish"—may be less an insult than he supposes.

In one crucial respect, then, Quentin's behavior grows out of his conviction that Caddy once held the full presence of love and coherence and that her loss must be perfectly redeemed. The loss of the successful supplement resembles the sense of lost origin. Because he does not confront the fact that Caddy is already a replacement, Quentin cannot imagine replacing her. Such an attitude betrays one of the components of Quentin's adolescent idiosyncrasies, and also helps to distinguish the larger attitudes of the novel toward this problem. For Quentin believes that time has turned presence into absence, while the novel—along with Faulkner's other mature fiction—seems to have won the recognition that there is never anything but the condition of already having lost. The state of diminishment or dispossession is the condition for articulation.

Quentin believes himself to be the victim of time. In addition to his celebrated combat with watches and clocks and his explicit meditation on the nature of time, Quentin remembers Caddy as being in dynamic synchronization with the natural time of sexual experimentation, pregnancy, and death. Caddy climbs the tree to see a funeral and earns Dilsey's affectionate diminutive "Minute" as a result. Caddy's 'death' by sexual initiation is the very embodiment of human change, and of the division between sexes that is the signature of a world fallen from atemporal unity. In the instant before his suicide Quentin remembers his father's intonation that "was[,] the saddest word of all" (222), is the undeniable proof of man's misfortune, time. Mr. Compson accuses Quentin of seeking the "apotheosis" of a temporary state of mind because he cannot bear to think that his grief someday "will no longer hurt you like this" (220). Against this sense of time as man's misfortune Quentin commits a memory devoted to saving Caddy herself. I propose that a discussion of articulation as supplement may enrich our understanding of this central, familiar issue in *The Sound and the Fury.* Quentin, unlike the novelist, refuses to accept language as loss because he identifies the supplementary nature of articulation as the death of the original plenitude. What he comes to intuit—and what makes his suicide so moving a creative gesture—is that even his hallowed memory deforms and substitutes for whatever was 'there' at first.

Language is that potent instrument which articulates loss as soon as immediacy has broken. But Quentin deeply distrusts words because he recognizes what Rousseau might see as their necessary danger: they seek to recover what their very existence proclaims is no longer self-sufficient. Something of a nearly logophobic attitude connects Quentin's stray thoughts about language. His furious silence rejects the "loud world," which mistakenly believes that saying something will bring it about: "They all talked at once, their voices insistent and contradictory and impatient, making of unreality a possibility, then a probability, then an incontrovertible fact, as people will when their desires become words" (145). Elsewhere he scornfully concedes that "people, using themselves and each other so much by words, are at least consistent in attributing wisdom to a still tongue" (146). He abruptly cuts off the jeweler's inquiry about his attire with "This is just a private celebration" and prefers Roskus' "diffident, secret, inarticulate and sad" demeanor to Deacon's "long pointless anecdotes" (104,121–122, 123). Silence guards Quentin's concentration on the lost Caddy. He risks no writing at all except the notes whose posthumous delivery cannot jeopardize the vitality of his commemoration; and he will never contribute to the librarian's "shelves of ordered certitudes long divorced from reality, dessicating peacefully" (155). The language of sexual difference already implicates Quentin in human discourse, but he once dreams of freedom from differentiation as if it would be an alien language: "It's not not having them. It's never to have had them then I could say O That That's Chinese I don't know Chinese" (143).

Quentin avoids words because he senses that they displace and substitute, but he also identifies his silence as a failure of nerve. The refusal to speak ensures his imprisonment in the memory of the dead Caddy. A complaint about his own impotence appears in the lament I quoted earlier ("if I'd just had a mother so I could say Mother Mother"), as if saying Mother would have been the way to solve her loss. Earlier in his section Quentin suggests a similar association between the fatal supplement (his sister) and the merely dangerous word: *"My little sister had no. If I could say Mother. Mother"* (177). In his various attempts to defend Caddy's honor, moreover, Quentin recognizes his voice as a weapon that he wields only haltingly and wishfully: *"Quentin has shot . . . Quentin has shot Herbert he shot his voice through the floor of Caddy's room"* (130). Quentin remembers his voice as a threat to intimacy with Caddy; once she asked him to pronounce Dalton Ames's name and to feel her pulse quicken. The episode summarizes Quentin's horror at the intrusion of the voice. Even as his voice arouses, penetrates, fills, possesses, and excites Caddy, it merely travesties their intimacy, for it is all the while proclaiming another. Every spoken word speaks for another—destroying and creating presence, invading immediacy.

The full maturation of his voice, as might have grown out of the trials of narrative in *Absalom* during the previous September, might have freed Quentin to articulate his responses to change and loss through language. He glimpses such an opportunity in his conflict with his father. To put Mr. Compson into words would be to invent him, to gain the authority of authorship over him, to reverse progenitor and son: "*Say it to Father will you I will am my fathers Progenitive I invented him created I him Say it to him it will not be for he will say I was not and then you and I since philoprogenitive*" (152).[27] Analogously, a fantastic memory from childhood spells out Quentin's sense of powerlessness before his parents:

> When I was little there was a picture in one of our books, a dark place into which a single weak ray of light came slanting upon two faces lifted out of the shadow. . . . It was torn out, jagged out. I was glad. I'd have to turn back to it until the dungeon was Mother herself she and Father upward into weak light holding hands and us lost somewhere below even them without even a ray of light.   [215]

The image of mother as dungeon of course suggests the regressive pull of Quentin's vision, since he yearns for the bliss of the womb, the most secure intimacy of mother, brother, and sister. But that the two faces of Caddy and Quentin are imprisoned in the darkened page of a book suggests that they are embryonically enclosed in the parents' book, incapable of speaking their deliverance. Quentin readily admits to his father that his confession of incest has been a feeble lie, for example, and consequently abandons the potential flight to a more elaborate fiction. In fact, the best measure of Quentin's willed silence occurs in the closing passages of his monologue. The conversation between father and son deliberately flouts the manner of an authentic exchange. It is cast in a stream-of-consciousness style that does not encourage the reader to distinguish the voices through setting, description, tone, gesture. Instead, the two voices are both versions of Quentin's own. No memory but an invention, as Faulkner confirmed later,[28] Quentin's thought does not fully create his father's voice at all. Unlike the rich detail of Sutpen's performance in *Absalom* that Quentin and Shreve concoct, this alien voice has nothing but a few well-worn ideas to call its own. Quentin seeks to silence his father's voice by internalizing it, and consequently what masquerades as a debate is actually a

27. Irwin emphasizes the struggle for narrative authority between Mr. Compson and Quentin (ibid., p. 120); but the mutual tellings of Sutpen's story also occasion moments of intimacy and tenderness between the narrators.
28. Frederick L. Gwynn and Joseph L. Blotner, eds., *Faulkner in the University: Class Conferences at the University of Virginia, 1957–1958* (New York, 1959), p. 262.

double-voiced soliloquy, the twin explanation of suicide as both surrender and defiance.

Quentin 'explains' his suicide to himself through an internal colloquy because he recognizes that any single gesture may express contradictory sentiments and arouse rival interpretations. (Compare the mysteries spun by Sutpen's unadorned gestures in *Absalom*.) The actual plunge into the Charles, although it is never recounted, might figure self-punishment, narcissistic reunion, exhausted frustration, and so on, as critics have suggested. But I am interested in what the imminence of suicide does to Quentin's memory before he dies. Faulkner's interest in Quentin's death does not involve the symbolism of the act or its direct consequences, but rather what is created by its looming. Sartre supposed that Quentin was like a man looking backward from a moving automobile; the past spread fully behind him, Quentin ignores the future.[29] Extending this idea, Peter Swiggart suggested that Quentin's suicide exerts a retrospective pressure on his experience of the present and his memory of the past which is able to impose a kind of obsessional order.[30] This seems the right approach to Quentin's suicide, since it is clearly a creative (though surely desperate) gesture.[31] If Quentin wants to erect an "apotheosis in which a temporary state of mind will become symmetrical above the flesh and aware both of itself and of the flesh it will not quite discard you will not even be dead" (220), if he seeks "to isolate [Caddy] out of the loud world" into a "hell" of his own making, he must envision his escape from time as the achievement *of* his life—and not some presumed ghosthood *after* it. The supernaturally eternal is irrelevant to Quentin; he aspires to a temporary state of mind that tricks itself into half believing its liberation from time. Quentin experiences such a state precisely during his suspended last moment, the moment during which he 'thinks' his monologue. Such a moment encloses a region populated with memories of childhood, with incidents from his last day

29. Identifying Quentin with his author, Sartre concludes that "Faulkner's vision of the world can be compared to that of a man sitting in an open car and looking backwards" (*Literary Essays*, p. 82).

30. Peter Swiggart, *The Art of Faulkner's Novels* (Austin, 1962), p. 96.

31. I urge a more sympathetic interpretation of Quentin's suicide than Bleikasten, who makes Faulkner's view of Quentin too strictly moralistic: "... Faulkner holds him [Quentin] at a distance, and subjects his loveless, life-denying egocentricity to ruthless exposure" (*Most Splendid Failure*, p. 143).

which compose an uncanny palimpsest of the past, with many varieties of the lie that Caddy had (had not) been taken by Quentin.

The artifice of imminent death is Quentin's necessary fiction. Imminent death is the supreme negation of time. Death arrests decay and loss: if grief for Caddy is only a "temporary" state of mind, as Mr. Compson avers, then Quentin wants to save at least that from time's dispossession. To think the annihilation of the future is to leave one's memories intact; it dreams an apotheosis of the temporary. It cheats the certainty that "someday it will no longer hurt you like this." Death gives peace to eyes exhausted by seeing the past through the present, by struggling to coerce the absent one to reappear in the flow of time:

> I could not see the bottom, but I could see a long way into the motion of the water before the eye gave out, and then I saw a shadow hanging like a fat arrow stemming into the current. [144]

Death contemplates the ending, completion; it resolves Quentin's fear of having to remember the past endlessly in order to preserve Caddy. "Finished. If things just finished themselves" (97); "Again. Sadder than was. Again. Saddest of all. Again." (118). Death by suicide kills time and death themselves: Quentin's gesture appropriates to himself the power of time to take away life.

If Sartre had been right about the power of the unchangeable past to invade the present and to occupy it wholly, Quentin's desperation would be difficult to explain. It is because "was" does *not* exist that there is grief. For all his furious devotion, Quentin still senses that his memory is incapable of reappropriating the lost Caddy. Critics have pointed to Quentin's 'recovery' of whole episodes from his childhood as testimony to his obsessive power of recall.[32] And we have begun to understand how the events of his last day subtly replicate features of his loss of Caddy, as if every present moment is a repetition of the original dispossession. But we may also discover that Quentin's memory necessarily disfigures, corrects, and structures the past so as to satisfy a fundamental ambivalence: he yearns to recover the plenitude, unity, and innocence of Caddy at the same time that he confronts the fact that to remember Caddy is to insist on her absence or death. Like Benjy, he can remember Caddy only

32. To Sartre, Faulkner's "past takes on a sort of super-reality; its contours are hard and clear, unchangeable" (*Literary Essays,* p. 82).

as the presence that has already begun to vanish. Similarly, the events of the last day, although they coincide with the past remarkably, nevertheless retain their stubborn difference. Incidents play in counterpoint across the years, but Quentin's imagination shapes the contingent present into a supplement of the past that is lost.

As Quentin spends his last afternoon trying to return a lost little girl to her family, his memory opens access to the moments of his own childhood that have witnessed the disappearance of a sister. Quentin's anxiety has been to evade sexual maturation because it constitutes initiation into a fallen world of sexual difference, procreation, and death, the fruits of time. When Caddy once discovers him in the barn with Natalie, he insists on their innocence: *"You know what I was doing? . . . I was hugging her that's what I was doing"* (170). Quentin evokes this moment precisely because it both creates the appearance of his own defection to adulthood and also deliberately denies it. It tests his power to call sexual passion mere brotherly affection and to convert an opportunity to lose his virginity into an occasion to defend it. The second phase of this incident elaborates the duplicity of Quentin's memory, for he remembers chastizing Caddy for her failure to care as much for his virginity as he does for hers. When she turns back to say, *"I don't give a damn what you were doing,"* he protests paradoxically by burlesquing an act of intercourse with her:

> She hit my hands away I smeared mud on her with the other hand I couldn't feel the wet smacking of her hand I wiped mud from my legs smeared it on her wet hard turning body. [170]

The performance expresses both Quentin's attempt to preserve Caddy's virginity and his recognition that he can remember her only as already contaminated by the filth of sex.[33] Moreover, it casts him as both defender and despoiler; his memory imagines a scene that satisfies the lie of incest. These divergent qualities are important because they confirm that Caddy may never be reappropriated as absolute innocence. The persistence of these memories derives from the beginning of difference; memory supplements as it recalls a past that is already dead.

A second arrangement of these tensions appears when Quentin

---

33. Both Irwin (*Doubling & Incest*, p. 45) and Bleikasten (*Most Splendid Failure*, p. 104) discuss Quentin's unnatural association of filth and human sexuality.

recollects threatening Caddy with a penknife. As many readers have noticed, this scene illuminates Quentin's neurotic identification of sex and death and prefigures the consummation of impotence in suicide.[34] But it also responds to Quentin's need to fuse the nostalgia for innocent prepossession to the knowledge of Caddy's disappearance. The moment begins by associating sexual exposure and death ("do you remember the day damuddy died when you sat down in the water in your drawers"). And, of course, the knife that murders is the phallus that penetrates. As the sequence of events presses toward climax, Quentin's impotence overrules:

> What is it what are you doing
> her muscles gathered I sat up
> its my knife I dropped it
> she sat up
> what time is it
> I dont know   [189–190]

The moment that Quentin recreates interrupts deathly intercourse before it can reenact Caddy's slaughter, but the long scene continues until Quentin eventually remembers passing his sister on to Dalton Ames, who does kill her ("*did you love them Caddy did you love them When they touched me I died*"). Almost-intercourse is exactly what Quentin might hope to imagine to himself endlessly. An eternal suspension at the instant between virginity and penetration, between childhood and adulthood, when no one asks what time it is, would enable Quentin never to lose Caddy because he had never possessed her. The incompletion, paradoxical tension, and displacement (substituting himself tentatively for the actual lover who kills Caddy) allow Quentin to play out his desire to possess Caddy while evading the murder by phallus. In these moments he possesses Caddy fully in her virginity; he enjoys an innocent incest.

Once Quentin has committed his memory to filling the vacuum of Caddy's loss, the supplemental properties of all substitution obstruct his naive efforts simply to reappropriate her. His memory persistently threatens to transform the sense of Caddy's absence

34. Irwin discusses this and the later penknife episode as examples of Quentin's neurotic linking of sexuality and death (*Doubling & Incest,* p. 46): the siblings' "conversation parodies that of sexual intercourse."

into the story of her loss. One may see the discursive qualities of Quentin's vision in the fictive image patterns of his section: the gulls of timelessness, the clocks of time-boundedness, for example. When he remembers his vain effort to banish Dalton Ames, moreover, he conjures a scene worthy of any Western melodrama. (Can we be sure Quentin hasn't even made up this outlaw suitor's name?) He finds Ames rolling a cigarette with one hand, demonstrating his sharpshooting, and smiling at Quentin's ultimatum to get out of town by sundown (198). Quentin locates their confrontation on a bridge; the two struggle over the branch about the body of Caddy. Ames picks bark chips from the bridge and shoots them as they flick into the water below, a taut image of the potency of his phallicism and the abandonment of Caddy (who smells like trees) to the flux. Quentin fails to hold his position on the bridge and faints like a girl after feebly voicing his objection to Ames's suit. The scene dramatizes Quentin's inability to bestride the waters of sex and time, and dooms him to flight. Satisfied with such symbolically charged vignettes, however, Quentin silences his voice just before it breaks into story.

The past that Quentin's memory represents is not the original, natural reality; it is the half-remembered, half-invented domain of a necessarily transfigured childhood. That transfiguration extends into Quentin's uncanny reliving of the past during his last day. Quentin's memory has been so magnetized by Caddy's loss that when he looks back from his last moment on the events of the preceding afternoon they seem to reenact her disappearance. His effort to restore the "little sister" to her home and his vain assault on the crowing Gerald Bland surely figure Quentin's childhood attempts to reclaim Caddy and to fight off Dalton Ameses and Herbert Heads. The narrative segments of the afternoon of June 2 occasion 'memories' of corresponding events in the sequence of Caddy's loss; the passages alternate, creating a sense of repetition. But if the episodes of the past fail to re-present the natural, innocent Caddy herself, as I have argued, the incidents of the afternoon also inevitably misshape the past. Quentin corrects the past as he relives it.

That Quentin calls the Italian child "little sister" leaves us no doubt about his association, but earlier in his monologue he has wondered about the "good Saint Francis that said Little Sister Death, that never had a sister" (94). The child embodies not the lost innocent sister but her ghost. Quentin sees her as unknowingly contaminated by sexuality: when she accepts coins from Quentin, her "fingers [close] about them, damp and hot, like worms" (157), an image that reflects Quentin's horror of the phallic and his usual attribution of masculine power to Caddy. After the shoplady's warning that the girl will "hide [the loaf] under her dress and a body'd never know it" (156), the child accompanies him through the rain with the tip of the loaf peering out of its wrapper ("the nose of the loaf naked," 168). Quentin's fumbling impotence in the rain with his penknife corresponds to his futile attempt to protect the loaf; as he looks at "the half-naked loaf clutched to her breast," he begins to "wipe the loaf, but the crust began to come off, so I stopped" (172). Quentin's gestures seem to resign custody of the phallus to the little girl and to accept its erosion by water. Perhaps the act figures the 'mutilation' and 'castration' that Caddy's loss means to Quentin. Quentin's dealings with this reincarnation of Caddy suggest that she is a substitute whose difference from the original prompts him to confirm rather than overcome the deadness of the past.

Shortly after this incident, Quentin experiences another moment that reveals the differences between past and present. He and "sister" surprise several boys swimming naked. As the two approach the water, Quentin chillingly predicts his suicide: "'Hear them in swimming, sister? I wouldn't mind doing that myself.' If I had time. When I had time. I could hear my watch" (170). To join Caddy, naked in the waters of death; to rejoin her in the mud of the river, in the branch of childhood; to master time finally and flee the ticking are suicidal fantasies. But Quentin recoils for the moment, as if yearning for a revision of the past that would pardon them from the original fall. The boys are embarrassed by their nakedness and shout:

> "Take that girl away! What did you want to bring a girl here for? Go on away!"
> "She won't hurt you. We just want to watch you for a while." [170]

If "sister" only watches the naked adolescents, she and Quentin can enact a past that never was. If only Caddy had never disrobed to enter the branch, the voices "o'er Eden" might still call to each other. When the boys threaten to "get out and throw them in," Quentin and little sister leave: " 'That's not for us, is it.' "

The entire climactic scene of little sister's shadowing Quentin resounds with echoes of his loss of Caddy. The little girl's refusal to leave her new love drives Quentin to long for parental responsibility ("if you could just slice the walls away all of a sudden Madam, your daughter, if you please. No. Madam, for God's sake, your daughter" [164]; and "your papa's going to be worried about you" [168]). After the child's brother finally spies the 'kidnapper' and his victim, he launches a pursuit, followed by two of the naked swimmers. "You steela my seester" elicits Quentin's hysterical laughter at the ironic repetition. Like Ames, Quentin makes off with a sister; but Julio, his two naked companions, and an older officer promptly seek her recovery. That quartet stands in mute antithesis to the trio of impotent brothers and the helpless father who witness Caddy's disappearance. The episodes of Quentin's last day are compelled by the focus of his memory to resemble the scenes of Caddy's loss; and yet they never become transparent replications of the past, nor do they even allow an untroubled reemergence of Caddy in memory. Instead, Quentin's monologue presents a Caddy who can be only a supplement to that illusory, originary presence. Memory, speech, and desire may be activated only by a sense of loss that can never know original possession; and their pleasures depend on the continued sense of difference, spacing, and death. These are the conditions for articulation.

iii

The toxic bitterness of Jason's voice in section 3 assaults us by ridiculing the highly unnatural sympathies that the novel has earlier asked us to cultivate. In Jason's "sane"[35] eyes, Benjy ought to be merely the asylum's star freshman, Quentin tried to go swimming without knowing how, Mr. Compson needed nothing so much as a one-armed straitjacket, and Caddy is—once and always—"a bitch." The willful, sullen child who trips through Benjy's section repeatedly rejects and is rejected by his siblings and father, and his

35. *The Sound and the Fury,* "Appendix," p. 421.

mother can manage no more than a formal acknowledgment of her preference for him. Jason fosters his pure defection from the core of the family by fighting with Caddy, by jealously destroying Benjy's toys, or by tattling on Caddy and Quentin. Such behavior naturally deepens into the isolation of Jason's adulthood, an isolation sealed by paranoia and festering with masochism. Though he believes himself excepted from the demented attachments of his brothers and though he prides himself in upholding the responsibility, respectability, and routine of a "civilised life," Jason has not solved the Compson crisis. He has only silenced it. Like his brothers, Jason articulates a response to loss and deprivation. But unlike them, he chooses a kind of speech—money—that pretends no referential ties. The pursuit of money, whether it is playing the stock market, earning a salary, or robbing his niece's piggybank, seems like a pure attempt to restore the family's depleted wealth. Finance, however, is not the nonsense language Jason thinks it is; it inadvertently reveals precisely what its speaker has failed to confront: the need for intimacy with his sister.[36]

Jason's economic rites prove to be a writing of his unconscious grief. The language of finance, like any language, is linked arbitrarily, rather than intrinsically, to what it stands for. For the reader of Jason's writing, its dislocated center is Caddy, who was never more than an absence in Jason's discourse. Jason's economy seeks, on the one hand, to establish an order for his life that differs from the disorder Caddy causes in Quentin's. Yet seeming to ignore her, on the other hand, Jason's writing also pursues—all the while deferring—a representation of Caddy in his life. Jason's language covertly manufactures the sister he never had.

Even to her favorite son, Mrs. Compson can offer no sustained warmth or security. Driven like his brothers to supplement her insufficiency, Jason finds Quentin in Caddy's arms and Benjy in her bed. As a result, he comes to depend on his grandmother for the attention he has been refused elsewhere. The connection is not one

36. I want to go beyond the view that Jason uses his niece as a surrogate to displace his repressed incestuous desire for Caddy. John L. Longley, Jr. (*The Tragic Mask: A Study of Faulkner's Heroes* [Chapel Hill, N.C., 1957]), suggests that Jason's "hatred is transference of his deeply repressed incestuous attraction toward Quentin" and, through her, toward Caddy (p. 147). But I see Quentin as only one denomination in Jason's elaborate financial articulation of sexual frustration.

that attracts much of the novel's attention because it serves chiefly to establish a more extreme version of the crisis of "filling the vacuum." For Jason's Damuddy dies at the very instant her most natural replacement, Caddy, also 'dies.' This is an excessive eruption of spacing and death at the origin, and it determines the third Compson brother's recoil from the obligations of creative supplementation.

Jason reacts violently to the loss of Damuddy:

> After a while even Jason was through eating, and he began to cry.
>   "Now you got to tune up." Dilsey said.
>   "He does it every night since Damuddy was sick and he cant sleep with her." Caddy said.   [31]

> "Do you think buzzards are going to undress Damuddy." Caddy said. "You're crazy."
>   "You're a skizzard." Jason said. He began to cry.
>   "You're a knobnot." Caddy said. Jason cried. His hands were in his pockets.
>   "Jason going to be rich man." Versh said. "He holding his money all the time."
>   Jason cried.   [42–43]

Jason never manages to replace the supplemental presence of Damuddy with another. Her absence condemns him to a perpetual sense of exclusion, diminishment, and impoverishment. For example, Mrs. Compson reminds him that " 'It was always her and Quentin. They were always conspiring against me. Against you too.... They always looked on you and me as outsiders' " (326). Over his father's grave he reflects about "when we were little and one thing and another and I got to feeling funny again, kind of mad or something, thinking about now we'd have Uncle Maury around the house all the time, running things like the way he left me to come home in the rain by myself" (252). Even the Compson name, which Jason equates strictly with the family fortune, is dead to Jason. "I reckon the reason all the Compson gave out before it got to me like Mother says, is that he [Mr. Compson] drank it up. At least I never heard of him offering to sell anything to send me to Harvard" (245).

To be angry with Mr. Compson for drowning himself in liquor

because such irresponsibility exhausts Jason's rightful patrimony might seem implausibly literal-minded—even for Jason—if it were not that he invariably interprets loss as financial setback. Caddy's pregnancy merely means the expense of a wedding; her divorce costs him the promised job in Herbert Head's bank; Quentin's suicide wastes the tuition money gained from the sale of Benjy's pasture. Jason's need for impersonal, collectible, hoardable money springs from his inability to speak his grief. Versh's joke, like so much else in Benjy's section, accurately forecasts the intimate connection between crying and pocket filling, between grief and reimbursement.

Jason recognizes that he can never afford the extravagance of suicide or cynicism: " 'I never had time to go to Harvard like Quentin or drink myself into the ground like Father. I had to work' " (224). At the same time that he resents his impoverishment, however, he also sees his "slavery" as a salvation from the intolerable self-indulgence he so scorns in the rest of his family:

> Well, Jason likes work. I says no I never had university advantages because at Harvard they teach you how to go for a swim at night without knowing how to swim and at Sewanee they dont even teach you what water is. I says you might send me to the state University; maybe I'll learn how to stop my clock with a nose spray. [243]

Work unambiguously establishes the value of time; each minute has a negotiable worth in tangible money. Surely one source of the strength of Jason's commitment to his work is that it protests against suicide's announcement that time is worth nothing. I shall discuss similar unspoken assertions of Jason's moneymaking shortly, but we should first notice that the realm of petty finance appeals to Jason precisely because it seems devoid of anything except intrinsic significance. Time, decay, desire, incest, and sexuality seem to have no place in the financial devotions of the one Compson who refuses to be mastered by the metaphysical.

> After all, like I say money has no value; it's just the way you spend it. It dont belong to anybody, so why try to hoard it. It just belongs to the man that can get it and keep it. [241]

Jason acts on the fatherly advice that Quentin refuses; money can displace grief, frustration, deprivation: "watching pennies has healed more scars than jesus" (221). And Job, after seeing Jason speed from check forging at lunch to stock jockeying to hardware huckstering, senses that Jason wants to leave something behind: "'You fools a man whut so smart he cant even keep up wid his-self. . . . Dat's Mr. Jason Compson . . .'" (312). Jason insists that his most profound disappointment in life is nothing more than the loss of his best financial opportunity, the promised clerkship in Herbert Head's St. Louis bank. He and Mrs. Compson are sure that at least Caddy would "have enough regard for the family not to jeopardize my chance after she and Quentin had had theirs" (246). Jason's entire "chance" for a future had rested on the missed job.

Jason's pronouncement of the neutrality of money fails to convince even as he says it, of course. But what needs to be examined more fully is the extent to which Jason's financial behavior thoroughly but mutely tries to fill the vacuum of loss. The very status of Herbert Head's desperately sought job conforms to the paradigm of loss in the Compson family. Just as Mrs. Compson is the mother whose children lose her before she ever allows them to possess her, so the clerkship is "the job in the bank of which he had been deprived before he ever got it" (382). Each is an illusory presence that can be known only in its loss, a dispossession at the origin.

At Damuddy's death, Caddy, too, becomes the object that is lost before it can ever be possessed. The problem for Jason is not how to preserve moments of intimacy with Caddy in his memory (as it is for Benjy and Quentin), but how to deal with her premature death to him. He does so by accepting the apparently dead substitute of money. Jason readily exchanges Caddy's absence for the opportunity to make money; accordingly, Herbert Head must be both the one who takes Caddy away and the one who reimburses her brothers for their loss. (Quentin, of course, repudiates so offensive a compensation: "To hell with your money. . . . you'd better stick to Jason he'd suit you better than I would," 136, 134.)

If Jason's decision were as uncomplicated as substituting cold cash for a cold sister, he would scarcely be inconsolable about the bungled clerkship. What Jason scarcely realizes is that the desire for money, rather than putting Caddy safely to rest, keeps the sense of her loss alive; and his irrational obsession with the single missed chance, with his doomed stock playing, and with his niece's purse strings unwittingly betrays an absolute absorption by his frustrated desire for Caddy. Quentin understands that Head's money offers more than mere compensation or diversion; to Quentin, it represents the brother-in-law's sexual potency and privilege. Even if Mrs. Compson had not virtually auctioned Caddy, Head's money would have symbolized sexual power. When he offers Quentin "a loan," he indirectly reminds him of his purchased right to intimacy with Caddy:

> No no come on I belong to the family now see I know how it is with a young fellow he has lots of private affairs it's always pretty hard to get the old man to stump up for I know havent I been there and not so long ago either but now I'm getting married and all specially up there come on dont be a fool listen when we get a chance for a real talk I want to tell you about a little widow over in town
>
> I've heard about that too keep your damned money   [136]

Quentin won't allow his sexual threat to Caddy to be bought off so easily, but Jason will because he can never muster a claim on her. The prospect of Jason's clerking in Head's bank is the very image of a brother's subordinate respect for the husband's purchase of his sister. Precisely such a job would have enabled Jason to enact the only incest available to him as outsider, that which Mr. Compson calls "the pure and perfect incest: the brother . . . taking that virginity in the person of the brother-in-law" (*Absalom,* 96). Jason's outrage at the loss of Head's job is hardly just the pique at bad business it might seem at first. It bemoans a failure to deaden passion into greed.

Money and sexual potency are associated throughout *The Sound and the Fury.* The opening scene of the novel presents a search for three things: Benjy hunts for Caddy and Luster looks for his missing quarter and stray golf balls. Luster's search comments antically on Benjy's, for the missing quarter reminds us both that Caddy's 'loss' in the branch leads to the sale of the pasture (now the golf course) and that the loss of money is related to the loss of "balls." Luster smirks to one of the wash women:

> "You all found any balls yet."
>
>   .   .   .
>
> "Aint you talking biggity. I bet you better not let your grandmammy hear you talking like that."   [17]

Benjy's castration constitutes the serious background of this banter; he has lost his manhood to his love for Caddy, and figuratively, he has no resources for recovery. (When Luster does manage to turn up a ball in the branch, a golfer tricks him into giving it up.)

As Quentin refuses the potency of Head's money, so he dramatizes his impotence in other financial transactions. He repeatedly gives away small sums of money in mimicry of his virginal consecration to the dead sister. On his way to the jeweler's, Quentin gives a nickel and a cigar to two bootblacks. He looks back and notices that "the one with the cigar was trying to sell it to the other for the nickel" (102). The prominent association of cigars with Herbert Head's phallicism ("Thanks I dont smoke" and "Keep your hands off of me you'd better get that cigar off the mantel" [132, 136]) might also suggest that the bootblacks play out the kind of deal Quentin refuses. Later, Quentin ironically purchases the little girl's companionship with his money; the moment poignantly travesties the forbidden intimacy.

By subtly renegotiating the terms of internal crises into capital quotients, Jason unwittingly invests all of his financial activities with expresssive content. For example, instead of letting his mother's investment in the hardware store mature toward a partnership for him, he secretly withdraws the money to buy a car. The decision has nothing to do with business acumen; the automobile gives him constant headaches (a reminder of his inescapable victimization); acquiring it protests the unnatural survival of his mother's authority over the family; and T. P. irrepressibly shows off for the town girls with it, perhaps signaling Jason's attraction to a disguised erotic flamboyance.

Jason's entanglement in the stock market similarly displaces without eradicating fundamental sources of anxiety and frustration. Despite perpetual setbacks, Jason persists with futile schemes. The more he loses, of course, the more deeply he is committed, since "I just want to hit them one time and get my money back. I don't want a killing ... I just want my money back ..." (292). Jason furiously believes that for every loss there will be an equal and opposite compensation. In fact, to the extent that the stock market both impoverishes and enriches, it is an analogue for Caddy, who first deprives Jason and then returns a kind of wealth to his embezzling hands. Stock transactions impersonalize for Jason the cycles of gain and loss that trouble each of the Compson brothers. And yet they also embody the very forces that have dispossessed Jason originally. Throughout his warfare with Wall Street, Jason is at two disadvantages: he is excluded from the center of power ("These damn jews... with all their guaranteed inside dope" 292) and he must endure comic lapses of time before he receives vital information ("'What are we paying you for'? I says, 'Weekly reports?'" 282). To suffer setbacks because he is an outsider and because he is behind time is unwittingly to reproduce the circumstances of his loss of Caddy. Perhaps a suggestion of his namesake's behavior can be found in one of Mr. Compson's tirelessly supplied metaphors: "it is hard believing to think that a love or a sorrow is a bond purchased without design and which matures willynilly and is recalled without warning to be replaced by whatever issue the gods happen to be floating at the time" (221).

Jason's blind devotion to finance seems on the surface to provide a refuge from the problems of lost love and sorrow that destroy his brothers. By reducing the stakes and by evading the expressive significance of his gestures, Jason constructs his own "reducto [sic] ad absurdum" as an alternative to suicide. Just as he trivializes Quentin's obsession with time through his incessant attention to being "on time" and never getting "enough time," so Jason shrinks the agony of loss to the annoyance of financial reverses. The most curious and revelatory commodity in Jason's complex economy, however, is neither his salary nor his stocks, but his niece.

The instant that Quentin Head enters the Compson household, Jason identifies her as the coin of an exchange: "'Well,'" he says, realizing that Head will withdraw the clerkship when he returns his counterfeit wife and child, "'they brought my job home tonight'" (246). Shortly after, he initiates his commercial custody by renting her to her mother for $100:

> And so I counted the money again that night and put it away, and I didn't feel so bad. I says I reckon that'll show you. I reckon you'll know now that you cant beat me out of a job and get away with it. [225]

Realizing a profit is always the kind of revenge that eases Jason. And surely his use of his niece and his willingness to keep her reflect her sheer monetary worth; so long as Jason possesses her, he can continue to deflect Caddy's checks into his private coffers. His swelling cache may literally replace the patrimony that Caddy's wedding and Quentin's suicide wasted, and Jason may enjoy the bonus of avenging his own disinheritance by stealing from the next generation. But like Jason's other economies, his manipulation of Quentin is an attempt to restore emotional wealth, too.

Quentin is not a faceless chip; she is a coin that bears the imprint of her maker. Although Jason refuses to deal with all of the ramifications of the fact, Quentin becomes the tangible token of her mother in Caddy's absence. "Just like her mother" (265), Jason fumes as he recognizes the willful eroticism of his sister in his niece. Quentin represents the only aspect of Caddy's passion that Jason could see as an outsider: her sexual appetite. And as Caddy's insatiability finally 'killed' her, Jason determines to oversee her delegate. All of Jason's unadmitted outrage at Caddy's infidelities (as she both nurtured his brothers and satisfied her lovers) focuses on Quentin's behavior. Frustrated because he seems to be the only male to whom Caddy has not been a whore in one way or another, Jason deplores her daughter's careless and alluring attire while noticing every effect ("Her kimono came unfastened, flapping about her, damned near naked" [228]). Later he hints that he needs to restrain himself in her presence: "I'll be damned if they dont dress like they were trying to make every man they passed on the street want to reach out and clap his hand on it" (289). When she threatens to rip her dress off, he stops her, as if reenacting the fatal moment of Caddy's disrobing; and later, when he chases Quentin and the stolen money, his role is mistaken for that of a cheated husband passing himself off as a brother. In these respects Jason treats Quentin like the seventeen-year-old sister he never had.

Jason's frustrated desire for Caddy also indirectly accounts for the violent zeal with which he 'fathers' Quentin. So far as his mother allows, Jason assumes the paternal responsibilities of the family once Jason Compson III has died. Mrs. Compson reminds Quentin that Jason "is the nearest thing to a father you've ever had" (324). And he regularly thinks of Quentin as something like a daughter: "If it was my own daughter now it would be different . . ." (307) and "I say it'd be bad enough if it was mine; I'd at least be sure it was a bastard to begin with, and now even the Lord doesn't know that for certain probably" (286–287). By playing a strong father to his niece, Jason secretly yearns to correct his own father's silent encouragement of Caddy's and Quentin's unnatural closeness, a closeness that steadfastly excluded him; Jason prides himself on being "a different breed of cat from Father" (250).

To the extent that he performs as Quentin's father, Jason serves as Caddy's remote, surrogate husband. The two quarrel about Quentin's money, clothes, schooling, and friends in a bizarre travesty of marriage. And yet Jason's frustration nearly brings his need for so implausible a relationship to the surface. When he speaks of Quentin as a bastard in the passage I quoted above, he implies that Quentin's paternity would be certain only if *he* had fathered her—on his own sister. This bitter suggestion of incest arises from one of Jason's darkest suspicions: that Quentin is the offspring of his brother Quentin and Caddy. Twice in conversations with the incomprehending Caroline Compson, Jason torments himself with the idea that he is looking at the very incarnation of his siblings' incest:

> "Sometimes I think she is the judgment of Caddy and Quentin upon me."
>
> "Good Lord," I says, "You've got a fine mind. No wonder you kept yourself sick all the time."
>
> "What?" she says. "I dont understand."
>
> "I hope not," I says. "A good woman misses a lot she's better off without knowing."   [325]

> "Do you think I need any man's help to stand on my feet?" I says, "Let alone a woman that cant name the father of her own child."
>
> "Jason," she says.
>
> "All right," I says. "I didn't mean that. Of course not."
>
> "If I believed that were possible, after all my suffering."
>
> "Of course it's not," I says. "I didn't mean it."
>
> "I hope that at least is spared me," she says.
>
> "Sure it is," I says, "She's too much like both of them to doubt that."   [327]

Mrs. Compson probably accepts Jason's last statement in the spirit of her earlier one, that Quentin displays the characteristic Compson shortcomings evident in her two most Compson-like children. But Jason toys rather with the thought that Quentin's personality may be more readily explained by biology than by metaphor. By being

the "nearest thing to a father" to Quentin, Jason insinuates himself
into a heavily disguised, disfigured intimacy with Caddy. His transactions with her enable him to maintain perverse contact with her;
and on one occasion he even experiences a flicker of what it must
have been like to know Caddy: "'Wait,' she says, catching my arm.
'I've stopped [her hysterical sobbing]. I wont again. You promise,
Jason [to show her Quentin]?' she says, and me feeling her eyes
almost like they were touching my face..." (261).

Virtually all of Jason's attitudes toward money reflect his central,
unspoken interest in Caddy. Even incidental annoyances correspond to deeper concerns. We might surmise that he disapproves of
paying money to the outsiders in the circus (the country folks "coming in in droves to give their money to something that brought nothing
to the town and wouldn't leave anything"[243]) because they echo
the menagerie of suitors who eventually carry Caddy away from
home. (Quentin literally steals off with one of the show people.)
And Jason is so preoccupied with what has been taken from him
that he sees thievery all around: "... any damn foreigner that cant
make a living in the country where God put him, can come to this
one and take money right out of an American's pockets" (239).
"'When are you going to spread the news that I stole it from my
mother?'" (284) he asks Earl, referring to his automobile.

The one market into which Jason has never been able to buy, of
course, is the one that deals Caddy. His frustration at her unavailability forces him to think of her as a kind of prostitute, who
refuses herself to him because he somehow has the wrong currency.
Discussing her offer of cash to buy back Quentin, Jason says,
"And I know how you'll get it.... You'll get it the same way you
got her" (260). As if to counter his exclusion from the favors of
such a "whore" (as even Quentin calls her [197]),[37] Jason purchases
"a good honest whore" (291).

Acquiring Lorraine epitomizes Jason's furious confidence in the
power of money to substitute. So far as Jason can understand his
need for her, Lorraine offers the pleasures of sexual intimacy ("if
you dont believe he's a man I can tell you how to find out she says"
[291]) without the danger of emotional engagement ("I never
promise a woman anything nor let her know what I'm going to give

37. Jason calls Quentin "that little whore" (p. 269).

her. That's the only way to manage them" [240]). She embodies the power of money to neutralize love and to preclude the sorrow of loss: "Here I says, giving her the forty dollars. If you ever get drunk and take a notion to call me on the phone, just remember this and count ten before you do it" (241). Lorraine can be repeatedly bought and lost; it is as if Jason wants to buy the power to possess and recover. What Jason may not recognize about his bought woman is that she fills all of the natural roles that Caddy's loss has disrupted. For example, Jason will never marry because he has become his mother's surrogate husband: "Like I say if I was to get married you'd go up like a balloon and you know it" (307). Such voluntary bachelordom at times suggests a kind of aversion to sexuality, and the one time we see Jason with Lorraine she seems more a protective mother than a lover: "He imagined himself in bed with her, only he was just lying beside her, pleading with her to help him, then he thought of the money again" (383). Perhaps Jason's unresolved desire for Caddy threatens him with the epithet he designed for Benjy: "The Great American Gelding." Almost antically, moreover, Lorraine becomes a daughter whose good behavior and fidelity may be purchased:

> I went on back to the desk and read Lorraine's letter. "Dear daddy wish you were here. No good parties when daddys out of town I miss my sweet daddy." I reckon she does. Last time I gave her forty dollars. Gave it to her. [240]

By attending strictly to finance, by maniacally interpreting and evaluating every event in terms of its monetary significance, Jason seeks to cleanse his world of the effects of Caddy's loss. Although his economies may seem self-enclosed systems, however, they articulate a deep analogue to his central deprivation. Rather than agonize over the deathly difference of the representation from the 'original,' however, as Benjy and Quentin do, Jason wants to escape through those very gaps. Money at first looks like the kind of supplement that could frankly deny its supplementarity and affirm its pure difference, resigning the original presence to dead irrelevance. Surely Jason renounces actual words because they dangerously carry the aura of absent love: "I make it a rule never to keep a scrap of paper bearing a woman's hand, and I never write them at all. Lorraine is always after me to write to her but I says anything I forgot to tell you will save till I get to Memphis again" (240). If I am right, however, Jason fails colossally to deaden himself completely after the breaking of immediacy. And his failure suggests that Faulkner seeks in *The Sound and the Fury* to confront both the absolute "differance" of articulation and also the necessary illusion that there is an originary presence or locus of full meaning with which writing plays.

Jason's divorce from the word affects the nature of his monologue's performance. Although his first-person narrative closes the distance between speaker and perspective that we noticed in Benjy's section, and although the oral rhetoric of the style creates the impression of a told story (as Quentin's did not), nevertheless Jason's narrative is no public performance. As readers we may sense that we are Jason's audience, but more often than not his furious soliloquy seems never to escape the theater of his own mind. Jason performs the story for himself. It is the largest of his closed economies. We might get a sense of this privacy near the end of his monologue. At one point he reproduces an exchange between him and his mother that, we eventually learn, has been 'said' only in his mind:

> "I don't know what else she'd do in there alone," she says. "She never did read any."
> "No," I says, "You wouldn't know. And you can thank your stars for that," I says. Only what would be the use in saying it aloud. It would just have her crying on me again. [328]

When Jason recounts his miseries, he speaks to himself: "He repeated his story, harshly recapitulant, seeming to get an actual pleasure out of his outrage and impotence. The sheriff did not appear to be listening at all" (378).

Jason will not see that his desperate economy supplements Caddy in her absence. His urgent denial of loss and frustration deprives him of the opportunity to grieve well, to mourn imaginatively. In fact, Jason steadily flees the responsibilities of creative articulation. About his stock market misfortunes he can shrug: " 'That's not my fault either. I didn't invent it; I just bought a little of it' " (305).

iv

So I wrote Quentin's and Jason's sections, trying to clarify Benjy's. But I saw that I was merely temporising; that I should have to get completely out of the book. I realised that there would be compensations, that in a sense I could then give a final turn to the screw and extract some ultimate distillation. Yet it took me better than a month to take pen and write *The day dawned bleak and chill* before I did so.... I knew that it was not anywhere near finished and then I had to write another section from the outside with an outsider, which was the writer, to tell what had happened.[38]

The Sound and the Fury is a novel that comes to yearn for an ending. None of the first three sections presents its protagonist as having defined a dilemma and acted to resolve it; none of the three brothers even arrives at a full understanding of his situation—that is, no section describes the career of a process of intellection, as in a James novel, for example. Nor does the work conduct the reader through a progressive initiation into the workings of three profoundly idiosyncratic minds; rather, each section fiercely clenches the sympathetic reader and seems to present everything all at once—with incessant repetition. The conclusion of each section insists on irresolution. The twilight of Benjy's suspended time will not fade so long as his relics retain the glow of Caddy's touch. Quentin's "temporary" state of mind has been arrested in a permanent "apotheosis" by the refusal of the narrative to follow his body into the Charles River. The suicide is the great unspoken fact of his monologue—a finality important only because it eternalizes the present by 'unthinking' the future. And as Jason bitterly throws out his closing words, he imagines someday getting that "even chance to get my money back. And once I've done that they can bring all Beale Street and all bedlam in here" (329). Jason, too, however, remains leaning aginst the future; the repetitiveness of his routine and rhetoric dooms him to a life that will endlessly unravel "like a wornout sock" (391). Quentin voices the common lament: "Finished. If things just finished themselves" (97).

In a novel so interested in the nature of articulation, the conse-

38. James B. Meriwether, ed., "An Introduction to *The Sound and the Fury*," *Mississippi Quarterly*, 26 (1973), 415.

quences of making an end to the fiction naturally come under self-conscious scrutiny. In the passage I quoted above Faulkner recalls both the urgent appeal of being able to tighten and secure *The Sound and the Fury*'s meaning and effects and the reluctance to begin the ending. The ambivalence informs many of Faulkner's other statements about the last section of the novel; for example:

> I finished it the first time, and it wasn't right, so I wrote it again, and that was Quentin, that wasn't right. I wrote it again, that was Jason, that wasn't right, then I tried to let Faulkner do it, that still was wrong.[39]

The virtual oxymoron of finishing repeatedly captures the dilemma. To finish is to get it right; to continue is to admit insufficiencies. But if the novel stops, must the story have reached its conclusive resolution? Faulkner suggests that it need not—that, in fact, it must not—for a variety of reasons. One is that the very integrity of writing depends on preserving the discourse's *différance* even at the conclusion. In the highly personal regions of *The Sound and the Fury* for Faulkner as writer ("and now I can write"), each telling seeks to present a sheerly different account. Section 4 resigns itself to an ending that does not arrive at the truth of the matter, does not enjoy special authority, deliberately defers perfect coherence and intelligibility. As a result, the novel reinvests the earlier tellings with equal merit. The joy of the discourse is its pain: there may always be another way to put the story as the novel takes pleasure in its differing and deferment. In addition, the achievement of fully resolved meaning and conclusiveness in the last stages of the novel would belie Faulkner's sense of time. Diminishment, deprivation, and loss—which comprise the site of articulation—may be dispelled or transformed temporarily (as we shall see in *Absalom*), but Faulkner's conclusions consistently revisit scenes of division, fraudulent order, and incomprehension. Time inexorably disfigures all that is shaped to protest or forget it.

Frank Kermode helps us to see that ordinarily the simple fact of an approaching end may enliven incident, gesture, tone; the conclusion necessarily completes the shape of the fiction's form and so

39. Gwynn and Blotner, eds., *Faulkner in the University,* p. 32.

retrospectively orders what precedes: "Ends are ends only when they are not negative but frankly transfigure the events in which they were immanent" (or, we might add, events in which the end is now seen *to have been* immanent).[40]

> No novel can avoid being in some sense what Aristotle calls 'a completed action.' This being so, all novels imitate a world of potentiality, even if this implies a philosophy disclaimed by their authors. They have a fixation on the eidetic imagery of beginning, middle, and end, potency and cause.[41]

> Time cannot be faced as coarse and actual, as a repository of the contingent; one humanizes it by fictions of orderly succession and end.[42]

The last section of *The Sound and the Fury*—"Faulkner's"—presents versions of completed actions, of fictions of orderly succession and end. Yet simultaneously it disturbs and complicates those closing procedures, accomplishing what Kermode calls the "difficult concords" of modern fiction, rich with "paradox and contradiction."[43] Dilsey's vision of "de beginnin" and "de endin" seems to promise an authorized context within which to resolve the Compson crisis. Similarly, the new authority of an 'omniscient' narrator marks the invocation of more customary narrative techniques. However, as Dilsey embraces her orthodox Christianity, and as the narrative quietly creates a sense of resolving intelligibility by relying on 'orthodox' aesthetics, the last section also puzzles over its own inability to get it "right."

Certainly the mood of closure permeates the last section. For Dilsey, the painful passage of the body through time will culminate in the resurrection of the spirit into eternity. Sainthood will reward martyrdom; blissful death will end "dis long time": " 'En I be His'n too, fo long, praise Jesus' " (396). Shegog's sermon, as we all know, draws her tears of future release down the "myriad coruscations of

40. Frank Kermode, *The Sense of an Ending: Studies in the Theory of Fiction* (London, 1966), p. 175.
41. Ibid., p. 138.
42. Ibid., p. 160.
42. Ibid., p. 160.
43. Ibid., pp. 176, 164.

immolation and abnegation and time" (368). Faith converts the passage of time from a process of attrition to one of accretion. Accordingly, Dilsey has allowed none of the Compson animosity toward time to infect her; she soberly attends to the rites of burial for the household, quietly hymning the disappearance of Quentin, the money, and Jason. And she adds her corrective voice to the words of the mangled Compson clock, expecting—even hastening— the day of the Lord: "a cabinet clock ticked, then with a preliminary sound as if it had cleared its throat, struck five times. 'Eight o clock,' Dilsey said" (341–342).

Jason and Caroline Compson juxtapose private senses of ending to Dilsey's eschatology. Jason "for the first time . . . saw clear and unshadowed the disaster toward which he rushed" (386): "So this is how it'll end, and he believed that he was about to die" (387). Mrs. Compson rallies fraily: "when faced at last by the incontrovertible disaster she exhumed from somewhere a sort of fortitude, strength" (373). All of the survivors seem to live under the sentence of sovereign chronology: "The clock tick-tocked solemn and profound. It might have been the dry pulse of the decaying house itself" (355).

Despite a creeping apocalypse, however, life persists. The events of the last section conjure the prospect of "de endin," of an "incontrovertible disaster," only to dispel it. Jason retrieves himself from death as he wrestles with "the fatal, furious little old man." Give me time, and I'll get out" (386), he pleads, recommitting himself to his clock-ruled world. And Dilsey's very capacity for endurance immediately enfeebles her glimpse of the transcendent, for she lapses into protecting her vision with silence. " 'Never you mind,' " she replies to Frony's effort to get her to elaborate a little on what she has seen (371),[44] as if eternal truth cannot be translated into a mundane idiom. Dilsey's Christian order is predicated on a denial of the inexplicable and the contingent. Faith in a beginning and an ending seems ultimately a faith in the necessary invention of closure and coherence. In the 1946 Appendix to *The Sound and the Fury*, Dilsey refuses to imperil her fiction of an ending by acknowledging that Caddy Compson's life might have continued. The librarian

44. Dilsey's fiercely protected privacy makes her Christian vision irrelevant, according to Kartiganer (see note 7), p. 638.

seeks confirmation that her photograph is of Caddy, but Dilsey has learned from the librarian's question that Jason will join her conspiracy of silence against the past. She does not see what she will not: "'My eyes aint any good anymore,' she said. 'I cant see it'" (418). Dilsey "humanizes" the coarseness of time by lifting a shape out of perpetual change.

Surely the theological aspects of Dilsey's Christianity have received adequate discussion, but the vision that renews its vitality for her is the result of a performance that has literary implications as well.[45] Reverend Shegog complexly figures the role of the author in his work as he strives to deliver the word that will interpret experience truly and establish the communion of speaker and hearer. Shegog's sermon creates a moment of transfigured vision for Dilsey; we might presume not only that she sees the beginning and ending of all human time in the example of Christ's death and resurrection, but also that she has fitted the rise and fall of her particular Compson family into the inevitable cycles of human history. She has accepted the end of the family. I suggest that her vision has been stimulated by the uncanny similarities between Shegog's inspired imagery and the Compson situation, and that such a transfiguration of the Compson story embodies one of the ambitions of the novel's concluding section.

A miracle of the St. Louis preacher's sermon is that it answers so much of what Dilsey calls the "Compson devilment" (344). Against Dilsey's sad sense of the house's decay, Shegog proclaims that only the "ricklickshun en de Blood of de Lamb" matters, for heaven is the only home and God's the only family worth thinking about. Though Benjamin may be "our lastborn, sold into Egypt" (Appendix, 423), yet the promised land redeemed the bondage of those who "'passed away in Egypt, de singin chariots; de generations passed away'" (368). Though Jason is the wealthy pauper, yet in heaven "'Wus a rich man: whar he now ... Wus a po man: whar he now ...?'" (368–369). Even the mournful, trying self-pity of

45. Bleikasten suggests that Shegog's triumph is Faulkner's, since the preacher is the "double" of the novelist (*Most Splendid Failure*, p. 201). Bleikasten contends that the novel coalesces and reaches a kind of authoritative version in the last section, just as Shegog's voice authorizes his sermon for Dilsey. But Shegog's sermon, as I shall argue, succeeds only because Dilsey hears (or reads) it correctly. It is a private and temporary manifestation of meaning.

Caroline Compson appears in " 'de weepin en de lamentation of de po mammy widout de salvation en de word of God' " (369).

Shegog's conjuring of the crucifixion scene touches remarkably on the death-plagued Compson past.

> "I sees hit, breddren! I sees hit! Sees de blastin, blindin sight! I sees Calvary, wid de sacred trees, sees de thief en de murderer en de least of dese; I hears de boastin and de braggin: Ef you be Jesus, lif up yo tree en walk! I hears de wailin of women en de evenin lamentations; I hears de weepin en de cryin en de turnt-away face of God: dey done kilt Jesus; dey done kilt my Son!' " [370]

Christ's death on the sacred tree may recall the fatal trees in which Caddy loses her innocence, dies to Benjy and Quentin, and provokes the eldest son's self-sacrifice. Caddy climbs the tree to see death, lies down among trees to surrender her virginity, and cloaks herself in their fragrance as her stigma. Calvary's tree is sacred, however, because it replaces Eden's tree of death; the second Adam redeems the site of the Fall. But Caddy's brothers have failed to resurrect her in their separate acts of "ricklickshun." Shegog inadvertently ironizes the contrast between the two deaths by confusing his scripture. He dramatizes the incomprehending taunts of those who challenge the dying Christ to prove his divinity: " 'Ef you be Jesus, lif up your tree en walk.' " Christ chooses to die before he can triumph over death, but Caddy remains simply powerless to deny crucifying, but natural, time. In the Gospels, the crowd never asks Jesus to lift up the tree and walk, but to "come down from the tree, if Thou art the Christ." The phrase Shegog is thinking of comes from an episode in Christ's earlier ministry, in which he challenges the faith of one infirm: "Take up thy bed and walk."[46] The lapse could be Faulkner's, of course (to the mortification of his grandfather, who made the Faulkner children recite their memory verses at the breakfast table); but if it is not, it neatly substitutes tree for bed, an ironic tailoring of the statement for Caddy, for whom trees have been a bed. The miracle of neither resurrection nor healing will save Caddy from her fatal infection by time (*"Sick how are you sick I'm just sick,"* she tells Quentin [138]).

Shegog's sermon figures the self-slain Quentin, too. We might

46. See, for example, Matthew 27:39–40 and Matthew 9:5–7.

recognize both Quentin's fantasy of punished incest and Mr. Compson's last grief in the picture of " 'de turnt-away face of God . . . dey done kilt my Son!' " The ecstatic word of one congregation member, "like bubbles rising in water," ironically recalls Quentin's water-stilled voice, as "de whelmin flood" that rolls between the generations evokes both the branch and the Charles River.

The achievement of Shegog's sermon stands at the very center of a novel's customary aspiration for its conclusion. The transfiguration of earlier events in which the end is immanent—that process Kermode locates in all legitimate ends—occurs for Dilsey as a result of Shegog's performance. She can see the pattern and has discovered a fiction of orderly succession and end. The moment epitomizes a climax of sense with which *The Sound and the Fury* might have ended, but does not. Shegog's sermon succeeds, moreover, because it rescues conclusiveness from irresolution. Shegog's first sermon casts a magnificent but distant spell on the congregation. The sheer "virtuosity" of the "cold inflectionless wire of his voice" creates the congregation's "collective dream" (366), but it does not erect an interpretive structure, as the second does. Dilsey prepares to leave when she senses the end of Shegog's first address: " 'Hush, now. Dey fixin to sing in a minute' " (367). Knowing that his sermon has not struck, however, Reverend Shegog dramatically modulates into his listeners' dialect. The sermon succeeds because it is willing to say, and then say again; it indulges its personal voice and then accommodates its audience. The result is spectacular. Speaker and hearers experience an "immolation" of the voice, "until he was nothing and they were nothing and there was not even a voice but instead their hearts were speaking to one another in chanting measures beyond the need for words" (367). The novel, like the sermon, might have striven for the revelation of comprehensive meaning; it might have attempted, like the passage from the first to the second performance, to resolve the pauses at the end of the opening three sections into a full cadence in the last. The idiosyncratic strangeness of the monologues' voices might have yielded utterly to the accommodating familiarity of the final section. Instead, the novel prefers a difficult concord, one that denies the possibility of absolute disclosure, that beclouds the prospect of the beginning and the ending, that signals the continuation of difference and deferment.

The last section of *The Sound and the Fury* explores the resources of conventional narrative discourse only to learn that they can compose no more authoritative telling of the story than the inside accounts that have gone before. The style, for example, bears much greater resemblance to traditional ones than the styles of the monologues.[47] We welcome syntactic regularity, descriptive passages, sequential action, dialogue, and so on. But if we examine the opening sentence closely—the sentence that reminds one critic of the confident voice of many Victorian novels[48]—we may notice as well a kind of laboring:

> The day dawned bleak and chill, a moving wall of grey light out of the northeast which, instead of dissolving into moisture, seemed to disintegrate into minute and venomous particles, like dust that, when Dilsey opened the door of the cabin and emerged, needled laterally into her flesh, precipitating not so much a moisture as a substance partaking of the quality of thin, not quite congealed oil. [330]

The extended syntax of this sentence suggests an impatience to refine and qualify in the very midst of the first saying, as if no simple statement can be trusted not to falsify the complexity of things. There are, for example, an immediate apposition ("a moving wall"), two restrictive modifying clauses ("which ... seemed to disintegrate" and "that ... needled"), two participial clauses, and a subordinate modifying clause. The elaborate artifice dramatizes the difficulty of saying. Action occurs, but at once qualification interrupts. The phrases "instead of dissolving" and "not so much moisture as" attempt to specify by a kind of negative circumscription. Faulkner's mature style remains attached to the idea that a thing may be described only between what it is and what it is not. (Addie reminds us that words never fit exactly what they are saying.) But these are also elements from which Faulkner takes pleasure. The need to qualify, to appose, to test all of the ways to say something, without the belief that any can succeed alone, coincides with the supplementarity of writing. The significance that writing produces 'begins' only in the movement of pure difference, and transparent meaning must remain deferred. We might also notice

47. Kartiganer (see note 7) sees this moment as a forecast of Faulkner's mature views of language (pp. 638–639).
48. Ibid., p. 634.

that Faulkner seeks strenuously to tap all of the resources for play in the language: casual assonance and consonance appear in "day"/"grey" and in "chill"/"wall"; but a more profound alliteration ties "Dilsey" to "day," "dawned," "dissolving," "disintegrate," "dust," and "door," which surely prepares for this Sunday of promised judgment, salvation, and resolution.

Like the style, other features of this "outside" narrator's discourse are concerned with presenting a more 'objective' account than the preceding monologues. The symbolism of this section tries to make itself explicit and to represent universal abstractions, but it proves as stiffly falsifying as Benjy's signs or Quentin's obsessive imagery.[49] For example, Benjy's howl "might have been all time and injustice and sorrow become vocal for an instant" (359), the "sound of all voiceless misery under the sun"(359); and, to Jason, Quentin is "the very symbol of the lost job itself" (383–384). When Quentin's treachery dawns on Jason, he paws at Mrs. Compson's "rusted keys on an iron ring like a mediaeval jailer's"; Jason's impotent imprisonment in the Compson house could be no more explicitly pictured. Similarly, one of the ruling puns of Benjy's section is flushed to the surface now:

"Here, caddie. Bring the bag."
... Ben went on at his shambling trot, clinging to the fence ...
"All right, den" Luster said, "You want somethin to beller about?"
"... Caddy! Beller now. Caddy! Caddy!" [394]

In the hope of getting the story right by virtue of the author's authority, the novel forswears reticence. Instead of the deeply submerged but mercilessly coherent systems presented in the three monologues, the last section offers broader contexts but shallower understanding. For example, we may be shocked to learn, after our intimacy with Quentin Compson's mind, that his mother has no idea why he committed suicide. Though her granddaughter would appear to have no motive either, she too may have taken her life as her uncle had: and "'what reason did Quentin have'" (374). Throughout the last section, the narrator's attention to explicit statement threatens to reduce the reader's search for meaning to a

49. Ibid., p. 635.

version of Mrs. Compson's hunt for "the note." We want the novel to divulge its meaning by its own hand, but Faulkner avoids both the note and the death at the ending. The last section has a status like Dilsey's church, framed but flat: "a weathered church lifted its crazy steeple like a painted church, and the whole scene was flat and without perspective as a painted cardboard set upon the ultimate edge of the flat earth" (364). *The Sound and the Fury,* in its first three sections, has already shown the need for more than the conventional, picture-making narrative. The fourth telling of the story sacrifices as much as it gains by its objectivity and detachment. Indirectly, it extends one of the abiding interests of *The Sound and the Fury:* a justification of its own radical innovativeness. The reader's customary demand for a conventional novel is mimicked by Benjy's concluding demand for the regular left-to-right flow of signboards past his eyes, like print on the page. The novel arrays itself against a too simple order by feigning conclusiveness and a conclusion. The structure of the story reflects this evasiveness.

The narrative, having apparently adopted the convention of linear chronology in section 4, avoids an ending even as it suggests the possibility of one. The sequence of Dilsey's morning climaxes in the vision of the beginning and the end, but the novel continues. The overall temporal restlessness of *The Sound and the Fury* (moving from Saturday to Friday to Sunday, from 1928 to 1910 and back again) erupts in a looping of chronology in section 4. Jason's morning starts after Dilsey's has ended: "He was twenty miles away at that time. When he left the house he drove rapidly to town, overreaching the slow sabbath groups" (376). For linear time to hold in the plot, the second sentence of this narrative sequence should begin with a past perfect tense—to bring us up to the narrative present: when he *had left* the house. Instead, the day's chronology begins over at a new location. The plot displays a seam that prepares for the centrifugal closing of *The Sound and the Fury.* The narrative preserves the momenta of several plot lines: first, there is Dilsey's expectation of the imminent, "incontrovertible disaster," her curious sense that Jason and Quentin will not be back and that a genuinely transfigurative "endin" looms. There are also Benjamin's dizzyingly repetitive rituals, which figure a desperate recoil from the unresolved. Both closures reflect an aspect of the novelist's desire to establish clarity and stability. But the plot also withholds resolution; Jason returns home delayed but not defeated, and his niece remains at large—the embodiment of the elusive future, her very name the sign of the past's devious capacity to persist.

The Sound and the Fury ceases while still faithful to the recognition that the act of articulation cannot successfully reappropriate what has been lost. The pain of grief, the folly of denying it, the hopelessness of recovery, the uneasy bliss of repetition and substitution, and the recognition of their failure all nourish the exceptional tensions of Faulkner's first unquestionably major novel. We might take Luster's saw playing as the closing figure of the artist's activity: like him, the author must try to recreate on his cruder implements the enchantingly, endlessly elusive music of last night's carnival.

CHAPTER 3

Marriages of Speaking and Hearing in *Absalom, Absalom!*

It remains, then, for us to *speak,* to make our voices *resonate* throughout the corridors in order to make up for [*suppléer*] the breakup of presence.... Rising toward the sun of presence, it is the way of Icarus.

And contrary to what phenomenology—which is always phenomenology of perception—has tried to make us believe, contrary to what our desire cannot fail to be tempted into believing, the thing itself always escapes.

—Jacques Derrida, *Speech and Phenomena*

Ultimately, one might say that the object of structuralism is not man endowed with meanings but man fabricating meanings, as if it could not be the *content* of meanings which exhausted the semantic goals of humanity, but only the act by which these meanings, historical and contingent variables, are produced. *Homo significans:* such would be the new man of structural inquiry.

—Roland Barthes, "The Structuralist Activity"

... don't be too certain of learning the past from the lips of the present. Beware of the most honest broker. Remember that what you are told is really threefold: shaped by the teller, reshaped by the listener, concealed from both by the dead man of the tale.

—Vladimir Nabokov, *The Real Life of Sebastian Knight*

i

Absalom, Absalom! is Faulkner's most accomplished, moving, and sustained meditation on the act of fabricating meaning. His ninth novel, it revisits the site of the crisis of articulation surveyed in

The Sound and the Fury; but it returns with a sure sense of the possibilities and limitations of language, a sense ecstatically discovered in that novel. "And now I can write," he had said in the 1933 preface to *The Sound and the Fury.* I have argued that *The Sound and the Fury* enabled Faulkner to come to terms with properties of language best described by Derrida's theme of the supplement whose movements are difference and deferment. Each section seeks to recover the thing itself, the elusive presence of the absent Caddy. Yet none of the separate performances arrives at a perfect reappropriation of what seems to have been lost; none succeeds in achieving an authorized, complete version of the loss; and each calls attention to the fact that it is strictly a simulacrum of Caddy's presence—a text that, in differing from her, replaces and thus presents her as already disappearing.

The situations of *The Sound and the Fury* and *Absalom* clearly resemble each other. Both Caddy and Sutpen are dead, absent centers whose full vitality remains an unrecoverable origin of the works. They are surrounded by those who experience their loss and strive to articulate responses to it. Rosa, for example, might be a Quentin Compson who lacked the nerve to kill himself; she is hostage to an endless remembering of lost love. Unlike the figures of *The Sound and the Fury,* however, the various witnesses of *Absalom* dedicate themselves to the painfully blissful, dangerously necessary methods of supplementing absence. They manipulate the supplements of speech and memory, and, through the simultaneous motions of difference and deferment, their narratives succeed in conjuring up a simulacrum of Sutpen.

That *Absalom* returns to crises that initiated and propelled *The Sound and the Fury* is suggested superficially by the reappearance of two members of the Compson family, Mr. Compson and Quentin. Faulkner confirmed the continuities between the two novels on several occasions. To a questioner at the University of Virginia he responded that the character of Quentin in both novels was "consistent" and that "Quentin was still trying to get God to tell him why, in *Absalom, Absalom!* as he was in *The Sound and the Fury.*"[1] And Ellen Schoenberg, in her recent study of the genealogy

1. Frederick L. Gwynn and Joseph L. Blotner, eds., *Faulkner in the University: Class Conferences at the University of Virginia, 1957–1958* (New York, 1959), pp. 274, 275.

of the Quentin figure in the early fiction, reports that one manuscript version of Chapter 2 of *Absalom* began with the words "That was the summer before Quentin died: that summer with wistaria everywhere . . . ,"[2] as if *Absalom* will deepen our understanding of Quentin's suicide.

In one sense, *Absalom* is yet another effort to tell the story of the Compson obsessions with time, incest, virginity, and tragedy.[3] If novels stand in a supplementary relationship to their ideal objects (figured by Caddy, Addie, Sutpen, and the rest), then every story may be retold, no matter how many times it has been told before. No substitute can fully replace the allegedly lost "thing itself." The idea of repetition governs Faulkner's view of the four tellings that comprise *The Sound and the Fury,* and he dramatized his conviction by trying to tell it a fifth time in the Appendix to the 1946 Viking Portable edition. In *Absalom* both Mr. Compson and Quentin—who are chief figures in *The Sound and the Fury*—try to tell a version of Sutpen's history. By studying their particular focuses, styles, and conclusions, I hope to show that each repeats a detailed version of his characteristic concerns. Faulkner suggests as much when he insists that the novel is Sutpen's story and at the same time the story of each of its narrators: "No it's Sutpen's story. But then, every time any character gets into a book, no matter how minor, he's actually telling his biography—that's all anyone ever does, he tells his own biography, talking about himself, in a thousand different terms, but himself."[4]

In a second respect, the story of Sutpen, as it is also told by Rosa Coldfield and Shreve McCannon, retells the story of lost love, lost coherence, and grief. The thematic centers of *Absalom,* in ways that I do not believe have been systematically investigated, are also chief concerns of *The Sound and the Fury.* Like Quentin, Rosa conse-

2. Ellen Schoenberg, *Old Tales and Talking: Quentin Compson in William Faulkner's "Absalom, Absalom!" and Related Works* (Jackson: University Press of Mississippi, 1977), epigraph (notes from the Jill Faulkner Summers Archive, University of Virginia).

3. John T. Irwin suggests that Faulkner's fiction embodies a particularly modern theory of tragedy, that man's tragic situation arises from the tantalizing sensation of nearly coalesced meaning—even from novel to novel. That meaning is repeatedly deferred defines the dilemmas of Quentin Compson and Charles Bon, for example (*Doubling & Incest/Repetition & Revenge: A Speculative Reading of Faulkner* [Baltimore, 1975], pp. 8–9).

4. Gwynn and Blotner, eds., *Faulkner in the University,* p. 275.

crates her memory to preserving, in impotent frustration, the dead object of her love. Like Quentin, Sutpen falls from the natural order and significance of his childhood into a world of division, paradox, and shadow. And he, too, seeks to deny such a change and to recover (through imitation) the lost plenitude of an origin. *Absalom* extravagantly displays how 'authors' use their fictions; it affirms that the substituting, differing, and deferring properties of narrative may console those who mourn. As Rosa reminds Quentin at the outset of the novel, Sutpen "died":

> Without regret, Miss Rosa Coldfield says—(Save by her) Yes, save by her. (And by Quentin Compson) Yes. And by Quentin Compson. [9; italics omitted]

The entire novel becomes an act of formal regretting.

The narrators' several attempts to fabricate meaning through the stories they tell have attracted thoughtful discussion. James Guetti's essay on *Absalom* in *The Limits of Metaphor* sees Sutpen's search for meaning as the core of the novel's problem and the synecdoche of the narrators' inabilities to tell his story successfully. As Sutpen failed to interpret his insult by the plantation slave and to devise a workable design, so the "inability of the narrators to understand the experience surrounding Sutpen may be an expression of a consistent theme: that human experience cannot be understood, that order cannot be created." Although Guetti concedes that Quentin's narrative, for example, creates a "vital, articulated vision," he emphasizes the pervasive failure of any interpretation—any metaphor, any telling—to master the mystery of Sutpen's career.[5] Guetti here makes the mistake of his chief critical predecessor, Walter Slatoff, by defining order and meaning as necessarily permanent, explicit, and unitary.[6] I argue rather than Faulkner's distinctive modernity involves an understanding of meaning as the infinite play of sig-

5. James Guetti, *The Limits of Metaphor* (Ithaca, 1967), pp. 70, 81.
6. Walter J. Slatoff, *Quest for Failure: A Study of William Faulkner* (Ithaca, 1960). Slatoff laments that paradox seems to destroy Faulkner's meaning: *Absalom*, for example, never forces Faulkner to "step beyond the sanctuary of the paradox, to make, himself, as do a number of his characters, the clarifying 'gesture.'" Consequently, Faulkner's "temperament" "makes the search for the meaning or design of his novels so enticing and yet so futile an occupation" (p. 201).

nifiers, and not as the attainment of an absolute signified, the "facts" of the story itself. Sutpen's demand for a clarified order and his attempt to reverse (or duplicate) the very moment of his fall appear in the novel as innocent, nearly tragic, demands on intelligibility. Sutpen's trouble was "innocence," General Compson insists, and that innocence is counteracted only by the vast knowledge of the various tellers about the impossibilities of conclusive accounting and the need to proceed with speculative fabrication anyhow. The supplemental properties of narrative replace the sterile demands of Sutpen's design as they persistently differ from that design (and from each other), and as they defer any assertion that they have gotten Sutpen's story entirely "right" once and for all. The narratives include their own failures, their own needs to be retold differently, their submission to a time that will make them obsolete and finally dead. The tellers master, by acknowledging, the very conditions that Sutpen defies, and so is mastered by. I shall argue that the narrators oppose Sutpen's rigidly phallic and dynastic language with a playful language that disseminates meaning.

I should also distinguish my argument from David Minter's analysis of the redemptive power of interpretation in *Absalom*.[7] He regards Sutpen's design (the aspiration to dynasty) as so significant culturally as to demand compulsive interpretation. The failures of Rosa and Mr. Compson to explain it are eventually surpassed when Quentin and Shreve manage to bring interpretive order out of the chaos that is Sutpen's design. But we are left with several important questions: How are the puzzlements of Rosa and Mr. Compson themselves a kind of remedy for Sutpen's infantile demand for conclusiveness? How is the imaginatively rich playfulness of all four accounts superior to Sutpen's closed "text"? Can we discover precise ways in which the manners and values of the tellings themselves replicate and transform elements of Sutpen's physical design?

The main channel of my approach is much closer to Hyatt Waggoner's and Arnold Weinstein's in their essays on the novel.[8] Each

7. David L. Minter, *The Interpreted Design as a Structural Principle in American Prose* (New Haven, 1969).
8. Hyatt H. Waggoner, *William Faulkner: From Jefferson to the World* (Lexington, Ky., 1959) and Arnold Weinstein, *Vision and Response in Modern Fiction* (Ithaca, 1974).

stresses that the novel presents scenes in which meaning is conferred through acts of loving partnership in telling rather than discovered through patient logical research.

> The inescapable infirmities of the private vision are honestly acknowledged, but there is an effort toward community. The value of selfless commitment and the embracing, creating vision of love are asserted against the claims of logic, evidence, and appearances.[9]

Weinstein's formulation of Faulkner's credo seems very near the heart of the matter, but I shall suggest a few departures in my own study. The possibilities of affective truth do not, as Weinstein may be suggesting, liberate the tellers from some obligation to the facts of Sutpen's story. We may finally never be able to judge what is fact and what fiction in the mutual tellings, as threatens to become an endless critical amusement;[10] but the desired state for the creative imagination seems to be a tense engagement with fact that fails to engage (to paraphrase Mr. Compson). That is, Sutpen's "real" story is something that can never be known in itself; it functions like the transcendent signifier of the metaphysics that Derrida questions. On the other hand, sheer improvisation would be the severest form of solipsism and despair since there could be no common ground between the fabricators. Instead, Faulkner creates partnerships that respect many (often unspeakable) certitudes in the narratives. What is important is not any fact itself but the mirage of its imminent presence deferred; this is precisely the movement of *différance* (as supplemental to Sutpen's absence) that allows a strange reappropriation of him and a coherent explanation of him. In addition, I question Weinstein's notion of "selfless commitment" in his otherwise shrewd formulation. I hope to show that precisely by deflecting the story through their considerable (but by no means absolute) differences, each teller enacts a version of the story that is

9. Weinstein, *Vision and Response,* p. 138.

10. See, for example, Cleanth Brooks, "The Narrative Structure of *Absalom, Absalom!,*" *Georgia Review,* 29 (Summer 1975), 366–394. In this article Brooks continues his campaign to establish the facts of *Absalom,* an enterprise begun in his *William Faulkner: The Yoknapatawpha Country* (New Haven, 1963). Carl E. Rollyson ("The Re-Creation of the Past in *Absalom, Absalom!,*" *Mississippi Quarterly,* 29 [Summer 1976], 361–374) disputes some of Brooks's facts.

personally and affectively "true," and which can at least temporarily be shared by the telling partner.

That the tellers of *Absalom* may arrive at moments of consent and affective truth helps to explain a striking formal feature of the novel, as well. Despite the certainty that we are meant to distinguish the four narrative performances (Rosa's and Mr. Compson's during separate hours of an afternoon in September 1909, and Quentin's and Shreve's in January 1910), every reader notices that the tellings are not set off by wholly individualized voices. Tones, emphases, topics, and manners may differ, but there is an essential sameness to the baroque prolixity, the nightmarish breathlessness, and the Latinate polysyllabism of the novel. Moreover, from time to time an ostensibly impersonal narrator's voice is heard, speaking in the third person, although it, too, can scarcely be said to have distinctive qualities. When it appears in Chapter 1, for example, it subtly takes on Quentin's viewpoint and gently wonders about the maniacal old Rosa. When it introduces Mr. Compson's narrative in Chapter 2, it impersonates his understated cynicism.[11] In addition to these difficulties, the reader is occasionally presented with passages that have no identifiable source: Chapter 5 is not Rosa's literal speech, nor is it the narrator's paraphrase or recounting, nor is it Quentin's remembered translation; it is more precisely some collaboration of all three. The effect produced by these interpenetrations of voice is of a variety of partnerships contracted on the common ground of Sutpen's story. That is, the hearing and speaking partners of each performance are seized by the intimacies of telling. Like Shegog's voice in *The Sound and the Fury,* the speaking instrument immolates, and teller and auditor disappear into the "text" itself. Such intimacies demarcate the space of writing in *Absalom,* the place where the novel escapes the simple dichotomies of presence and absence, being and nonbeing.

ii

I have taken the title for this chapter from a familiar passage in *Absalom, Absalom!* (1936) which marks a critical transition in the

---

11. See Gerald Langford, *Faulkner's Revisions of Absalom, Absalom!* (Austin, 1971). Langford observes that Faulkner frequently reassigned portions of the narrative by moving quotation marks around; one voice seems to fit all (p. 21).

narrative of Sutpen's career. Quentin and his Harvard roommate, Shreve McCannon, have recounted the origin and growth of Sutpen's design and are about to explore Charles Bon's threat to it when the narrator announces the new topic of love:

> ... all that had gone before just so much that had to be overpassed and none else present to overpass it but them, as someone always has to rake the leaves up before you can have the bonfire. That was why it did not matter to either of them which one did the talking, since it was not the talking alone which did it, performed and accomplished the overpassing, but some happy marriage of speaking and hearing wherein each before the demand, the requirement, forgave condoned and forgot the faulting of the other—faultings both in the creating of this shade whom they discussed (rather, existed in) and in the hearing and sifting and discarding the false and conserving what seemed true, or fit the preconceived—in order to overpass to love, where there might be paradox and inconsistency but nothing fault nor false. [316]

Though Quentin's and Shreve's collaboration is the most vigorous and evenly distributed in the novel, the narratives that precede theirs—by Rosa Coldfield and Mr. Compson—also celebrate marriages of speaking and hearing. In several respects marriage is one of the chief figures for storytelling in *Absalom,* and I want to argue that a peculiar, perhaps even parodic, version of marriage embodies the intimacy and pleasure of narration, and also suggests how fiction makes its meanings.

The first two tellings of Sutpen's story are usually dismissed by critics as varieties of irrelevance.[12] Rosa Coldfield, moldering for forty-three years in black outrage at Sutpen's insult, and Mr. Compson, steeped in a sardonic cynicism, both seem to offer accounts

---

12. Olga Vickery, for example, in *The Novels of William Faulkner* (Baton Rouge, 1959), argues that Rosa presents the most "distorted" account, a "rank melodrama" that constructs a world wholly divorced from 'reality' (pp. 87–88). Rosa's role is important to Michael Millgate (*The Achievement of William Faulkner* [New York, 1963]) only as it prepares for Quentin's major responsibility in recreating the past (pp. 153–154). Cleanth Brooks (*William Faulkner*) also subordinates Rosa by concentrating on Sutpen's mythic career, as does Melvin Backman in *Faulkner: The Major Years* (Bloomington: Indiana University Press, 1966). James Guetti (*Limits of Metaphor*) accounts for Rosa's difficulty by calling it a "psychological problem" and does not attend to the features of Rosa's language. Richard P. Adams better understands that Rosa's situation resembles the artist's: both aim to arrest life in their

that are not fully coherent. As Mr. Compson once puts it, " 'It's just incredible. It just does not explain' " (100). We may expect greater intelligibility from Quentin's and Shreve's versions; they seem to possess more 'facts'; they speak with greater urgency and a deeper devotion to getting it "right"; and they overpass to love, where there is "nothing fault nor false." We underestimate *Absalom's* richness, however, if we fail to appreciate the truths of Rosa's and Mr. Compson's narratives. I want to follow the contortions of Rosa's language because the tale she tells Quentin, the poems she writes to Confederate soldiers, and her love for the *words* Charles Bon and Thomas Sutpen—all these uses of language are weddings of speaking and hearing. Rosa Coldfield conjures a life for herself and her subjects through her words; she may tell us something about the writer's consecration to desire, bereavement, and memory.

Rosa's romance of the word does not begin on the eve of her sortie to Sutpen's Hundred when she tells Quentin her story; nor does it originate on the night her father locks himself in the attic to protest the Confederate cause and she writes her first war poem. Rather, Rosa's first breath inspires her worded life. Born into her parents' old age at the price of her mother's life, Rosa guiltily tries to deny her own presence by living in an imagined world, what she calls a "might-have-been which is more than truth" (143): "so that instead of accomplishing the processional and measured milestones of the childhood's time I lurked, unapprehended as though, shod with the very damp and velvet silence of the womb, I displaced no air, gave off no betraying sound, from one closed forbidden door to the next and so acquired all I knew of that light and space in which people moved and breathed as I (that same child) might have gained conception of the sun from seeing it through a piece of smoky

---

representations, but Rosa makes the mistake of trying to "live in the dream of art" (*Faulkner: Myth and Motion* [Princeton, 1968], p. 202). More recently, Richard Forrer ("*Absalom, Absalom!:* Story-Telling as a Mode of Transcendence," *Southern Literary Journal,* 9 [Fall 1976]) largely ignores Rosa as he studies the moments of "transcendence" in the narratives. My argument makes Rosa's failure to transcend herself consonant with the function of language in the other narratives. Rosa's narrative attracts more interesting attention in Irwin's *Doubling & Incest.* Irwin notices some similarities between Rosa and Quentin—their incestuous desire, impotence, and hatred of their fathers—but he does not analyze the nature of Rosa's telling or the verbal strategies by which she leads her life.

glass" (145). Rosa's desires learn to frustrate themselves, to respect the barrier of the closed door even as they picture what goes on behind it. Rosa's chief instrument for fashioning such a life is her language, for she recognizes how rumored love both affirms desire and protects against its satisfaction. This economy of desire resembles Derrida's model for the general economy of language. The motions of difference and deferment comprise the activity of language that moves away from the absent object of representation and postpones its reappearance. Rosa's various languages of love display these characteristics; her words substitute for the lovers she will not permit herself and they safely defer the satisfaction of her desire, thereby extending its life. This aspect of Rosa's performance is enunciated early by the narrator when he notices that Rosa seems to be grieving in black for some "sister, father, or nothusband" (7). "Nothusband" is a word that defines the paradox of Rosa's language; she is wedded to those who have been negated or erased even as they have become her husbands. Shreve McCannon surmises that Rosa has been "irrevocably husbanded" to Sutpen precisely because they do not marry.

For too long, critics of *Absalom* let Shreve McCannon do their reading. When Quentin's roommate offers his hasty synopsis of the Sutpen story at the beginning of Chapter 6, he plausibly (if somewhat theatrically) explains Rosa's voluntary "ghosthood" as her hysterical reaction to Sutpen's suggestion that "they breed [like?] a couple of dogs together." It was a proposal that "would not only blast the little dream-woman out of the dovecote but leave her irrevocably husbanded . . . with the abstract carcass of outrage and revenge." Before he and Quentin have begun their elaborate meditation on Sutpen's career, Shreve overestimates the force of Rosa's "Puritan righteousness" as he tries to understand the South in terms of its conventions. To him, Rosa's incredible forty-three years of "demonizing" must be the aghast complaint of the Methodist spinster maddened by Sutpen's disregard for morality. But Quentin's first impression of Rosa suggests that something more than simple hatred accounts for her inexhaustible devotion to Sutpen's memory:

> She was talking in that grim haggard amazed voice until at last listening would renege and hearing-sense self-confound and the

long-dead object of her impotent yet indomitable frustation would appear, as though by outraged recapitulation evoked, quiet inattentive, and harmless, out of the biding and dreamy and victorious dust. [7–8]

The atmosphere in Rosa's room is charged with sexual frustration, rife with "the rank smell of female old flesh long embattled in virginity" (8), and darkened by the "eternal black" worn for the "nothusband" who has become the dead object of desire. Rosa's "impotent frustration" speaks a tale not of offended morality but of thwarted love: "And that's what she cant forgive him for: not for the insult . . . but for being dead" (170).

Rosa talks endlessly about love to Quentin, and her idea of it is what we might expect to find in a spinster's "mausoleum." Despite her incontestable virginity, however, she recalls an adolescence that had awakened the "root bloom and urge" of passion. She knew that she was only a "warped bitter pale and crimped half-fledging" leaf that would never draw "to it the tender mayfly childhood sweetheart games or . . . the male predacious wasps and bees of later lust" (144; italics omitted), but she never denies the fact of her desire. Instead, she celebrates a kind of love that defers sexual gratification and physical possession. In "the unpaced corridor which I called childhood" (144), Rosa imagines a special order of love that will leave her virginal isolation from experience intact, that will accomplish the necessary frustration of desire: she loves Charles Bon "because I asked nothing of him, you see. And more than that: I gave him nothing, which is the sum of loving" (147). Such a love may protect her from the "maelstrom of unbearable reality" (150); it reaches toward its object without hoping to gain it.

Rosa repeatedly returns in her conversation with Quentin to descriptions of a love that recoils from full mutual possession and depends instead on the absence of its object. The soldiers of the Confederacy go off to their slaughter, "dying not for honor's empty sake, nor pride nor even peace, but for that love they left behind. Because he [Bon] was to die; I know that . . . else how to prove love's immortality" (150). Similarly, Bon's separation from Judith paradoxically constitutes and preserves the life of their love even as it postpones its consummation: "if even deferred love could have supplied her with the will to exist, endure for this long, then that same love, even though deferred, must and would preserve Bon until the folly of men would stalemate from sheer exhaustion" (87). The awakening of passion in Rosa at age fourteen created a world of "living marriage" that is uncontaminated by physical sexuality, that "moment which only virgins know: when the entire delicate spirit's bent is one anonymous climaxless epicene and unravished nuptial" (145).

The conflicting demands of Rosa's "unravished nuptial" are met perfectly by her love for Charles Bon. To Rosa, the mysteriously seductive suitor of her niece seems only the trace of an actual presence. Rosa can afford to love him precisely because his absence makes him unattainable: "I never saw him. I never even saw him dead" (146; italics omitted); she "had only Ellen's word for it that there was such a person" (146); and she loves him because he is her invention—"a picture seen by stealth, by creeping (my childhood taught me that instead of love and it stood me in good stead; in fact, if it had taught me love, love could not have stood me so) into the deserted midday room to look at it" (147; italics omitted). Rosa dreams about marriage "on the nooky seat which held invisible imprint of his absent thighs" while she fondles the name of the lover who is simply a word to her: "Charles Bon, Charles Good, Charles Husband-soon-to-be" (148; italics omitted). Mr. Compson accents Bon's status as a word when he tells Quentin how Rosa "had got the picture from the first word, perhaps from the name, Charles Bon" (75). Rosa balances the paradoxes of desire in the language of love.

Bon's proximity would have been ensured by his marriage to Judith, a marriage that would have allowed the spinster aunt an eternally vicarious possession of him. Had Bon married Judith, Rosa could have enjoyed the perpetual deferment of her own desire by a vicarious interest in her niece's. As she awakens to the prospect of "marrying" Bon through Judith, Rosa conceives a role that will preserve her fearful seclusion: "I who had learned nothing of love, not even parents' love . . . became not mistress, not beloved but more than even love; I became all polymath love's androgynous advocate" (146; italics omitted). This identity is composed through the agency of Rosa's voice, as the etymology of "advocate" reflects. Bon's murder by Henry, however, converts the charged absence into a corpse, the mirage, the rumor, into a mere gravesite; Bon's death constitutes his absolute absence and makes him the subject not of desire but of memory. Wash Jones's message summarizes his demystification: " 'Air you Rosie Coldfield? Then you better come on out yon. Henry has done shot that durn French feller. Kilt him dead as a beef' " (133).

The extraordinary demands that Rosa places on her artifice of loving may help to explain the nature of her attraction to Sutpen. In retrospect, she understands her love for Bon as a preparation for Sutpen; it was a chance "to renew, rehearse, the part as the faulty though eager amateur might steal wingward in some interim of the visible scene to hear the prompter's momentary voice" (147; italics omitted). Ultimately, Sutpen can no more be possessed than Bon. Rosa protests to Quentin that her frustration is not simply sexual disappointment; it originates in Sutpen's essential unreality—the sense that he is only "articulated flesh":

> I never owned him; certainly not in that sewer sense which you mean by that and maybe think (but you are wrong) I mean. That did not matter. That was not the nub of the insult. I mean that he was not owned by anyone or anything in this world, had never been, would never be. . . . Because he was not articulated in this world. He was a walking shadow. [171]

Sutpen's stature and mystery make him a suitable successor to Bon in Rosa's paradox of desire. As she does in her love for Bon, Rosa seeks to haunt the unpaced corridors of passionate possession. She moves into Sutpen's mansion when he goes to war because Ellen asks her to protect the children; but, evasively, she pretends to the positions of wife and mother for the absent Sutpen. After Bon, Rosa seems to "renew" the deferment of desire by attaching it to the remote and disinterested Sutpen.

Rosa's fragile desire for an essentially absent beloved—a shape, a walking shadow—is nearly overthrown by the contrasting energy of Sutpen's own design. Sutpen's marriage proposal threatens to end Rosa's arrested adolescence. His desperate innocence conducts Rosa out of the unpaced corridor of her childhood and into the bedroom from which Judith had earlier excluded her. As if calling her into physical existence, Sutpen lays his hand on her head and proposes marriage. Rosa broods on this event as a sign that her ideal of frustrated desire is about to change. She wonders about the "touch of flesh with flesh . . . which enemies as well as lovers know because it makes them both—touch and touch of that which is the citadel of the central I-am's private own" (139). On this very threshold of Rosa's passage from a vicarious into an actual life, Sutpen 'refines' his initial offer and Rosa gathers up her morality, like soiled crinoline, in retreat. His subsequent death, like Bon's, condemns Rosa to the life of the "crucified child" (8), to imprisonment by "that engagement which did not engage, that troth which failed to plight" (13).

Rosa's tortured, paradoxical love of Bon and then Sutpen seeks to fill a void. Rosa's youth, as I have been arguing, aspires to constitute a life through the power of an imaginative supplement, a supplement that both intimates and frustrates desire. Rosa's embryonic passions fill a gap that opens at her birth. Her life, bought with her mother's, initiates an unending chain of debts: Rosa can never help but "see in the fact of her own breathing not only the lone justification for the sacrifice of her mother's life, not only a living and walking reproach to her father, but a breathing indictment, ubiquitous and even transferable, of the entire male principle" (59–60). A life that so fully doubts its worth and despises its origins may continue only by being profoundly disfigured. Rosa seeks a mother but finds only an aunt (who also abandons her); she lacks a lover in adolescence but invents a Charles Husband-soon-to-be; she hates her father and watches his tedious suicide, but she attempts to replace him with a Sutpen who flamboyantly differs in every respect from Goodhue Coldfield. (Rosa even interprets Sutpen's death as chastisement for attempting to supplement her father: "as if she had been instinctively right even as a child in hating her father and so these forty-three years of impotent and unbearable outrage were the revenge on her of some sophisticated and ironic sterile nature for having hated that which gave her life" [170; italics omitted].)

Since Sutpen has long been dead by the time of Rosa's narration, we learn of her youthful desires only through the mediation of a second discourse of desire in the novel—the desire of memory or speech for its object. Sutpen's death, like Bon's, dispels the illusion of vicarious or deferred possession; it erases the "invisible imprint of absent thighs" and converts hope into mourning. Rosa's memory, for the forty-three years since Sutpen's 'death' to her, serves as a mausoleum within which she conducts private rites of commemoration. When Quentin begins listening to her narration, he assumes that she is giving it to him "because she wants it told," presumably for the first time (10; italics omitted). This is, as I shall discuss in a moment, an important aspect of her performance for Quentin, since Rosa represents the ghosthood of an imagination, the absolute consecration of the mind to remembering the past. Rosa's grief so fiercely concentrates on the loss of love that at first it scorns what she takes to be the shallower consolations of language or image, of "thought." The following passage, for example, suggests that every effort to represent the past necessarily inscribes its loss, that the mind pictures only what it will never possess again:

> Once there was—Do you mark how the wistaria, sun-impacted on this wall here, distills and penetrates this room as though (light-unimpeded) by secret and attritive progress from mote to mote of obscurity's myriad components? That is the substance of remembering—sense, sight, smell: the muscles with which we see and hear and feel—not mind, not thought: there is no such thing as memory: the brain recalls just what the muscles grope for: no more, no less: and its resultant sum is usually incorrect and false and worthy only of the name of dream. . . . Ay, grief goes, fades; we know that—but ask the tear ducts if they have forgotten how to weep. —Once there was (they cannot have told you this either) a summer of wistaria. [143; italics omitted]

Rosa's grief fades into impotent frustration and petrifies into black widowhood for her "nothusband." The state of mind that she seeks banishes all but the lost object of love. Rosa dies to Jefferson, dies to time, and welcomes a deathlike trance in which she can dream about "a might-have-been which is more than truth" (143): "my life was destined to end on an afternoon in April forty-three years ago, since anyone who even had as little to call living as I had had up to that time would not call what I have had since living" (18). The stifling, sweetly sick air of Rosa's office entombs a ghostly and grotesque substitute for the marriage that never was: " 'Rosie Coldfield, lose him, weep him; caught a man but couldn't keep him' " (168). But not even that: "I had not lost him because I never owned him" (171).

Rosa's narrative, which she apparently tells for the first time to
Quentin, is an outgrowth of her memory. As we may have expected
after seeing Quentin's futile efforts to recall the 'original' Caddy,
Rosa's language succeeds only in representing a simulated Sutpen.
One of the most striking qualities of the Sutpen who emerges from
Rosa's tale is his deadness. Quentin notices that the "long-dead"
demon "would appear, as though by outraged recapitulation
evoked, quiet inattentive and harmless, out of the biding and
dreamy and victorious dust" (7–8). Sutpen's commanding potency
and violence necessarily drain out of the supplement that comes to
stand for him. Rosa's voice willingly sacrifices itself to the ardors of
recollection, but Sutpen nevertheless retains an inertness that corresponds to the "visibility, spacing, death" that mark all speech:

> Meanwhile, as though in inverse ratio to the vanishing voice, the
> invoked ghost of the man whom she could neither forgive nor revenge
> herself upon began to assume a quality almost of solidity, perma-
> nence. Itself circumambient and enclosed by its effluvium of hell, its
> aura of unregeneration, it mused (mused, thought, seemed to possess
> sentience, as if, though dispossessed of peace—who was impervious
> anyhow to fatigue—which she declined to give it, it was still irrevoca-
> bly outside the scope of her hurt or harm)....   [13]

The narrator's "as though" and "as if" caution us that any recovery
of immediacy and intelligibility will be the product of a fiction that
acknowledges itself as such. The accumulating flesh and 'presence'
of Sutpen, as the several tellings of *Absalom* unfold, must be seen as
the mirage of presence in speech.

Absalom, even more explicitly than *The Sound and the Fury,*
encourages the reader to understand the desire of a character for the
absent body of his or her beloved as analogous to the desire of the
storyteller for his subject's representation and for the achievement
of natural sense. Any narration confronts both the absence of what
is represented and the desire for its reappropriation. What Derrida
states about the trace—that which language produces—resonates
with Sutpen's status in Rosa's story: "The trace is not a presence
but is rather the simulacrum of a presence that dislocates, displaces,
and refers beyond itself. The trace has, properly speaking, no place,
for effacement belongs to the very structure of the trace.... [The
text] proposes *both* the monument and the mirage of the trace, the

trace as simultaneously traced and effaced, simultaneously alive and dead, alive as always to simulate even life in its preserved inscription."[13] On the one hand, Rosa understands that her narrative is something left behind Sutpen's original presence, that it is a monument and an inscription. For example, Rosa realizes that Sutpen's peremptory marriage proposal will stand in her memory as "a ukase, a decree, a serene and florid boast like a sentence (ay, and delivered in the same attitude) not to be spoken and heard but to be read carved in the bland stone which pediments a forgotten and nameless effigy" (164). Rosa's forty-three years of ghosthood stand as that carved pediment over Sutpen's grave. Sutpen is the product of a kind of writing in Rosa's discourse.

Rosa's story firmly creates the sense of a remote Sutpen, an object that must be spoken about and remembered in the stubborn monument of language. At the same time, however, Rosa demonstrates how the deferment of a fictional character's presence may conjure up "the mirage of the trace." For Sutpen undeniably reappears through Rosa's telling, just as he does in the other accounts. Faulkner is exploring the deepest springs of narrative's resources—uncompromisingly testing the tensions between the original absence and the represented presence. Rosa demonstrates a number of narrative techniques that—through the motion of deferment—help to create the illusion of a reappropriated Sutpen.

Rosa's narrative habitually seeks the places of puzzlement and mystery in Sutpen's career. It does so because such moments of apparent enigma capture an impression of Sutpen while hinting at a realm of action beyond the power to explain, the illusion of a life not exhausted by descriptions of it. For example, Rosa repeatedly testifies to the stature of Sutpen's superhuman will and ambition by citing his disruption of Bon's courtship: "I saw Judith's marriage forbidden without rhyme or reason or shadow of excuse" (18). Rosa does not want to explain this puzzle; she prefers rather to recite it as a place where her words cannot fully replace Sutpen's life. As she warns Quentin, her narrative will "take that many sentences, repeat the bold blank naked and outrageous words just

13. Jacques Derrida, *Speech and Phenomena and Other Essays on Husserl's Theory of Signs*, trans. David B. Allison (Evanston: Northwestern University Press, 1967), p. 156; first published as *La voix et le phénomène* (Paris: Presses Universitaires de France, 1967).

as he spoke them, and bequeath you only that same aghast and outraged unbelief I knew when I comprehended what he meant; or take three thousand sentences and leave you only that Why? Why? and Why? that I have asked and listened to for almost fifty years" (166–167; italics omitted). Rosa's narrative mystifies Sutpen and defers his full presentation.

Mystification as deferment also explains Rosa's "demonization" (as Shreve puts it) of Sutpen. Rosa withholds logic and genuine inquiry from Sutpen's career so that she may be free to ornament it poetically. Quentin notices that the source of Sutpen's potent life in Rosa's discourse is his inscrutability: "Out of quiet thunderclap he would abrupt (man-horse-demon) upon a scene peaceful and decorous as a schoolprize water color" (8). Rosa performs for Quentin a fictional *complication* of Sutpen's story that possesses "that logic- and reason-flouting quality of a dream," whose credibility for the dreamer consists not in fact but in "verisimilitude," and which aims not at information but at "horror or pleasure or amazement" (22). In his early impatience, before Quentin realizes that the process rather than the product is the goal, he wonders why the "getting to it . . . was taking a long time" (13).

Rosa's memory and speech negotiate a wedding in words with Charles Bon and Sutpen, her "nothusbands." As creations of her language, they are represented by traces of their presence. Rosa's words are their monuments and their mirages. In a second respect, Rosa's narrative is produced by a wedding of her story and that of her auditor's. The surprising intimacy between the old maid Rosa and the young Quentin grows largely out of the shared crisis of lost love. Quentin at first wonders why Rosa has chosen him to receive the tale and comes to discard his initial hypothesis that she simply wants it told to someone. Mr. Compson later reasons that Quentin's involvement had been predetermined by Grandfather Compson's singular befriending of Sutpen; Rosa may simply want to keep the skeleton in the family closet. But Quentin's behavior under the spell of Rosa's voice reveals that the story holds him—whatever the original bond—by the power of its similarity to his own. For example, we know that Quentin is twice stopped by the same incident in Sutpen's history: Henry's murder of Bon. Obviously, the spectacle of a brother executing his father's wishes to defend his sister's honor and to kill her lover would transfix Quentin's attention. But Rosa's story is rich in resemblances to Quentin's and they suggest how profoundly all narratives are marriages of hearing and speaking.

Rosa might easily be a portrait of Quentin as an old man. The outline of Rosa's story is Quentin's, pressed to grotesque boundaries. For example, the premature 'death' of Caroline Compson to her son is exaggeratedly reflected in Mrs. Coldfield's death at Rosa's birth. Goodhue Coldfield hides himself from the war and suffers a coward's suicide, darkly figuring Mr. Compson's conviction that "no battle is ever won" or "even fought" and that the "field only reveals to man his own folly and despair."[14] Fittingly, Mr. Compson, too, dies a prisoner of lonely principles, though his are a cynic's. Like Rosa, Quentin invents a tortured paradox of desire to satisfy a fear of maturation, time, and sexual identity. Each inserts a forbidden object of desire into the emotional vacuum of childhood. Rosa's innocent, vicarious love of her half-invented Bon corresponds to Quentin's memories of Caddy's childhood intimacies, intimacies that are irrevocable once he admits her loss. Quentin's paralysis before Caddy's disappearance similarly finds a description in Rosa's incapacity to accept Bon's death: "There are some things which happen to us which the intelligence and the senses refuse just as the stomach sometimes refuses what the palate has accepted but which digestion cannot compass—occurrences which stop us dead as though by some impalpable intervention, like a sheet of glass through which we watch all subsequent events transpire as though in a soundless vacuum, and fade, vanish; are gone, leaving us immobile, impotent, helpless; fixed, until we can die" (151–152; italics omitted).

Rosa's frustrated love for Sutpen duplicates aspects of Quentin's adolescent passion for his sexually mature and rapidly 'dying' sister. At the verge of Rosa's surrender to Sutpen's sexual possession, he threatens her with a trial copulation. Caddy, similarly, offers to satisfy Quentin. Both Rosa and Quentin invoke an external morality to shield them from upsetting the fragile balance of suspended passion. Rosa recoils into her mausoleum of "Puritan righteousness," while Quentin blends "some concept of Compson

14. William Faulkner, *The Sound and the Fury* (New York, 1929; Vintage ed., 1946, 1956), p. 93.

honor" with "some Presbyterian concept of . . . eternal punishment" to explain his refusal to commit incest.[15] Rosa and Quentin are both aged twenty when they suffer the beloved's 'death'; and each settles into the hellish solitude of "impotent frustration" and "embattled virginity." That Rosa is "female old flesh" (8) to Quentin may deepen her hold on her young listener, since Quentin already senses that his virginal devotion to Caddy has unmanned him. In *The Sound and the Fury* he once broods on self-mutilation; in *Absalom* he takes Rosa as an incarnation of his future—a eunuch faithful in the service of the past.[16]

iii

Rosa's breathless nightmare of a story seizes Quentin, but it scarcely invites his fully active participation. Mr. Compson's performance also assumes his son's passivity as he fills the evening of Rosa's sortie to Sutpen's Hundred with his own version of the legend. John Irwin, in his deeply rewarding study of the Freudian model of family romance in Faulkner's fiction, argues that Quentin and his father struggle with each other over the problems of paternal priority, virginity, and incest as first one and then the other proclaims mastery of Sutpen's story.[17] And he notices that the accounts reflect the particular anxieties of the tellers; for example, "the dialogue between Quentin and his father about virginity that runs through the first part of *Absalom* appears to be a continuation of their discussions of Candace's loss of virginity and Quentin's inability to lose his virginity contained in Quentin's section of *The Sound and the Fury*."[18] One of the ways in which Mr. Compson differentiates his story from Rosa's is by consciously shaping it to warn Quentin about his dangerous obsessions. Quentin's despair at Caddy's loss of virginity encourages Mr. Compson to editorialize at the appropriate points in Sutpen's history: he says, for instance, that the ceremony of Sutpen's wedding to Ellen Coldfield has noth-

15. Ibid., Appendix, pp. 406–407.
16. Irwin notices that the Biblical Candace is attended by a eunuch (*Doubling & Incest*, p. 52).
17. According to Irwin (ibid.), Quentin struggles for authority over his father by appropriating the authorship of Sutpen's story.
18. Ibid, p. 114.

ing to do with ostentation, but rather with the need to ritualize the loss of innocence. Women who have been deprived of such a formal ceremony may feel "actual frustration and betrayal" since "to them the actual and authentic surrender can only be (and has been) a ceremony like the breaking of a banknote to buy a ticket for the train" (49). Mr. Compson persistently devalues the physical state of virginity—which "must depend upon its loss, absence, to have existed at all" (96)—so as to press Quentin toward a mature reconciliation with the loss of childhood.

In just as obvious a response to the configurations of Quentin's sorrow, Mr. Compson suggests a model for a brother's liberation from incestuous desire: "In fact, perhaps this is the pure and perfect incest: the brother realizing that the sister's virginity must be destroyed in order to have existed at all, taking that virginity in the person of the brother-in-law, the man whom he would be if he could become, metamorphose into, the lover, the husband" (96). He also warns Quentin, however, that vicarious fulfillment turned Rosa into a comic excrescence; Rosa was "projecting upon Judith all the abortive dreams and delusions of her doomed and frustrated youth . . . (it was Ellen who told this, with shrieks of amusement, more than once)" (71). In telling Sutpen's story, Mr. Compson draws character, attributes motives, and invents dialogue to present Quentin with an exemplary drama. He conjectures that "it was Henry who seduced Judith" (97) through Bon, who was merely a necessary invention, "shadowy: a myth, a phantom: something which they engendered and created whole themselves; some effluvium of Sutpen blood and character, as though as a man he did not exist at all" (104). At this point, of course, Mr. Compson wants to urge that the imagination has the capacity to surmount obsession.

Because he can sense the tension that will breed Quentin's fantasy of incest in *The Sound and the Fury,* Mr. Compson imagines a moving confrontation between Henry Sutpen and his father. When the conflict of honor and love forces Henry to deny Bon's earlier marriage, Mr. Compson allows that "at the instant of giving the lie he knew that it was the truth" (90), as if he can appreciate Quentin's pitiful attempt to say that he had committed incest and give his own father the lie. Moreover, Mr. Compson must grimly respect Quentin's indirect threats of suicide. He carefully constructs his story so that it will climax with an account of Bon's letter to Judith. As I shall discuss shortly, this Bon and Judith represent Mr. Compson's firmest convictions about the absence of transcendent meaning and the need to confer significance. But for Quentin, he stresses that Bon and Judith, for all the tragic impediments to their love, will not let the past take away their lives: Bon is free to begin over "because what WAS is one thing, and now it is not because it is dead" (131); and Judith, when she realizes that Grandmother Compson has misinterpreted her gift of the letter as a preparation for suicide, protests, "No. Not that. Women dont do that for love. I dont even believe that men do" (129). In much the same ways as he warns about the follies of denial and suicide, Mr. Compson also counsels Quentin against too nice a sense of morality. He imagines a scene in which Henry, "the grave provincial" (113), first learns about dueling over the honor of a disputed woman: Bon, the "mentor," observes that " 'that was never my way' " (113) as he tries to temper Henry's rigid puritanism. In the near background of this passage stands Mr. Compson's disapproval of Quentin's ludicrous challenges to Dalton Ames and Herbert Head.

Whenever *The Sound and the Fury* and *Absalom, Absalom!* are discussed together, the resemblances between the Compson story and the Sutpen story emerge: Mr. Compson's concentration on the principal themes of Quentin's mind constitutes one way in which every telling is a marriage of speaking and hearing. What readers have not readily attended to is the way in which Mr. Compson tries to tell his own story through Sutpen's, just as Quentin will try to tell his. The full complexity of his narrative may be seen as he tries to solve a problem that Rosa has chosen to leave a mystery, Bon's murder by Henry. On no discernible evidence, Mr. Compson suggests that Henry objected to Bon's marriage to his octoroon mistress, a marriage that to Bon means nothing but to Henry portends bigamy: "It would be the fact of the ceremony, regardless of what kind, that Henry would balk at: Bon knew this" (109). Mr. Compson's Henry, like his Sutpen, strongly respects the authority of ceremony to authorize the loss of virginity. Henry balks because Bon's marriage is a ceremonial declaration of his lost innocence, and a sign of his dangerous potential for contaminating (sexually) Henry's sister and excluding the rival brother. One thrust of Mr. Compson's explanation is toward Quentin. Charles Bon becomes a portrait of the prospective brother-in-law, a sexual sophisticate and older mentor whose intercourse with a literal dark lady (the octoroon mistress) in decadent New Orleans figures the world of adult sexuality into which the virginal Quentin ought to be initiated. Mr. Compson wants to encourage Quentin to forfeit his juvenile attachment to his own and Caddy's virginity; he must reconcile himself to the loss of his sister, to the loss of his own virginity, and to the psychic bigamy of repeated engagements and disengagements with experience. As we have seen, however, Quentin rejects the strain of repetition: "again" is sadder than "was."

The figure of bigamy is central to Mr. Compson's view of life. He understands that Bon's willingness to contrive a ritual or ceremony to fit the particular demands of the moment must be the essence of surviving in a world that has been deprived of natural, transcendent meaning. Mr. Compson invents a scene in which Bon explains to Henry why he has married the octoroon: she was "a sparrow which God himself neglected to mark" (116), the useless waste of slavery that those like Bon choose to "save" if they can. Bon insists that such a ceremony does not fulfill a divine providence but rather is a "formula, a shibboleth meaningless as a child's game, performed by someone created by the situation whose need it answered" (117). Charles Bon loves Judith and wants to marry her, despite the fact that "this was not the first time he would have gone through a ceremony to commemorate it" (94). Mr. Compson deeply admires Bon's response to a universe whose omnipotent deity, its Father, is now too old ("though he must have been young once") to sustain order: imagination must repeatedly improvise answering rituals.

In the mythical past, when gods and fathers were strong and young, the world may have enjoyed simple, virginal virtues; but the modern state is marked by fragmentation, diminishment, and repetition:

> . . . that day and time, of a dead time; people too as we are, and victims too as we are, but victims of a different circumstance, simpler and therefore, integer for integer, larger, more heroic and the figures therefore more heroic too, not dwarfed and involved but distinct, uncomplex who had the gift of loving once or dying once instead of being diffused and scattered creatures drawn blindly limb from limb from a grab bag and assembled, author and victim too of a thousand homicides and a thousand copulations and divorcements. [89]

To be "author and victim" both is to create one's own rituals, to write one's own parts. Mr. Compson celebrates Bon's ability to do this, and, as we shall see, imitates such self-authorship in his own story. This is the strategy forced on weaker sons by the decay of the world of stronger fathers.

Throughout Mr. Compson's narrative Sutpen appears at the zenith of his success. Rosa's, Quentin's, and Shreve's attraction to the disintegration of Sutpen's dream may lessen our appreciation of Sutpen's achievement, but Mr. Compson reminds Quentin that Sutpen "was the biggest single landowner and cotton-planter in the county now, attained by the same tactics with which he had built his house—the same singleminded unflagging effort and utter disregard of how his actions which the town could see might look," and "he was accepted" (72). Sutpen's strong performance is all the more estimable because Mr. Compson knows that mastery over circumstance is only a temporary illusion, a performance *as if* one is in control: Sutpen possesses "that alertness for measuring and weighing event against eventuality, circumstance against human nature, his own fallible judgment and mortal clay against not only human but natural forces, choosing and discarding and compromising with his dream and his ambition like you must with the horse which you take across country, over timber, which you control only through your ability to keep the animal from realizing that actually you cannot, that actually it is the stronger" (53). Mr. Compson does not expect to see the nerve of such heroism again; instead, he sympathizes with Henry and Charles, who must endure Sutpen's futile attempts to resist the natural decay of his achievement. Mr. Compson seeks out the moments of slippage in Sutpen's career because they confirm his sense of lessened opportunities. Thus, even while Sutpen relaxes in a cadence of success, "while he was still playing the scene to the audience, behind him Fate, destiny, retribution, irony—the stage manager, call him what you will—was already striking the set and dragging on the synthetic and spurious shadows and shapes of the next one" (72–73). Sutpen's career attracts Mr. Compson because it encompasses the passage from the larger heroism of the dead past to the "diffused" and complex victimization of the present.

The decay of what the fathers have built is the very substance of the Compson story, as well; Jason Compson, Quentin's father, already represents the virtual end of the family. Jason Lycurgus Compson, Mr. Compson's grandfather, accomplishes prodigies of the will: he arrives at the site of the future Jefferson in 1811 with two pistols, a saddlebag, and a horse—just as Sutpen does.[19] But, like Henry, Charles, and Sutpen's anonymous grandchild, Compson's son and grandson oversee the collapse of the domain. Clearly Mr. Compson displaces and explores the nature of dynasty building in his South, the process of decay, and the strategies for survival amid the ruin as he tells Sutpen's history to his own son. His sympathy for Bon appreciates that "air of sardonic and indolent detachment like that of a youthful Roman consul making the Grand Tour of his day among the barbarian hordes which his grandfather conquered" (93).

Throughout his telling, Mr. Compson is attracted to the figure of Bon: "He is the curious one to me" (93). Mr. Compson's tone toward a more splendid (or at least more vigorous and violent) past seems occasionally elegiac, but it is also cynical, bemused, and detached as it confronts the sense of lost stature. Tirelessly Mr. Compson returns to Bon's protective isolation; he is "a mere spectator, passive, a little sardonic, and completely enigmatic" (93); he is the "indolent fatalist" (105), sharpened by "that pessimistic and sardonic cerebral pity of the intelligent for any human injustice or folly or suffering" (115). Such descriptions of the overaged law student who imperils Sutpen's design may clearly be read as Mr. Compson's wry squints at his own life as a satirist in Latin, as a retiree from his training in the law. To Mr. Compson's mind, Bon's willingness to improvise ceremonies and to mark his own meaning arise from a cerebral, amused fatalism that leads the way out of the never-ending consequences of the past's failures. Bon strikes Mr. Compson as just the sort of outsider who can incarnate his own feelings of the alienation and weak despair suffered by the sons of the South. Mr. Compson does not know that Bon is Sutpen's first son, and so he remarks Bon's impressive liberation from the past: a "personage who ... must have appeared almost phoenix-like, fullsprung from no childhood, born of no woman and impervious to time" (74). And yet he nearly makes the connection between the prospective son-*in-law* who seeks Sutpen's acceptance and Sutpen's lawful first

19. Faulkner, *The Sound and the Fury*, Appendix, pp. 406–407.

son ("the one before Clytie and Henry and Judith even" 62), who mysteriously has been set aside and made a dispossessed heir, as he has been.

Because he feels exiled from a "larger, more heroic" age, Mr. Compson steadily tries to persuade himself that diminishment is actually enhancement, loss actually gain: he defends Mr. Coldfield's retreat on principle from the war ("he was no coward" [82]) as a higher morality; and he insists that the French architect turns Sutpen's monstrous plan into a success precisely by reducing it. Like the architect, "an artist" (38), Mr. Compson hopes to rescue a purely formal elegance from the colossal events of the past. An artifice erected at the site of loss, like Absalom's pillar, pediments the doomed efforts to act and the equally doomed efforts to make sense of those actions. Mr. Compson hollows out his performance finally by suggesting that the sheer effort to create order outweighs the merits or flaws of any personal solution. Both Charles Bon and Judith articulate this position in Mr. Compson's closing passages. Bon marks the sparrow that God neglected to mark, and Judith passes her love letter to Mrs. Compson purely "to make that scratch, that undying mark on the blank face of the oblivion to which we are all doomed" (129). Mr. Compson's Judith voices an ethic of desperate invention: "five or six people all trying to make a rug on the same loom only each one wants to weave his own pattern into the rug; and it cant matter, you know that, or the Ones that set up the loom would have arranged things a little better, and yet it must matter because you keep on trying and then all of a sudden it's all over and all you have left is a block of stone with scratches on it . . . and after a while they dont even remember the name and what the scratches were trying to tell and it doesn't matter" (127). Mr. Compson offers his own narrative as a marking on oblivion, as the fatalistic, cerebral affirmation of significance in the face of utter senselessness.

Mr. Compson executes a narrative that is a sophisticated equivalent of Charles Bon's answering rituals. Recognizing the aptness of the occasion of Quentin's summons by Rosa, Mr. Compson ceremonializes his performance so as to imitate aesthetically the actions he narrates. Mr. Compson's story, like the other tellings of *Absalom*, has its own emphases, themes, subjects, and tone; and, as I have argued, they may be explained by Mr. Compson's efforts to express himself and also address Quentin. The distinctive features of his narrative compose what Judith calls the "pattern in the rug." Traditionally, critics have noticed that Mr. Compson's pattern is set off by a fondness for classical allusion (as we might expect of one who sits "all day long with a decanter of whiskey and a litter of dogeared Horaces and Livys and Catulluses" [*SF*, Appendix, 409–410]). His consistent use of dramatic metaphors to describe Sutpen's hubristic career (the town as chorus "in steady strophe and antistrophe: *Sutpen. Sutpen. Sutpen*" [32] is his introduction of this element) exemplifies the ways in which Mr. Compson draws on Greek drama, for example, to provide a pattern for the Sutpen tragedy. And yet what troubles his telling is that the pattern in the rug never gets completed, the order and sense that a narrative ought to bestow on its subject never emerge:

> They are there, yet something is missing; they are like a chemical formula exhumed along with the letters from that forgotten chest, carefully, the paper old and faded and falling to pieces, the writing faded, almost indecipherable, yet meaningful, familiar in shape and sense, the name and presence of volatile and sentient forces; you bring them together in the proportions called for, but nothing happens; you re-read, tedious and intent, poring, making sure that you have forgotten nothing, made no miscalculation; you bring them together again and again nothing happens: just the words, the symbols, the shapes themselves, shadowy inscrutable and serene, against that turgid background of a horrible and bloody mischancing of human affairs. [101]

Such a situation corresponds exactly to Mr. Compson's analysis of both Bon's and Judith's fatalism; Bon contrives rituals that create their own significance, as Judith makes the mark on "the blank face of oblivion." Mr. Compson dramatizes, for himself and for Quentin, the necessary play between the loss of absolute meaning and the power of the mind to create its own: "It's just incredible. It just does not explain. Or perhaps that's it: they don't explain and we are not supposed to know" (100).

In *The Sound and the Fury* we saw Quentin's loss of Caddy as a synecdoche for the intrusion of time into innocence and the disappearance of full, natural significance. Quentin was unwilling to supplement Caddy's absence with articulations of her loss and chose instead to coerce her representation in his memory. Such memories themselves proved to be supplements already, subtle replacements, distortions, and corrections of a Caddy who could never be recovered, who did not exist until she was lost. Mr. Compson's performance attempts to show Quentin a higher resignation to loss. Judith, her lover murdered by her brother, stoically proceeds with her life; she comes to Grandmother Compson with the cold but consoling assurance that passing Bon's letter to another will be a scratch to pediment their love: "at least it would be something just because it would have happened, be remembered even if only from passing from one hand to another, one mind to another, and it would be at least a scratch, something, something that might make a mark on something that *was* once for the reason that it can die someday . . . " (127). These are precisely the circumstances under which Mr. Compson passes that same letter on to Quentin, and he repeats the gesture when he sends his memorial letter about Rosa's death to Quentin. On that one occasion, Quentin and Shreve fulfill Mr. Compson's faith in the value of taking the written document and meditating on it until what is "almost indecipherable" becomes "meaningful."

Mr. Compson labors to make Sutpen's story the site of an intimacy between his son and himself. It may be that father and son struggle in mortal combat over the body of the story, as Irwin argues,[20] but the antagonism of several hands trying to impose their own patterns on the rug also produces moments of tense but tender union. Later, Quentin despairs that he has listened too long, as Shreve's voice turns into his father's; but Quentin's familiarity with the substance of the Sutpen legend also allows his father's performance of it to reach him more deeply and intimately: remembering his father's explication of the grave markers, Quentin thinks "that what your father was saying did not tell you anything so much as it struck, word by word, the resonant strings of remembering" (213; italics omitted). The graveyard scene, like Mr. Compson's ritualized telling, serves as an invitation to an initiation. Father attempts to show son the power of making the mark, the scratch on the blankness; and he encourages Quentin to reanimate that meaningless past with love and imagination, "smoothing with his hand into legibility the faint lettering, the graved words" (191).

20. Irwin, *Doubling & Incest*, p. 120.

iv

At the climax of their telling of Sutpen's story, Quentin and Shreve excitedly discover a 'mistake' in Mr. Compson's version; it was not Bon but Henry who was wounded at Shiloh, and not Henry but Bon who saved a brother's life: " 'Because your old man was wrong here, too! He said it was Bon who was wounded, but it wasn't. Because who told him?' " (344). The two roommates, in their youthful eagerness to appropriate personal and cultural histories for themselves through the stories they tell, retain a respect for criteria of evidence, fact, and truth. Shreve goes on to show how Mr. Compson's view is based on undocumented assumptions and how his own interpretation fits better. But the narrator's voice periodically interrupts Quentin's and Shreve's initial scruples to assure us that what matters is the quality of their invention, and not any attainable factuality. The characters that the two evoke to execute their narrative are "probably true enough" (335), the narrator says. Differing accounts of Bon's murder or the battlefield wounding create significance by differing over them; *Absalom*'s meaning emerges not as the novel excludes interpretations but as it multiplies them.

Bon's wounding at Shiloh accords with the pattern of Mr. Compson's story. For him, Bon is the sophisticate whose worldly wisdom gets him elected to a lieutenancy, but whose world-weariness makes the rank unsought. His wound is the sign of a presumed psychic anguish that has formed the scar tissue of cynical fatalism, a deep sympathy, in Mr. Compson's eyes, with incoherent victimization. And Henry, responding to Bon's threat of bigamy, "carried him to safety apparently for the sole purpose of watching him for two years more" (124). Mr. Compson's Bon constitutes the brother-in-law whose sexual possession of the sister must be dealt with by the brother. Mr. Compson emphasizes Henry's puzzled watchfulness during the four years of "probation" because he expects Quentin to endure a similar period of indecision—indecision between denying and accepting the loss of his sister to another. Mr. Compson wants Quentin to keep the brother-in-law's acceptable claim alive.

When Quentin and Shreve contradict the earlier account, they act out of a different understanding of Bon's threat and Henry's desires. Because the roommates present Bon as the half brother who broaches incest, critics have customarily seen him as Henry's (and by implication Quentin's) shade, a darker, repressed self. Irwin marks the position: "In the doubling between Bon and Henry, Bon plays the role of the shadow—the dark self that is made to bear the consciously unacceptable desires repudiated by the bright half of the mind."[21] In the stages of the story when Bon represents the desire for the sister (Judith) and Henry represents moral restraint, Quentin is manipulating the drama to investigate his corresponding self-division. Shreve, improvising out of these anxieties, with Quentin's help, arrives at a moment when Bon must have rescued Henry from a wound. The rescue is the equivalent of Quentin's inability to let the prohibition of incest die; he can never, as we remember from *The Sound and the Fury,* simply take his sister's body, and so the part of him that is Henry must live. Bon, leaning over his bleeding half brother, tries to force Henry to confess his desire for Judith in the person of Bon's body: " 'Say you do want me to go back to her. Maybe then I wont do it. Say it . . . ' " (345). Here Shreve makes his own contribution to Quentin's use of the story; knowing, or intuiting, his roommate's obsession with his sister, Shreve presses Quentin toward speaking and perhaps exorcising incestuous desire.[22]

For a moment I wish to follow the added differences of Quentin's and Shreve's narrative. Although one does not learn a great deal about Shrevlin McCannon from either *The Sound and the Fury* or *Absalom,* one may see idiosyncratic interests in his contribution to Sutpen's history. Shreve's chief invention is Charles Bon's past. As Terrence Doody has argued,[23] Shreve wants to provide Bon with what he lacks: a father, mother, childhood, and motivation; consequently, he spells out Bon's tutelage in revenge by Eulalia and the sinister lawyer, and he founds Bon's challenge to Sutpen on his demand for paternal acknowledgment. These are obvious attractions to Shreve, since he too seeks patriation in an adopted new land. As an outsider to the story, Shreve also sympathizes with the

21. Ibid., p. 30.

22. Shreve resembles Mr. Compson in this regard; in *The Sound and the Fury* Quentin mocks his father's faith in talking it out by imagining the scene in which he confesses his incest with Caddy. Even in Quentin's imagination, however, Mr. Compson cannot be troubled by mere words; he immediately spots his son's confession as the lie it is.

23. Terrence Doody, "Shreve McCannon and the Confessions of *Absalom, Absalom!,*" *Studies in the Novel,* 6 (Winter 1974), 461ff.

general dilemma of Bon's plight: everyone is confronted by both too much personal history (like Eulalia's memories) and not enough (like Sutpen's indifference). Bon is "held for a minute or five minutes under a kind of busted water pipe of incomprehensible fury and fierce yearning and vindictiveness and jealous rage [which] was part of childhood which all mothers of children had received in turn from their mothers and from their mothers in turn from that Porto Rico or Haiti or wherever it was we all came from but none of us ever lived in" (298–299). Shreve, through Bon, sees "all boy flesh" "stemming from that one ambiguous eluded dark fatherhead and so brothered perennial and ubiquitous everywhere under the sun" (299). Bon embodies the search of every individual for paternity, for an intelligible personal history that fathers one's independent identity. Bon's demand for his father's acknowledgment is a search for self-comprehension, "almost touching the answer . . . just beyond his reach, inextricable, jumbled, and unrecognizable yet on the point of falling into a pattern which would reveal to him at once, like a flash of light, the meaning of his whole life, past" (313). By using Bon's story, Shreve may begin to understand how one defines oneself emotionally in the crucible of fictional history. Shreve's encounter with the Sutpen story resembles an initiation into the process by which any reader creates the fiction, and creates himself in the fiction.

Of course, Shreve also wants to learn specifically about the country that will furnish his education. Like his classmates, Shreve never tires of making Quentin "tell about the South" (174). Shreve knows that "the Canadian and the Mississippian are joined, connected after a fashion in a sort of geographical transubstantiation of that Continental Trough, that River which runs . . . through the physical land of which it is the geologic umbilical" (258). Shreve is mystified by the South's uncommon solidarity; his initial references to "Aunt" Rosa Coldfield betray his senses of the South as a vast family and of his own need for adoption. And, as a new undergraduate, Shreve also explores the universal issues of young adulthood: for example, his sophomoric conclusions about romantic love and incest fend off a premature disillusionment:

'And who to say if it wasn't maybe the possibility of incest, because who (without a sister: I dont know about the others) has been in love and not discovered the vain evanescence of the fleshly encounter; who has not had to realize that when the brief all is done you must retreat from both love and pleasure . . . and retreat . . . the *was-not: is: was:* is a perquisite only of balloony and weightless elephants and whales: but maybe if there were sin too maybe you would not be permitted to escape, uncouple, return.—Aint that right?' [323–324]

As a novitiate in the story, Shreve tends either to help Quentin hear his deep resonance with the Sutpen legend or to draw from it wider generalizations about the South, love, and so on.

The principal themes of the Compson story—sexual maturation, incest, suicide, and filial rebellion—occur as regularly in Quentin and Shreve's mutual history of Sutpen as they do in Mr. Compson's. Their reappearance undoubtedly justifies the familiar critical judgment that Quentin formulates a private understanding of himself out of the Sutpen legend.[24] But we may also notice that it is precisely by dissenting at crucial points from his father's (or Rosa's) explanation that Quentin's version acquires its personal authority. For instance, Shreve—as he reflects Quentin's anxieties and information—consistently identifies Henry's worries as Judith's fornication and threatened miscegenation, and *not* as incest. In his hasty summary, Shreve portrays Sutpen's desire to have Henry protect Judith's honor: "the demon must turn square around and run not only the fiance out of the house and not only the son out of the house but so corrupt, seduce and mesmerize the son that he (the son) should do the office of the outraged father's pistol-hand when fornication threatened" (179). Shreve's mocking tribute to Sutpen's power reflects Quentin's exasperation—voiced periodically in *The Sound and the Fury*—with his own father's refusal to prevent Caddy's dalliance. The same exasperation informs the scene in which Shreve imagines the lawyer suggesting to Bon that he go ahead and take Judith, "a nice little piece" (338). The invented lawyer becomes a grotesque parody of Mr. Compson (the failed lawyer), who permits both Quentin's declaration of his incest and Caddy's fornication. Bon is made by Shreve to attack the lawyer savagely; as he does so, Bon becomes a version of Quentin, who wishes that his

24. Vickery, *Novels of William Faulkner*, pp. 91ff.

chastity might somehow preserve Caddy's virginity. Bon signals a kind of phallic restraint ("holding the pistol by the barrel against his leg" [338]) as the lawyer "did the heavy father" (310).

In his telling of the Sutpen story, Quentin seeks to present a version of incestuous desire that challenges his father's confidence in a brother's vicarious identification with his brother-in-law. That Charles Bon is Sutpen's oldest son and that he possesses black blood are facts known only to Quentin and Shreve. Quentin uses them to turn Mr. Compson's interpretation of Bon's threat into a massive irony. Mr. Compson's model for perfect incest is the brother who takes his sister's virginity in the person of the brother-in-law; but Quentin reduces this idea to absurdity by 'discovering' that the potential brother-in-law is actually a lawful brother. Such a reversal makes Mr. Compson the unwitting advocate of the very incest that his version sought to forbid. (Quentin and Shreve are the only tellers in *Absalom* who know the facts of Bon's paternity and race; they discover or invent those facts out of their special interests in the story, and not out of better research. In Faulkner's original conception of *Absalom,* Bon's history was to be known by both Rosa and Mr. Compson.)[25] In his compulsion to justify incestuous desire, Quentin has Henry accept Bon's proposal to marry Judith: "And then Henry would begin to say 'Thank God,' 'Thank God' panting and saying 'Thank God,' saying 'Dont try to explain it. Just do it' and Bon: 'You authorize me? As her brother you give me permission?' and Henry: 'Brother? Brother? You are the oldest: why do you ask me?' '... Write. Write. Write'" (349). Through Henry, Quentin comes to terms with probated incest, with the spoken or written declaration of longing for one's sister. And to Quentin, Judith would have been an ideal Caddy, a sister who would have desired her brother: "because they both knew what Judith would do when she found it out because they both knew that women will show pride and honor about almost anything except love..." (341).

Quentin's model of perfect incest, as we may remember, is eternally unconsummated intimacy, a fragile paradox of desire. Quentin's Henry encourages Bon to state his intention, but balks when

---

25. Langford, *Faulkner's Revisions,* p. 3.

Bon actually threatens sexual possession of Judith. This ambivalence plays out the paradoxes of Quentin's own complex solution, for Bon represents the necessary yet dangerous displacement of incest. Bon exists as a shadowy emanation of Henry-Quentin, a *fictional* self who may both desire and be prevented from taking the sister. Psychoanalytic readings of Bon make his blackness a sign that he is the darker, repressed self.[26] But the novel especially stresses that Bon's darkness has to do with his being a fiction, a figure consciously invented to execute a vicarious life. Quentin and Shreve's characters are called "shades" in whom as tellers they "exist" (316); Mr. Compson refers to Bon as a "shadowy character. Yes, shadowy: a myth, a phantom: something which they engendered and created whole themselves; some effluvium of Sutpen blood and character, as though as a man he did not exist at all" (104). Henry (like Quentin) writes his incestuous desire into Bon ("You authorize me?" Bon puns. "Write," Henry replies.) But the written shadow is safe only so long as it suspends and encodes desire; when it broaches consummation it also constructs its own barrier. Bon becomes a Negro only when he threatens to take Judith: " 'I'm the nigger that's going to sleep with your sister' " (358). The specter of consummation transforms incest into miscegenation by casting a shadow across the virginal space. And so Henry futilely attempts to enforce a boundary: *"Dont you pass the shadow of this post, this branch, Charles; and I am going to pass it, Henry"* (133).

As an account of fatherly response to the threats of incest, miscegenation, and the rebellion of children, Sutpen's story obviously attracts Quentin as a way to explore, even to author, a relationship with his own father. Complexly, Sutpen becomes a fictionalized version of a stronger Mr. Compson who would enforce family law and taboo, while Shreve's invented lawyer represents their enfeebled corruption. Because all of the 'facts' of the Sutpen history are in a certain respect made up, however, Quentin is free to use the fiction repeatedly and differently. Not only does he tell and discover his story in Bon's desire, Henry's restraint, and Sutpen's authority, but he also appropriates Sutpen's youth as his own.

This phase of Sutpen's story requires a modulation of tone and key. In Chapter 8, Quentin and Shreve are said to reach the "mar-

26. Irwin, *Doubling & Incest*, p. 92.

riage of speaking and hearing" that accomplishes an apparent immediacy in their telling. But before this moment, the narrative that they alternately and collaboratively tell depends on a kind of antagonism and rivalry. The tension between Quentin and Shreve is not an outright struggle, however, since most of the occasions on which Quentin or Shreve pleads for the other to stop talking, or wards off the other's interruption, are moments of creative dissension. It is not so much that either wants to talk the other into extinction, but that each wants to perform, to create, to specify for the other, to speak in the common voice of both. For example, Shreve stops Quentin once because he does not realize that the child Sutpen murders is a daughter; but Shreve allows Quentin to finish the narrative sequence of Wash's revenge and his arrest before he breaks in (292). And he permits Quentin's momentum to shrug him off misleadingly ("'You mean that he got the son he wanted...' 'Yes...'" [292]) until he finally gets a clarification ("'*Will you wait?*'" [292]). But Shreve is not trying to wrest the story away from Quentin here; he is trying to pin Quentin's impressive effects to an interpretive pattern, to in-form their extended performance of the fiction. At such moments Shreve impedes Quentin's rush because he cares about the internal coherence of the version they are constructing.

Earlier in the collaboration Shreve does the principal talking. The legends of the South have turned Quentin into a commonwealth of voices and he fears resurrecting them because he suspects that "I shall have to never listen to anything else but this again forever" (277; italics omitted). At the outset (Chapter 6) Shreve charges into the story, hastily completing a preliminary version of the entire Sutpen history while Quentin assents monosyllabically and privately thinks his own version. When Quentin reluctantly contributes, he speaks with "that curious repressed calm voice," "that overtone of sullen bemusement, of smoldering outrage" (218). Quentin's silence, his inattention to Shreve's early performance, and the repressed deadness of his voice function to enrich the tension between the two roommates. However, Shreve's sardonic amusement with Mississippi's Ben Hur and Quentin's despairing auditorship evaporate into moments during which each is genuinely moved by the story they tell. The high emotional stakes of exposing themselves to each other demand that they monitor the energy of confabulation: Quentin pleads with Shreve to " 'wait, I tell you!' " in a "voice with its tense suffused restrained quality" (277); and Shreve likewise prevents Quentin from transgressing on the suspense of the story by saying prematurely whom he found at the mansion. The effects of deferred climax and postponed revelation are immense in the final movement of the novel toward a "marriage of speaking and hearing." The restraint, dissension, pauses, waits, and struggle all turn our attention (and the tellers') to the making of meaning, and not to its achievement. Such an emphasis is also suggested by our understanding that the story's performance is not a simple exchange of information. Shreve knows much of Sutpen's history before Mr. Compson's letter arrives: "that not Shreve's first time, nobody's first time in Cambridge since September: *Tell about the South*" (174). Shreve himself tells a quick version of the story in its entirety before he and Quentin elaborate on it—deepening, complicating, enriching it. (At one point Shreve tries to recreate the Sutpen graveyard; " 'How was it?' Shreve said. 'You told me; how was it? you and your father shooting quail . . . ' " [187].) Telling the Sutpen story demands loving, violent play; the moments of significance arise out of the repetition and revision of the story.

That Quentin and Shreve may be drawn into a special kind of marriage by the stories they share is a possibility that flickers through *The Sound and the Fury*. Shreve's eagerness to share Quentin's past and to defend his roommate's moodiness sets them apart; when Quentin finished his suicide letter, he "propped [it] against a book on the table so I would see it. Calling him my husband" (*SF*, 213). The ambiguity suggests both that their classmates have tagged this odd couple and also that Quentin actually addresses Shreve as his husband when he attempts to explain his virginal sacrifice to his sister's unfaithfulness. Shreve once jokes about Mrs. Bland's attempt to separate them: " 'Well, I'll say a fond farewell. Cruel fate may part us, but I will never love another. Never' " (131). The imagery of marriage and sexual intercourse appears more explicitly in *Absalom* to explain the quality of their creative, loving partnership in telling. Their attempt to make a story initiates them into a world of mature, imaginative creativity; gaining one's first narrative experience seems to be like gaining one's first sexual experience. Quentin and Shreve "looked at one another, curious and quiet and profoundly intent, not at all as two young men might look at each other but almost as a youth and a very young girl might out of virginity itself—a sort of hushed and naked searching, each look burdened with youth's immemorial obsession not with time's dragging weight which the old live with but with its fluidity" (299).

What does the figure of marriage suggest about the nature of Faulkner's narrative in *Absalom?* First, we recall that Rosa's narrative—as it voices her desire and articulates its objects—does not merely express her identity; rather, her language constitutes her selfhood. Both as she weds the word of her beloved and as she later embodies that love in her story, Rosa's life is her language. The narrators of Sutpen's story do not merely "discuss" the "shades" of the tale, they "exist" in them. More broadly, I might suggest that the novel poses a view of identity as language; no character lives beyond the moment of his or her voice since all thought and consciousness appear to Faulkner as kinds of talk.[27] Quentin, in *The Sound and the Fury,* defines death as an "isolation out of the loud world" of voices, as if to escape speaking is to escape living, remembering, and thinking. That talk constitutes identity also accounts for the persistent air of discovery, surprise, horror, and improvisation in the various tellings; Quentin and Shreve are never quite prepared for the moments when they suddenly see themselves as Henry Compson and Charles Bon. We may remember Faulkner's remark that "every time any character gets into a book, no matter how minor, he's actually telling his biography."[28]

Second, the marriage of speaker and hearer questions our usual notion of the economy of truth in a discourse. The author does not 'have' a story that he 'gives' to the auditor or reader; rather, marriage suggests the necessity of exchange. The teller tells her story as the reader hears his own. The coincidence of Rosa's story and Quentin's, for example, confirms that the truth of a narrative arises from the way it is created and shared, and not strictly from its content. The partners who make a story consent to differ and hesitate, making the climaxes of sense all the more convincing. Frequently the auditors or co-authors of *Absalom*'s narratives contribute only reluctantly, or do not listen at all, or meditate privately

27. For a similar view of *As I Lay Dying,* see Stephen M. Ross, "'Voice' in Narrative Texts: The Example of *As I Lay Dying,*" *PMLA,* 94 (March 1979), 300–311.

28. Gwynn and Blotner, eds. *Faulkner in the University,* p. 275.

on another aspect of Sutpen's career; but their inattention, hostility, or indifference impede the achievement of meaning while empowering its production.

The temporary successes of *Absalom*'s tellings depend on their differences from each other. The apparent conflicts of fact or interpretation between the several accounts do not require resolution. Each teller makes his or her meaning precisely by selecting incidents important enough to dispute; Mr. Compson, we remember, believes that Bon has been wounded during the war and been rescued by Henry, but Quentin and Shreve argue that it must have been the reverse. Each view enforces the coherence of its own telling.

The narratives of *Absalom* behave as rival offspring of the novel; the marriages of speaking and hearing issue in contending interpretations whose legitimacy or illegitimacy cannot finally be judged. *Absalom* challenges more traditional views of what we might call the paternal, phallic authority of a text's meaning. Edward Said provides a lucid account of how Derrida's contrasting idea of *dissémination* may bear on literary texts:

> For rather than being mystified by the obvious analogy between the production of writing and the production of organic life (as the similarity is permitted to stand in the parallel between *seme* and *semen*, for example), Derrida breaks the similarity down, reverses matters. . . . Dissemination *maintains* the perpetual disruption of writing, *maintains* the fundamental undecidability of texts whose real power resides not in their polysemousness . . . but texts whose power lies in the possibility of their infinite generality and multiplicity.[29]

Absalom is not inseminated by a single closed meaning or a discrete set of meanings, but must disseminate the seed, fostering a family of tellings. This is a kind of play with the semantic properties of language, what Derrida has called a "hymeneal" model of truth[30]—hymeneal not only because it celebrates or hymns apparent consummations of the text's meanings, but also because the scattering of the seed paradoxically protects the "virginity" of the text. *Ab-*

29. Edward W. Said, "The Problem of Textuality: Two Exemplary Positions," *Critical Inquiry,* 4 (Summer 1978), 693.

30. See Gayatri Chakravorty Spivak's discussion of Derrida's "hymeneal" fable of meaning in the preface to her translation of *De la grammatologie* (Paris: Editions de Minuit, 1967), translated as *Of Grammatology* (Baltimore, 1974), p. lxvi.

salom suggests that the marriages of speaking and hearing are importantly different from corporeal unions. They are versions of Rosa's "unravished nuptials," "climaxless" in their refusal to conceive and authorize a single meaning. The imagery associated with Rosa's and Quentin's interview suggests that their intimacy is a kind of awkward erotic play rather than a verbal consummation: "the loud cloudy flutter of the sparrows like a flat limber stick whipped by an idle boy, and the rank smell of female old flesh long embattled in virginity" (8). The past is "evoked now out of the airless gloom of a dead house between an old woman's grim and implacable unforgiving and the passive chafing of a youth of twenty" (14). Mr. Compson might also be describing the narrators' marriages when he describes the "engagement which did not engage" (13).

Since the narrators of *Absalom* all seem afraid of life and morbidly attached to their senses of loss, one might wonder if Faulkner is not depreciating their absorption by the play of language and the ceremonies of talking. However, the complex achievements of the marriages of speaking and hearing in the novel gain authority as they reply to Thomas Sutpen's ruination. Sutpen's notorious design rests on a naive use of language; once his innocence is called an "impediment" by General Compson, and I suggest that this innocence directly confounds Sutpen's efforts to articulate himself.

"Sutpen's trouble was innocence," General Compson insists to his grandson Quentin. Sutpen's chief intention is to construct a statement of his identity, a "design" that will de-signate him as author and avenger. But Sutpen's innocence acts as an "impediment" to his speech by suggesting only the simplest aims of language. Sutpen's reliance on the innocence of phallic, singly inseminated meaning governs at least three phases of his career: (1) Sutpen accepts without adjustment his nostalgic memories of perfect coherence, equality, and order in childhood; (2) Sutpen believes that there was a discernible moment in space and time when he "fell" from innocence into knowledge, from a fully significant world to a contradictory and indecipherable one; and (3) he constructs his design expecting to annul this loss, confident that some word or gesture will reappropriate the original state. In one sense, then, Sutpen's tragic blindness darkens the nature of language to him;

unlike his narrators, he does not appreciate paradoxes—that his childhood is always clouded over by the memory's images of loss, for example, or that the passage from innocence is never recognized except as already transgressed, and that every articulation must accommodate the play of failure and repetition. Sutpen's own account of his frustration to General Compson also reflects the speech impediment that troubles Sutpen's other efforts to articulate himself; his story is the novel's stillborn fiction.

When Sutpen tells his story to General Compson, he looks back on his mountain childhood as a place beyond social differentiation, moral ambiguity, and complexity: "where he lived the land belonged to anybody and everybody," for example (221). Sutpen suffers a metaphysical concussion when the slave bars his entrance to the mansion and directs him to the back door. The privileges of social, racial, and financial standing, the law of property, the blight of accumulation, all seem to burst on Sutpen in the moment of the insult. Yet Quentin Compson's narrative, as it repeats General Compson's version, suggests that innocence may be known only in its loss. Before he ever arrives at the mansion door, Sutpen has already fallen. As he unwittingly presents it, his childhood has always been deprived of absolute innocence. For example, the tales of private landownership and personal fortune penetrate his boyhood and "when he got to be a youth and curiosity itself exhumed the tales which he did not know he had heard and speculated on, he was interested and would have liked to see the places once" (222). Compson mitigates the Tidewater trauma when he remarks that Sutpen "had hardly heard of such a world until he fell into it" (222). And before his insult, Sutpen begins "learning that there was a difference between white men and white men, not to be measured by lifting anvils . . . " (226). The death of his mother, which precipitates the decline of the family, Sutpen deliberately understates, as if to suppress the fact that everything he remembers about a simpler, purer time is already contaminated with an aura of loss: "He said something to Grandfather about his mother dying about that time . . . " (223). The principle of social distinction Sutpen has always already begun to learn: "he had begun to discern that without being aware of it yet" (226). Sutpen believes that the insult has robbed him of a kind of moral virginity, the slave "looking down at him from within the half-closed door during that instant in which, before he knew it, something in him had escaped" (234). But even as Sutpen recounts his childhood before the presumed fall, his language subverts its innocence.

Sutpen erects his design on a trauma whose arbitrary nature he cannot detect. The perpetual loss of innocence compromises the significance of the mansion door episode, but Sutpen identifies it as the very passage from virginity to maturity. Grandfather Compson, echoing Sutpen, believes that Sutpen has lost something at the door, but the consequences say differently. Compson himself suggests that Sutpen's innocence is never jeopardized by the episode. His description of Sutpen's sudden understanding of what has happened to him is curious because it relies on a rhetoric of revelation to say that nothing has happened:

> It was like that, he said, like an explosion—a bright glare that vanished and left nothing, no ashes nor refuse; just a limitless flat plain with the severe shape of his intact innocence rising from it like a monument; that innocence instructing him as calm as the others had ever spoken. [238]

Sutpen's innocence remains intact, instructing him, presumably, as it has before. Later, Compson admits that it was "an innocence which he had never lost . . . after it finally told him what to do that night he forgot about it and didn't know that he still had it" (240). Sutpen is innocent because he cannot understand that no one is ever fully innocent; to become conscious of lost innocence is to know it only as lost. Or, as Mr. Compson puts it more concisely: " . . . virginity must be destroyed in order to have existed at all" (96).

Sutpen's lifelong obsession with reconstructing the scene of his dispossession demonstrates a colossal ignorance about the nature of origins and loss. Sutpen contrives his design as if he has been robbed of the innocence of childhood by the plantation owner and as if he may be able to recover and correct that lost child's future. Quentin pictures Sutpen's ambition: "now he would take that boy in where he would never again need to stand on the outside of a white door and knock at it: and not at all for mere shelter but so that that boy, that whatever nameless stranger, could shut that door himself forever behind him on all that he had ever known . . . riven free from brutehood" (261). Sutpen's design aspires to reverse his loss, to recover the moment before his apparent fall and to avert it.

The design protests the alleged passage from innocence to experience and aims to restore childhood. Sutpen's first response to his insult is to withdraw to a kind of womb: "He said he crawled back into the cave and sat with his back against the uptorn roots" (233). Once he conceives his plan, Sutpen pursues it with childlike singlemindedness. Quentin marvels that "destiny had fitted itself to him, to his innocence, his pristine aptitude for platform drama and childlike heroic simplicity" (246), and later he quotes Sutpen's perplexity that his design will require a new beginning once he has prevented Bon from marrying Judith: the dilemma presents "'a mockery and a betrayal of that little boy who approached that door fifty years ago and was turned away, for whose vindication the whole plan was conceived and carried forward to the moment of this choice, this second choice devolving out of that first one ... '" (274). Such an infantile allegiance to innocence makes Sutpen faithful to his ideal of psychic virginity, too. At twenty he is, like Quentin, still a virgin because "that too was part of the design which I had in my mind" (248). Grandfather Compson eventually despairs at Sutpen's incomprehension by asking him, "What kind of abysmal and purblind innocence could that have been which someone told you to call virginity?" (265). And his design exposes him to the risk of a permanent childhood: "He showed Grandfather the scars, one of which, Grandfather said, came pretty near leaving him that virgin for the rest of his life too" (254).

However, Sutpen's design implicates him in paradoxes that he cannot accommodate. To recover the past through his speech and gestures, Sutpen must devise substitutes for what has been lost, and he cannot do so without recognizing that a supplement can neither fully recover the original nor fully come to stand for it. Consequently, his design breaks apart because of his innocent expression, his impediment. Sutpen decides that he must have a wife, a son, land, slaves, and a mansion in order to "combat" his insulters and to reverse the child's misfortune. The language of Sutpen's design wants to make a simple statement; it tries to restore the aura of total coherence that marks Sutpen's childhood. It depends on making one "right" marriage, having one firstborn son, and establishing a legitimate dynasty. Dictated by the "pillar" of Sutpen's innocence, erected in the middle of a limitless plain, the design honors a phallic, paternal model of meaning. But *Absalom, Ab-*

salom! dismantles Sutpen's statement of dynastic sense because it disregards the complexities of language. Sutpen's insemination of a legitimate line is imperiled by Charles Bon, who arrives at the mansion door to announce that the father's seed has been disseminated. Henry, who was the firstborn, instantly becomes the younger brother; an original repetition. Charles insists that he is the darker, differing, rival son, the one before the first who erases the distinction between legitimacy and illegitimacy. Charles Bon yearns in vain for a "sign" from his father, a sign that will declare his origin and paternity. But Sutpen cannot acknowledge Charles Bon without accepting a world in which origin and priority have lost their privilege, in which rival sons claim the same father, differing signs the same signified. Sutpen refuses one son and remains loyal to the false authority of dynastic speech.

Sutpen's own effort to narrate his history amplifies his impediment. Despite its fascination, Sutpen's firsthand telling by no means constitutes the most authoritative or richest version. What strikes Quentin about Sutpen's own narrative (and what must have struck Grandfather Compson) is that it is dead to itself. When Sutpen and Compson pause overnight in their pursuit of the French architect, Sutpen passes the time with a curiously detached autobiography:

> ". . . he telling it all over and still it was not absolutely clear—the how and the why he was there and what he was—since he was not talking about himself. He was telling a story. He was not bragging about something he had done; he was just telling a story about something a man named Thomas Sutpen had experienced, which would still have been the same story if the man had had no name at all, if it had been told about any man or no man over whiskey at night.
>
> "That may have been what slowed him down. But it was not enough to clarify the story much. He still was not recounting to Grandfather the career of somebody named Thomas Sutpen. . . . " [247]

Sutpen divorces himself from his fiction, deliberately suppressing the possibility that he might invent, explore, or reconstitute himself through narrative. Later, when he comes to Grandfather Compson with the ruins of his design, he continues to treat the story as a mere recording of the facts of the case. He wants Compson's legally trained mind to help him discover his "mistake," but he is blind to his story's cultural, psychological, and aesthetic tragedy: "And he not calling it retribution, no sins of the father come home to roost; not even calling it bad luck, but just a mistake... " (267).

Sutpen's inability to author himself is suggested by his stunning lack of invention as he concocts his design. Sutpen depends desperately on his history books and his teacher, unable to escape his conviction that life can be only repetition: " 'I learned little save that most of the deeds, good and bad both, incurring opprobrium or plaudits or reward either, within the scope of man's abilities, had already been performed and were to be learned about only from books' " (241–242). Sutpen slavishly copies the rhetoric and vocabulary of his design from accounts of how things were done in the past; he performs with "that attitude that nobody ever knew exactly who he had aped it from or if he did not perhaps learn it too from the same book out of which he taught himself the words, the bombastic phrases... because of that innocence which he had never lost... " (240). Throughout his career Sutpen succeeds remarkably in imitating the archetype of the American settler that he has read about. After his 'fall' into Tidewater decadence (the exhausted Europe of his career), Sutpen discovers the West Indies with the eye of an Adam ("set out into a world which even in theory he knew nothing about" [53]). Drawing on French colonial design (35) and Spanish coin (34), Sutpen reenacts in miniature the entire history of America.[31]

Sutpen never manages to lose himself in his own tale. Absorbed by the story they fashion, however, Quentin and Shreve learn that the process of transforming oneself temporarily into a fictional character is both exhilarating and painful. Quentin's and Shreve's identification with Henry and Bon ("the two become four") serves as a model for the way in which author inhabits character: each creates the other. But such inventions are also disfigurements, and the anguish of existing in the shades of the imagination permeates

31. Ilse Dusoir Lind ("The Design and Meaning of *Absalom, Absalom!*," *PMLA*, 70 [December 1955], 887–912, as reprinted in Frederick Hoffman and Olga Vickery, eds., *William Faulkner: Three Decades of Criticism* [New York, 1960]) contends that Sutpen is an "incarnation" of the Old South (p. 300). Vickery believes Sutpen to be a "mirror image" of the old South, though at the same time an anachronistic one (*Novels of William Faulkner*, p. 93). A good summary of the growth of the Old South is provided by Melvin Backman, *Faulkner: The Major Years* (Bloomington, 1966), pp. 88ff.

Quentin's and Shreve's telling too. On the one hand, they enjoy the clarity and vitality that making up a story offers; Quentin understands that "If I had been there I could not have seen it this plain" (190; italics omitted); and the two tellers conjure up "Quentin's Mississippi shade . . . who dead remained . . . somehow a thousand times more potent and alive" (280). On the other hand, they recognize that investing in a narrative is a kind of willed self-diminishment: the narrator affirms that the details of the Sutpen story do not matter to Quentin and Shreve because they are, like their fictional subjects, "free now of flesh" through the power of the imagination. The authors give away self-presence to their stories. The formal expression of such necessary invention is the chill that settles into the Cambridge dormitory room. It is as if Quentin and Shreve expose themselves to the strange nakedness of self-divesting and re-creation: "First, two of them, then four; now two again. The room was indeed tomblike: a quality stale and static and moribund beyond any mere vivid and living cold" (345). The moment of intimacy is dangerous and costly. The two take their very existence from their creation, "this shade whom they discussed (rather, existed in)" (316). And they absent themselves in order to be more fully present: "Shreve ceased again. It was just as well, since he had no listener. Perhaps he was aware of it. Then suddenly he had no talker either, though possibly he was not aware of this. Because now neither of them were there. They were both in Carolina and the time was forty-six years ago . . . " (351). The price of repeatedly meeting in the shadows of fictions, of living in the imagination's "shadowy, paradoxical" world, proves too great for Quentin, as we remember from *The Sound and the Fury*. In the earlier novel he excludes everyone except Caddy from his concentration; even his conversation with Mr. Compson is strictly imaginary. *Absalom* outlines the conditions under which he flees a world of words since his re-creation of the Sutpen story represents immersion in the alterity of fiction—in its repeatability and shared proprietorship. Shreve is no mere convenience for Faulkner or a spectral double of Quentin,[32] he is a distinct character whose irony, sarcasm, hyperbole, and ignorance are attractively different to Quentin. The roommates' difference emphasizes all that may be over-

32. Cf. Irwin, *Doubling & Incest*, pp. 121–122.

come in the temporary intimacies of speaking and hearing: "since it did not matter (and possibly neither of them conscious of the distinction) which one had been doing the talking" (334). The only respect in which Shreve is Quentin's creation is that he is telling Quentin's story through Sutpen's. The situation resembles the novelist's, whose characters invent his story as their own. Novel writing may be a kind of suicide from the psychoanalyst's point of view, but it is also a reconstitution of the self into Shreves, those tellers and readers of their informers' lives.

Absalom ceases amid the clearest demonstration that its meanings have been made: that they must be unmade. The metaphor of sexual intercourse oversees the disengagement of the tellers in Chapter 9. Earlier Shreve refers to the *"was-not: is: was"* (324) of intercourse; by the beginning of the last chapter, the two roommates already experience their excited intimacy as a memory. Their certitude at the conclusion of Chapter 8 ("'Aint that right? Aint it? By God, aint it?' 'Yes,' Quentin said" [359]) lapses into doubt ("'Do you understand it?' 'I dont know,' Quentin said" [362]). As the sun rises, the room warms, replacing the chill of narrative displacement with the fever of obsession. Their antagonism revives as Quentin sinks back into the personal mysteries of his life: "'You cant understand it. You would have to be born there'" (361). The impulse to share and to tell subsides as Quentin opens his private memory to the evening of his visit to Sutpen's mansion. The discovery of Henry represents, in Derrida's terms, the apparent thing itself. Narratives and memories are dispelled by the presence of a living Henry; even Rosa abandons her commemoration and accepts the conflagration of the house; "And she went to bed because it was all finished now, there was nothing left now ... " (376). Quentin's direct questioning of Henry, of course, yields far less than his imaginative "ratiocination," but their circular conversation does not parody the novel's processes; it rather confirms them.[33] Truth is a matter of invention, not inquiry. Henry's riddles endorse the necessary return of the novel to the state of puzzlement and mystery. The voices that have temporarily grown articulate and meaningful are replaced by Jim Bond's elusive howl. The rites of disengagement are concluded by

33. Guetti (*Limits of Metaphor*) argues that the conversation epitomizes the "futile circularity" of the novel's narratives.

Shreve's feeble, false summary. His racial calculus reduces and distorts the terms of the novel, and his closing question to Quentin ("'Why do you hate the South?'") is significant not simply for its content—which likewise exaggerates a minor dimension of the novel—but primarily for its function. By introducing another question as the last ("one thing more"), Shreve dramatizes the perpetual open-endedness of the fiction-making process. And by surprising Quentin in his hatred, Shreve pins Quentin into his hysterical solitude. His imminent suicide, as we have seen, urges Quentin's passage from a world of perpetual creation to one of dead peace. The conclusion to *Absalom* deliberately disfigures the expected achievement of authoritative meaning so as to protect the supplementary properties of the narrative even in its cessation. This phase of the novel conforms to Derrida's alternative definition of deferment, which "carries desire or will out in a way that annuls or tempers their effect."[34]

Faulkner celebrates the narrators' marriages of speaking and hearing in *Absalom* because they complicate, trouble, and challenge the offenses of Sutpen's tragic innocence. The novel weds the narrators' words to Sutpen's stammered design, that sentence which begins repeatedly but cannot conclude itself. All of the tellers are "irrevocably husbanded" by the carcass of Sutpen's failure.

34. Derrida, *Speech and Phenomena*, p. 136.

CHAPTER 4

The Hamlet:
Rites of Play

i

The Hamlet (1940) suggests a novelist awakened from *Absalom*'s reverie about the nature of fiction. Present taste for self-conscious literature contributes to the high esteem accorded *Absalom*, the novel in which Faulkner most nearly writes a book about writing books. How one fashions narratives; how stories fill the voids of grief; how they substitute for what is lacking; how fictions differ and defer, repeat and disfigure, and create truth without fact—all are questions that power *Absalom*'s breathless ride over the grounds of its own existence. *The Hamlet* appears uninterested in such questions. Rather than "the best of all ratiocination" (*AA,* 212), we find "the science and pastime of skullduggery";[1] rather than Sutpen's dream of an articulated dynasty, we find Flem's silent, froglike leaps toward the Jefferson Bank; rather than Rosa's acute sentience, we find Eula's dumb allure; rather than the meditative stillness of Jefferson and Cambridge, we find a violent ferocity that devours the "Federal officers [who] went into the country and vanished" (4). Nor does V. K. Ratliff's "humorous concern" to counter the Snopes invasion match the hysterical devotion with which Rosa and Quentin seek to narrate the histories of Sutpen and the South. I have argued that those narratives, as they explore their origins, truthfulness, and satisfactions, follow the movements of *différance.* The plays of difference and of deferment—which comprise the double action of supplementarity—inspire both the fearful

1. William Faulkner, *The Hamlet* (New York, 1940), p. 83. I shall quote throughout from this edition.

evasiveness of *The Sound and the Fury* and the uneasy cheer of *Absalom, Absalom!* To construct a narrative is to arrange a game that will produce significance through the play of signifiers. This view of play suggests the common ground that novels as different as *Absalom* and *The Hamlet* might share. Every reader of *The Hamlet* recognizes its celebration of sport in the rituals of barter, courtship, and taletelling that spin through its pages. Such common forms of play correspond to the cerebral play of *Absalom,* and I hope to show that the conditions that stimulate narrative invention in *Absalom* also foster the rites of play in *The Hamlet*.

Play in *The Hamlet* becomes charged with the same desperate urgency as the taletelling in *Absalom*. In both cases the edge on play derives from the absence of a larger structure of values within which to accommodate the tides of advantage or ruin. As in Derrida's view of discourse, the play of systems in Faulkner's fiction does not imply a center:

> The field is in effect that of *play,* that is to say, a field of infinite substitutions only because it is finite, that is to say, because instead of being an inexhaustible field, as in the classical hypothesis, instead of being too large, there is something missing from it: a center which arrests and grounds the play of substitutions. One could say ... that this movement of play, permitted by the lack or absence of a center or origin, is the movement of supplementarity.[2]

Such slippages and decenterings permit play in *The Hamlet,* where games playing structures society. Ratliff comes to understand that the centers of meaning in the community are strictly arbitrary; they lack contact with the origins of authority or truth. Nature, the supernatural, romantic love, finance, law, and language—all potential "grounds" for human society—are exposed as systems of play that float around missing centers. Such play produces sense and coherence by organizing conventions of exchange, opportunities for intimacy, and various economies of lack and substitution. But they are not centered, they do not signify prior or hidden sources of authority, and they prove defenseless against Flem Snopes's patently lawful exploitation of them.

2. Jacques Derrida, *Writing and Difference,* trans. Alan Bass (Chicago, 1978), p. 289; first published as *L'écriture et la différance* (Paris: Le Seuil, 1967).

On these grounds I distinguish my approach from both Olga Vickery's and Warren Beck's, whose readings of *The Hamlet* masterfully open the discussion of play, economy, and social organization in the novel. Vickery argues that Faulkner explores the conflict of sex and economics—"the one natural and the other social"—as the "two primary modes of human survival."[3] The perversions of economic man, embodied by Flem, are offset by the exaggeration of the natural man, represented by Ike and Eula. Though their conflict has grotesque proportions, they constitute a fundamental dispute between what is "necessary and eternal" (sexuality) and what is "contingent and historical" (economy). Ratliff, of course, champions the middle way of mediation between extremes. Vickery's view suggests that the natural, sanctioned ground for human behavior is sexuality, which subsequently grows subject to the perversions of economic organization. But even the most radical innocence in the novel—the love between Ike and the cow—is presented as already under the marks of civilization. Ike's courtship implicates him in rites of romance that are founded on value, acquisition, ownership, and corporeal exchange. *The Hamlet* displays a world unalterably established on the discourses of society; there are no natural centers from which to measure the fall into civilization. Similarly, Beck's view that Ratliff has a traditional moral purchase in his combat with Snopesism raises some problems. Beck argues that the "key is ethical. Curiosity, Faulkner shows, need not be idle, and its scrutiny may be extended to all phases of *what is* and *what goes on* with the most serious reference not only to *how so* but to *what should be* or *should not be,* under the aspect of humanistic presuppositions."[4] But Ratliff regularly relies on the power and violence of his actions—his trades, stories, and gestures—to contest Flem. " 'I am stronger than him. Not righter,' " he insists, and the provocation of such an insight is Flem's exposure of the foundations of human ethics as arbitrary and noncentered. Flem plays according to the rules, but even if he did not, there are no umpires.

Ratliff is the player in *The Hamlet* who learns that games are predicated on "the lack or absence of a center or origin." Flem's disturbance of the community precipitates a series of crises in which

3. Olga Vickery, *The Novels of William Faulkner* (Baton Rouge, 1959), pp. 167ff.
4. Warren Beck, *Man in Motion: Faulkner's Trilogy* (Madison, Wis., 1963), p. 41.

the perfect noncenteredness of the hamlet appears to Ratliff. I shall discuss shortly the novel's major unmooring of natural innocence, romantic love, spoken language, and commerce by barter, but two less important examples may introduce the process. Readers have agreed that *The Hamlet* revives Faulkner's early interest in the rhythms, imagery, and moral force of nature.[5] The painful crossings of human affairs seem to pollute the simple impersonality of the natural background. The cycles of the day and the seasons, the gentle rhythms of the body and the earth, mutely chastise the fevered schemes, the passionate tempers of the hamlet. Yet nature's significance is never presented as a given truth, as an open book; instead, it is held open to designated meaning. The values ascribed to nature are produced by the literary play of the text; the novel specifies the significance of natural setting by making it a commentary on the action of the plot. For example, in the following passage the fall of evening 'occurs' strictly to express a metamorphosis within those who have purchased the spotted horses:

> The moon was almost full then. When supper was over they had gathered again along the veranda, the alteration was hardly one of visibility even. It was merely a translation from the lapidary-dimensional of day to the treacherous and silver receptivity in which the horses huddled in mazy camouflage. [280]

Dusk is the state of mind in which afternoon dreams are about to turn into nightmare. Similarly, winter in the novel primarily serves as a correlative for the absences from the hamlet of Eula's fertility and Flem's supervision. Mink's wife wonders about Flem's icy silence at his cousin's incarceration, but Ratliff encourages her:

> "Maybe he might answer a letter," he said. "After all, blood is blood."
> The freeze could not last forever. On the ninth of March it even snowed again and this snow even went away without turning to ice. "She's back home again," Bookwright said. "Got in last week." [268]

5. Vickery, for example, argues that the highest values of the novel reside in "the natural and timeless world of love" (*Novels of William Faulkner*, p. 168). Eula's natural innocence and the land's simple fertility are associated by Viola Hopkins in "William Faulkner's *The Hamlet*: A Study in Meaning and Form," *Accent*, 15 (Spring 1955), 125–144.

I do not mean to suggest that all events in nature derive their status from other spheres in the novel, or that they should be understood as monstrous pathetic fallacies. But the novel, in the play between 'artificial' plot and 'natural' phenomena, prepares us for the intuition that any system of sense is decentered fabrication, even the grammar of nature.

Ratliff's faith in God is unmoored in a similar way. He and Bookwright wonder about the kind of deity that could create the idiot Ike Snopes and subject him to the abuse of the barnyard spectacle. In the following passage, Bookwright challenges God's goodness by citing him as the necessary author of evil; but Ratliff suggests two arresting refinements:

> "And yet they tell us we was all made in His image," Ratliff said.
> "From some of the things I see here and there, maybe he was," Bookwright said.
> "I dont know as I would believe that, even if I knowed it was true," Ratliff said. [83]

Bookwright turns God's own declaration—that we are all made in his image—against him, but Ratliff cites the sacred text only to discard it. The authority of what "they tell us" crumbles before Ike's silent indictment, and Ratliff prefers to substitute an acceptable belief for an intolerable truth—that Ike is not made in God's image. Untruth successfully revolts against the tyranny of authority; Ratliff invents a supplement to the original scripture, and in so doing he cuts faith free from any responsibility to its original grounds or authority. Part of his solution, moreover, severs the bond between the original and its representation. Ratliff suggests that Ike may not be a faithful or true impression of the original. Ike is a bad copy, a forgery, and if copies cannot reflect their models, then Ratliff must deal with a world deprived of the authority of origins, condemned to the play of *différance* over missing centers.

Chiefly through Ratliff, *The Hamlet* recognizes that the substance of play—which provides the essential organization of the hamlet's community—arises from the absence of origins or grounds for behavior. More simply, the turbulent rounds of financial transactions, the circulation of tales, the customs of courtship, even the extravagant repetition of nearly identical narratives steadily present a world in which all meaning is produced by a play of exchange and repetition, by structures that do not reflect sense but fabricate it. Ratliff celebrates the rites of play in the novel as he practices or underwrites all of its significant forms. The ordinary rituals of yarn spinning, horse swapping, and marrying generate everyday equivalents for the heady exhilaration inspired by Quentin and Shreve's effort to articulate through their narrative a response to the lost centers of love and history. Ratliff is the champion of fabricated meaning in *The Hamlet;* his very profession—seller of sewing machines—evokes the metaphor of fabrication that Barthes uses in my epigraph for Chapter 3. When Barthes speaks of "man fabricating meanings" he precisely describes Ratliff's function in his community: the narrator introduces Ratliff as a tradesman, "retailing from house to house the news of his four counties with the ubiquity of a newspaper and carrying personal messages from mouth to mouth about weddings and funerals and the preserving of vegetables and fruit with the reliability of a postal service" (13). Ratliff stitches the counties together by both his words and his commerce. He promotes the life of the community's discourse as he carries messages as if they were letters. His mouth-to-mouth deliveries perpetually resuscitate the community; they also suggest that, like a priest, Ratliff distributes the elements of communion through his "retailing." The narrator puns on Ratliff's chief occupations when he chooses "retailing," for Ratliff both retails his personal knowledge of the news and also retells the tales of the community as he circulates. As I hope to show, speaking and swapping are analogous systems of play, serious games that produce meaning, values, and intimacies. Ratliff is one of Faulkner's favorite characters, and his moral and literary brokerage in the Snopes trilogy resembles the novelist's own activity. Derrida's thoughts about the etymology of *text* might confirm Ratliff's status. Text derives from two Latin words, *textus* (cloth) and *texere* (to weave). Ratliff sews the text together with his anecdotes, trades, and eyewitness accounts; he fabricates its meaning. We remember as well that his partner and coplotter is Bookwright.

Even as he recognizes that he can play only when such centers of established meaning as Will Varner's law, Eula's feminine ideal, divine providence, and the courts have been unsettled, Ratliff nevertheless suffers from nostalgia for lost origins and authority. In a familiar passage in "Structure, Sign, and Play," Derrida distinguishes two attitudes toward play:

> Turned towards the lost or impossible presence of the absent origin, . . . [the] thematic of broken immediacy is therefore the saddened, *negative,* nostalgic, guilty, Rousseauistic side of the thinking of play whose other side would be the Nietzschean *affirmation,* that is the joyous affirmation of the play of the world and of the innocence of becoming, the affirmation of a world of signs without fault, without truth.[6]

At first one might assume that a choice between these two views of play in the discourse of the human sciences would be necessary, but Derrida advises a more deliberate investigation of their common ground, "the *différance* of this irreducible difference." Within *The Hamlet* I hope to locate a similar tension. On the one hand, Ratliff witnesses the exposure of absent centers in his community. Flem fully masters the rules of commercial and legal usage, mechanically usurping and exploiting them. As Ratliff wards off Flem's advances, he learns that the presumed foundations of value—Varner's authority, Eula's commanding beauty, Ike's innocent purity, the rules of free enterprise, and so on—are wholly baseless, radically uncentered. He discovers that the economies of the hamlet are floating systems of signification. The goats, mules, ponies, harnesses, anecdotes, cows, food, cash, and bodies that flow from hand to hand or mouth to mouth have little value in their own right; only their exchange inscribes meaning in the community. Commerce, conversation, and courtship resemble languages, whose terms signify through difference and consensus. At moments Ratliff displays a "Rousseauistic" nostalgia for lost origins, immediacy, and varieties of self-presence, such as speech or barter. His anguish over Eula's sale, Ike's victimization, and Flem's joyless transactions arises from a nostalgia for natural authority. On the other hand, Ratliff abandons himself to the adventures of play; he accepts the manipulation of systems that are arbitrary: barter is no better than sale, speech no more trustworthy than writing, value no more intrinsic than extrinsic.

Ratliff's nostalgic mood accounts for a familiar aspect of *The Hamlet,* its apparent preoccupation with the future. Most interpre-

6. Derrida, *Writing and Difference,* p. 292.

tations of the novel agree that it deals with some sort of social transformation represented by the Snopes invasion. Ratliff appears to oppose Flem's renegotiation of the hamlet's values, and through him Faulkner seems to lament the 'modernization of the South.' Surely *The Hamlet* does present an age in which the heroic designs of the antebellum South are obsolete. The opening pages find Will Varner puzzling over the remains of the old Frenchman place: even the "chief man of the country" has trouble " 'trying to find out what it must have felt like to be the fool that would need all this' " (6). So much for "baronial splendor" (6). Flem seems to be the cutting edge of social metamorphosis, and the population parades through Varner's store just to "look at the man whose name a week ago they had never heard, yet with whom in the future they would have to deal for the necessities of living . . . " (52). Identifying Snopesism as a pollutant, Ratliff watches in outrage as Ike's innocent love becomes a sideshow, and as Eula Varner, who ought to be held above the play of commerce, is foully sold by her father to a nickel-and-dime prince. Yet Ratliff's tremendous effort to ward off the threatened dispossessions and usurpations of the Snopeses rests on an assumption that new, alien ways are about to ruin what is now good. Flem's power in the hamlet, I shall argue, depends rather on his strict conformance to the conventions of the society as it exists. Flem is less a character in the novel than a reflection of the deathly, impersonal conditions of play. He reflects the noncenteredness of all play and exposes unwittingly the fragile agreements that weave a society together. His patient literalism leads him to unmask commerce, the law, marriage, speech, and writing as consensual authorities in a community. The absence of centers permits the play of supplements throughout the hamlet; Flem does not represent the new, only the previously concealed. Ratliff's nostalgia causes the rhetoric of the novel to perspire with a dread of the future, but nothing in the hamlet evokes a sense of origin or privilege. Instead, Ike's pure love, Eula's supernal sex, the arcadia of barter, the intimacy of speech, all appear in the novel as always already lost. Like the other sites of origins in Faulkner's fictions, they may be known only in their loss, spoken only amid the movements of "visibility, spacing, death."

If Ratliff ponders the coincidence of missing centers and the possibilities for play, his adversary ponders nothing. Flem voids both nostalgia and joy, both the negative and affirmative uses of play. Like Ratliff, he practices the rites of the tradesman, but Flem is a despoiler because he manipulates commerce, speech, and romance strictly for their "benefits," and not for the pleasure of an aroused imagination, or for the opportunity to improvise, originate, squander, or dream. His power to focus the hamlet's attention derives from his perversion (through exaggeration) of the chief dangers of human economies. Flem embodies the noxious effects of a world deprived of higher authority, filled with representation, substitution, and consensual meaning.

ii

Flem Snopes's status in *The Hamlet* may remind us of those other absent centers in Faulkner's fiction: Caddy Compson, Addie Bundren, and Thomas Sutpen. Unlike them, however, Flem is shadowy not because he has been lost to the past but because he has apparently made himself a part of the dark future. The entire community, with Ratliff as its champion, regularly finds itself a move or a step behind Flem's advances. Flem makes a career of surprising the hamlet, and it is repeatedly forced to try to determine his course by looking at his wake. Here is the account of his "advent" before Jody Varner:

> One moment the road had been empty, the next moment the man stood there beside it, at the edge of a small copse—the same cloth cap, the same rhythmically chewing jaw materialised apparently out of nothing and almost abreast of the horse, with an air of the completely and purely accidental which Varner was to remember and speculate about only later. [22]

The third-person, mostly omniscient narrative voice in this passage conspires to make Jody's surprise the reader's too ("materialised apparently out of nothing").[7] But the presiding point of view is Ratliff's, who takes it on himself to explain Flem and to counter his plots. The voice of the novel modulates considerably; sometimes Ratliff himself relates incidents (and the narrator quotes him);

7. Joseph W. Reed (*Faulkner's Narrative* [New Haven, 1973]) discusses the old-fashioned, "loquacious" narrator who seems to tell *The Hamlet*'s story (p. 218).

sometimes Ratliff's thoughts are reproduced or paraphrased, as when he imagines Flem's assault on the underworld in Book 2. At other points, the omniscient voice betrays its assumption of Ratliff's vantage; for example, when Flem is said to have a "broad still face containing a tight *seam* of mouth" (52; emphasis added), we might recognize the eye of a sewing machine salesman. Throughout these modulations, Ratliff's voice rises to divine Flem's mystery.

Ratliff's voice and the general narrative with which it intertwines try to weave an account that will explain and arrest Flem. From the outset, however, their words prove incapable of anticipating Flem's movement; the narrative persistently demonstrates that its language may name an event only after it has happened. Language is incapable of pre-diction for that would be to have the word intersect with the deed itself, and yet the deed *is* nowhere until it is worded. Articulation only acts as if to fill the void opened by the breakup of presence. The novel demonstrates Faulkner's coincidental position with Derrida's when it repeatedly skips ahead of its own account so as to see Flem in retrospect:

> Then in September something happened. It began rather, though at first they did not recognise it for what it was. [59]

> But that was to be sometime in the future yet. Now they just watched, missing nothing. [61]

> But that all appeared later. All they saw now was... [67]

> Within another year it would be the morning's formal squire in a glittering buggy drawn by a horse or mare bred for harness, and the youths of this year would be crowded aside in their turn. But that would be next year; now... [131]

> That was the fall before the winter from which the people as they became older were to establish time and date events. [263]

The discourse of the novel insists that presence and speech, event and knowledge, possession and articulation cannot coexist.

Ratliff's stake in trying to resist Flem's intrusion is fairly substantial, although he conceals (and presents) his interest "behind his faint constant humorous mask" (81). By insinuating himself into

Will Varner's clerkship, Flem effectively cancels Jody's legal son-ship: "It was Snopes who did what Varner had never even permitted his son to do . . . " (89–90). But Jody is not the only victim of Flem's "usurpation of an heirship," for Ratliff himself is the next thing to a son to Will; the older Varner realizes that Ratliff "was a good deal nearer his son in spirit and intellect and physical appearance too than any of his own get" (160). When Flem moves into the barrel-stave chair, he becomes the son entitled to Varner's land, profits, and daughter; these are usurpations that Ratliff feels with a dispossessed son's hurt. And yet because Ratliff is not an actual son, his dispossession is more abstract than Jody's. Ratliff loses the pleasure of sharing Varner's schemes; he sees his reputation as being a little too smart jeopardized by Flem; and he deplores the loss of the hamlet's collective dream about Eula's virginity. That Flem impoverishes the imaginative wealth of the hamlet is what worries Ratliff; early in the novel the narrator remarks Ratliff's "hearty celibacy as of a lay brother in a twelfth-century monastery—a gardener, a pruner of vines, say" (43). Like a medieval monk, Ratliff seeks to be the custodian of the hamlet's unwritten scriptures, its garden, and its blessed virgin. I shall argue that Ratliff opposes Flem's dull utilitarianism with a "hearty" sportiveness. The actual (Ratliff would say "active" and not be wrong) stakes in the struggle are imaginative, and Ratliff begins his engagement with Snopesism by thinking of it as a game, a test, a con-test:

"I think the same as you do," Ratliff said quietly. "That there aint but two men I know can risk fooling with them folks. And just one of them is named Varner and his front name aint Jody."

"And who's the other one?" Varner said.

"That aint been proved yet neither," Ratliff said pleasantly. [28]

Ratliff wants to "beat" Flem with grace, wit, skill, and ethics; he might succeed except that Flem is not playing.

Ratliff fosters or practices three kinds of game in *The Hamlet*: taletelling, trading, and the rites of love. They have common denominators that explain how they are endangered by Snopesism, and how they are exercised by Ratliff in an attempt to combat it. In the first place, games provide pleasure. For example, even though Ratliff knows that the pleasure of trading can become an intoxicant or a dangerous "disease," he admires the legendary Pat Stamper, who "played horses against horses as a gambler plays cards against cards, for the pleasure of beating a worthy opponent as much as for gain" (30). Pleasure is part of the profit for Ratliff, too: "He was looking forward to his visit not only for the pleasure of the shrewd dealing which far transcended mere gross profit, but with the sheer happiness of being out of bed and moving once more at free will ... " (68). The opportunity to trade again constitutes Ratliff's recovery. Ratliff loves talk for its own sake as well: " 'You fellows dont know how good a man's voice feels running betwixt his teeth until you have been on your back where folks that didn't want to listen could get up and go away and you couldn't follow them' " (80). The romantic attachments in the novel, grotesque as they are, also furnish stubborn, rude, but indispensable pleasures. Ab Snopes, for example, forfeits his pride when his wife is forced to renegotiate the return of her milk separator, yet he allows, with surprising tenderness, that " 'it looks like she is fixing to get a heap of pleasure and satisfaction outen it ... ' " (48).

Games not only please, they also excite the imagination and enrich the mundane. Stamper and his sidekick are legends because they make magic out of horsetrading: the "Negro hostler ... was an artist as a sculptor is an artist, who could take any piece of horseflesh which still had life in it and retire to whatever closed building or shed was empty and handy and then, with a quality of actual legerdemain, reappear with something which the beast's own dam would not recognise, let alone its recent owner ... " (30). " 'But that nigger was a artist' " (38), Ratliff never tires of telling us. Trade, like talk, traffics in black magic, dreams, and fantasy. Flem understands this and uses it to victimize the hamlet when he sells his spotted ponies. The men dreamily congregate as Flem's "circus" parades into the community, and their thirst for excitement and novelty turns the Texas horses into "transmogrified hallucinations" (277), "gaudy phantoms" (286), and "harlequin rumps" (278). Even Ratliff, when he shows up later, respects what he takes to be Flem's Stamperlike artistry:

> "But me, I'd just as soon buy a tiger or a rattlesnake. And if Flem Snopes offered me either one of them, I would be afraid to touch it for fear it would turn out to be a painted dog or a piece of garden hose when I went up to take possession of it." [283]

This seems to me a misjudgment by Ratliff; as I shall argue shortly, Flem has no interest in games, art, magic, talk, passion, or romance—all of the forms of play that enliven the mind.

One might wonder how Ratliff's pleasure in gamesmanship accords with his clear moral opposition to Snopesism. Why does the "faint constant humorous mask" dissolve "into baffled and aghast outrage"? (201). Ratliff's morality is not orthodox, formulaic, or divinely sanctioned; instead, it arises from the conventions of fair play, from faith in the inalienable rights of the imagination. To Ratliff's mind—and to Faulkner's too, I think—an imagination that recognizes the fictionality of reality will enact a sound morality. If truth is a matter of loving difference, value a matter of conferred significance, intimacy a matter of perpetual exchange, then transgressions against another's sense of things, however idiosyncratic, are morally censurable. The text describes this ethic when it tries to explain Ratliff's anger and his acts of charity. Mrs. Littlejohn charges Ratliff with caring more about the mystery than the immorality of Ike's stock-diddling: " 'So that's it,' she said. 'It aint that it is, that itches you. It's that somebody named Snopes, or that particular Snopes [Lump], is making something out of it and you dont know what it is' " (201). Sharp words, but Ratliff invokes no absolute moral standard to defend his closing of the barnyard engagement: " 'I know that the reason I aint going to leave him have what he does have is simply because I am strong enough to keep him from it. I am stronger than him. Not righter. Not any better, maybe. But just stronger' " (201). Lump and the gallery crowd brutalize Ike because their spectatorship turns his innocent love into a vulgar joke. Ratliff reads moral weakness as imaginative poverty; he and Tull debate Flem's usury:

> "What could we do?" Tull said. "It aint right. But it aint none of our business."
> "I believe I would think of something if I lived there," Ratliff said. [72]

The Hamlet becomes a splendid record of Ratliff's attempts to "think of something."

Ratliff's early story about Ab Snopes's encounter with Pat Stamper concentrates in part on the ethical overtones of trade.

Stamper's victory stuns Ab and the young Ratliff when they realize that a day's trading has managed to get them "the same horse we had left home with that morning and that we had swapped Beasley Kemp the sorghum mill and the straight stock for two weeks ago" (44). Two lessons seem to emerge from these early trades in the novel: nothing has intrinsic value; and the essence of finance is that one can buy what one already owns. Flem reflects the second principle when as clerk he makes Will Varner pay for a plug of tobacco from his own store. Commerce excludes an unmediated relationship between an owner and his possessions. And Varner himself points to the 'unmotivated' or arbitrary nature of value when he laments to Ratliff that the Old Frenchman Place must have no worth because it cannot be sold: " . . . my one mistake. This is the only thing I ever bought in my life I couldn't sell to nobody" (6). On the other hand, these qualities are the very ones that liberate trade to a realm beyond "gross profit." Ab, even though he is beaten, practices horse trading as he ought, with "the entire honor and pride of the science and pastime of horse-trading in Yoknapatawpha County depending on him to vindicate it" (35), "doing it not for profit but for honor" (36). It is a game of imaginative and not simply material satisfactions.

The anecdote of Ab Snopes and Pat Stamper introduces Ratliff's repertoire of yarns and exemplifies how his voice rises to the menace of the Snopeses. The shaggy stranger who limps into the hamlet puzzles the gallery, but Ratliff has a story to explain (away) every move Ab makes. The point of Ratliff's tales is to mitigate and control the unexpected by immediately making sense of it in a rhetoric drawn from the past; Ratliff's mythology is a homespun fabric of intelligibility. When word of Ab's barn burning catches up with him, Ratliff eases the gallery's dread by recounting the history of Ab's alienation. Snopes, like any of the rest of them, began with accepted values, subscribing to the hamlet's conventions, even naming his son after Colonel Sartoris. But his series of degrading defeats by DeSpain, the courts, and Pat Stamper leave him subversive. Ratliff assures the gallery that Ab's vicious course is predictable because " 'he aint naturally mean. He's just soured' " (27). The metaphor of souring is apt (Ratliff repeats: " 'Because he wasn't curdled then' " [48]) to express Ratliff's faith in process as explanation. The present and future may be extrapolated from the past:

"This would be exactly the chance he must have been waiting on for twenty-three years now to get his self that new un-Stampered start" (49), Ratliff figures.

Ratliff's histories are designed to defuse change by suggesting predictive patterns. After reminding the gallery of the Stamper legend, Ratliff uses it as a frame for Flem's career; he wonders if Ab hasn't "done caught the Pat Stamper sickness just from touching" the horse (32) and much later wants to see Flem's circus as a relapse of "that Texas disease" (313). Disease is a consoling metaphor because it convinces the recovered patient that time can sometimes bring beneficial changes. Of course, Ratliff's own gall operation (the injury is psychic—galled as Ratliff will be by the Snopes plague) figures the comfort of "convalescence in which time . . . did not exist . . . , time now the lip-server and mendicant to the body's pleasure instead of the body thrall to time's headlong course" (69). Ratliff's historical anecdotes never quite succeed in encompassing Flem, although the disease analogy inadvertently predicts Ratliff's ultimate fate. Joking that the surgeon may have cut out his pocket-book by mistake (69), Ratliff foreshadows Flem's final triumph over his finances—especially since Flem's whittling is said suggestively to draw "neatly along the board, the neat, surgeon-like sliver curling before it" (316–317).

Ratliff's narratives grow more desperate and labored in their ambitions as Flem proves an increasingly more virulent antagonist. The urge to confine Flem's career to a fictional pattern is nowhere more clear than in Ratliff's private fantasy about Flem's assault on the underworld. The passage concludes Book 2 ("Eula") and expresses outrage at Flem's overreaching success in purchasing the hamlet's magnificent goddess. The novel speaks through Ratliff's anxieties at this moment; Ratliff seeks limits and the first words are: *"Until at last . . . "* (151). The fantasy imposes a comic extreme on Flem's design ("What do you want? Paradise?" . . . "Is it yours to offer?" . . . "Take it! Take it! . . . "). But the question in Ratliff's dream is whether there is a boundary or a goal at all. The Prince first tries to bribe Flem by showing him all "temptations, the gratifications, the satieties"; but Flem only spits in disgust after "watching his self performing them all, even the ones he hadn't even thought about inventing to his self yet" (154). The Prince offers a final bargain; Flem is intent on eternal acquisition. That opposition precisely reflects Ratliff's deepening worry. He also sees that Flem sneers at "gratifications" and "satieties" since pleasure has no value to him, and that Flem has reduced commerce to its hollowest form: "He says a bargain is a bargain" (151). Ratliff's adversary is becoming an unbeatably inhuman trade machine. Flem's defiance of any effort to explain or stop him enables him to escape Ratliff's nightmare untouched: the fantasy attempts to see Flem as a Faust who sells his soul to the devil, but the pattern is hopelessly scrambled. The reader cannot tell whether the Prince is Christ or Lucifer, whether the underworld is hell, paradise, or limbo, or whether the story of Flem's ambition will have an ending "at last" or not. Book 2 collapses into a puzzled, furious ellipsis. The fantasy fails to supply a limit or a pattern for Flem's movement.

Ratliff tailors his performances to the varieties of Snopesism they challenge. When I. O. Snopes's offenses against language attract Ratliff's notice, he satirizes him mercilessly. I.O.'s shower of aphorisms especially galls Ratliff because proverbs travesty the relevance of the past to the present. I.O.'s sayings are a kind of false currency, borrowed without interest from common knowledge (as his name proclaims, he "owes"); aphorisms reduce experience to inane generalization. In addition, they confess a mind's impoverishment since they are ready-made thoughts. Ratliff turns his verbal abilities against the imaginative sterility of Snopesism: in the following passage he uses one of I.O.'s own mottos to warn the gallery, and he coins the verb "to Snopes" as his original contribution to the game of naming the metamorphosis:

> "Well well," Ratliff said. "Well well well. So Will couldn't do nothing to the next succeeding Snopes but stop him from talking. Not that anymore would have done any good. Snopes can come and Snopes can go, but Will Varner looks like he is fixing to snopes forever. Or Varner will Snopes forever—take your pick. What is it the fellow says? off with the old and on with the new." [164]

Ratliff's pun in this passage on "succeeding" (merely following Flem ensures success) also suggests Ratliff's ability to enrich exhausted or misused language by doubling its meaning. The salvo of punning in the following aphorism demonstrates his technique:

"Waste not want not, except that a full waist dont need no prophet to prophesy a profit and just whose." Now they were all watching him—the smooth, impenetrable face with something about the eyes and the lines beside the mouth which they could not read. [164]

Another of Ratliff's tales reaches the edge of moral despair as it attempts to compel Flem to return Mrs. Armstid's money. Ratliff realizes that Flem will never act out of his own charity, but he seeks to incite the gallery's sympathy and outrage by narrating a miniature melodrama about the Armstids' suffering. Shrewdly he provokes the gallery's recognition of the Armstids' misfortune by airing any dissent himself:

"Sholy," Ratliff said. "I've heard laziness called bad luck so much that maybe it is."

"He aint lazy," the third said. "When their mule died three or four years ago, him and her broke their land working time about in the traces with the other mule. They aint lazy." [318]

Ratliff negotiates this spoken defense from the gallery, and he masterfully pictures the pitiable helplessness of Mrs. Armstid as she figures her chances with Mrs. Littlejohn: "'He wont give it back to me'" (319) becomes a refrain. He also sketches the admired Mrs. Littlejohn's rage as he imagines her having "taken up the dishes and pans and all and throwed the whole business at the cookstove" (319). This climax of pathos and anger is timed to coincide with Mrs. Armstid's arrival at the gallery to petition Flem; it embodies Ratliff's persistent hope that the imagination possesses its own persuasive ethics. Flem escapes Ratliff's melodrama, however, with a surprisingly nice irony, offering Mrs. Armstid an exaggerated tithe—precisely one one-hundredth of the sought five dollars—in the form of a nickel's worth of candy.

Ratliff's retailed stories, like the other games in the novel, are systems that require several participants; they are occasions for intimacy and verbal exchange; they seek to incorporate what is novel or chancy into a structure of relationships and rules; and they organize experience by fabricating sense. Yet Ratliff's general situation in his games worsens as the novel proceeds, and we can trace his waning verbal powers too. When the dispossessed Prince of the underworld recognizes the scale of Flem's ambition, his very capacity to speak is endangered: "... *he can feel his self grabbing and hauling at his throat to get the words out like he was digging potatoes outen hard ground*" (153–154). Ratliff's fears are fulfilled later, when he suddenly cannot find the word for Lump's resemblance to Flem: "'... I said encore,' he cried. 'What I was trying to say was echo. Only what I meant was forgery.' He ceased having talked himself wordless, mute" (201). Eventually he has to leave his insights blank: "'He come back,' Ratliff said. 'I misjudged his... nerve aint the word I want, and sholy lack of it aint. But I wasn't wrong'" (325).

Ratliff's narratives are only one kind of speech in the hamlet; trade, too, is a game that yields pleasure, makes statements, and fabricates meaning. We have already seen how Ratliff makes deals more for the pleasure of shrewd bargaining than for "gross profit"; and Varner reminds Ratliff that one buys only to sell (6). After the auction of the spotted ponies, the "Rabelaisian" Varner laughs away the men's misery in chasing the phantoms: "'They'll get the money back in exercise and relaxation. You take a man that aint got no other relaxation all year long except dodging mule-dung up and down a field furrow. And a night like this one, when a man aint old enough yet to lay still and sleep, and yet he aint young enough anymore to be tomcatting in and out of other folks' back windows, something like this is good for him'" (313).

Trade not only laughs, it talks. In discussing the customary valorization of oral language as a self-presence and the depreciation of written language, Derrida suggests that money is similarly treated as a mere notation of the self-presence of things themselves: "Money replaces things by their signs, not only within a society but from one culture to another, or from one economic organization to another. That is why the alphabet is commercial, a trader."[8] I shall argue shortly that *The Hamlet* refuses to valorize the barter of things, just as it refuses to valorize oral speech; all of these economies depend on pure substitution, the play of signifiers rather

8. Jacques Derrida, *Of Grammatology,* trans. Gayatri Chakravorty Spivak (Baltimore, 1976), p. 300; first published as *De la grammatologie* (Paris: Editions de Minuit, 1967).

than the presence of signifieds. For the moment, however, I want to concentrate on the simpler ways in which Ratliff uses his trade to make statements. When Ratliff first apprizes that the clerk wants to impersonalize transactions in Varner's store and regulate every sale himself, he deliberately gestures his dissent. He defies Flem's new-found authority by choosing his candy in the old style: " 'Howdy, Jody. Howdy, Flem. Dont bother; I'll get it myself' " (78). He also picks over the candy, refusing to concede his rights of judgment and whim; and he pays for it in the traditional manner, a method that depends on the purchaser's integrity: "He moved to the cheese cage and put a coin into the cigar box" (79). In the episode, these are understated gestures, but they stage a dumbshow of Ratliff's vigilant, symbolic resistance to Flem's ways. Because Ratliff identifies Flem's chief danger as his obsession with gross profit, Ratliff also uses his trade to express alternative values. Ratliff wants to "beat" Flem in their various deals by throwing him for financial losses, but he also wants to forswear profit when doing so will serve a higher symbolic end. The most memorable example is the goat-farm scheme; as Cleanth Brooks explains,[9] Ratliff concludes his bout showing a total profit of $16.80 and inflicting $7.50 in damages to his opponent. Yet Ratliff renounces greater profit when he burns a note worth $11.80 rather than let Flem trade in the future on his guardianship of Ike's finances, and he later gives Mrs. Littlejohn the $16.80 for Ike's care. Charity and extravagance are values that give the game of trade back to its players. By choosing to squander profit or make a contribution to the correction of all "injustice," Ratliff can act imaginatively, morally, and personally within the structure of the game's rules.

Ratliff's "hearty celibacy" suggests a general gusto without a strong sexual appetite, yet he consistently protects the rites of romantic love—like those of talking and trading—from Flem's deathly exploitation. The way he imagines Ike's innocent love for the cow, his outraged closing of the barnyard "engagement," his worship of Eula's awesomely erotic virginity, and his tender assistance of Mink's wife all show his respect for passion and his disgust with mere lust. Physical ownership of another's body without imag-

9. Cleanth Brooks, *William Faulkner: The Yoknapatawpha Country* (New Haven, 1963), pp. 403ff.

inative, spiritual, and sentimental possession is thoroughly debasing and unjust in Ratliff's eyes. It turns bodies into dead coins, things to be owned and sold. (As we shall see, this view is exposed as a touching naiveté; Faulkner knows that innocence is already experience, possession already ownership.) The novel celebrates Ike's innocent romance of his cow, but when he 'buys' her sexual favors, Ratliff feels that he must put a halt to what I.O. calls "stock-diddling" (204). The collapse of Ike's dreamy, ideal affection into a crudely sexual assault precisely reflects Ratliff's estimation of what Flem Snopes stands for. Though wrongly (in view of Flem's apparent impotence), Ratliff sees Flem's aggression as a sexual attack, a rape of the hamlet. Flem's brutal obsession with material profit and use turns the community into an inert body with which he has his way. The very icon of his rapacious success is his purchase of Eula's body, but Ratliff offers other warnings about the prodigies of Flem's lust. For example, after Flem interrupts Varner's dirty joke to make him pay for his own tobacco, Varner distractedly asks the gallery, " 'Where was I?' " (55). With an eye on what Flem has just done to the hamlet's "chief man," Ratliff coyly answers, " 'The fellow had just begun to unbutton his over-halls.' " Ratliff makes several other remarks about the hamlet's taking down their pants to Flem,but his most extreme version of Flem as rapist occurs in a little fantasy that he seems to tell to himself. Ratliff's frustration and anger at Flem's marriage to Eula have provoked him to imagine the circumstances of Flem's sexual apprenticeship. He pictures a poor black girl coming into the store to trade her sweaty body for a tin of Flem's canned fish, " 'laying there and looking up at them every time his head would get out of the way long enough, and says, "Mr Snopes, whut you ax fer dem sardines?" ' " (166). Ratliff rages at Flem's debasement of the human body and love; when he remembers Eula's marriage, he suggests that " 'any sign-painter can paint him a screen to set up alongside the bed to look like looking up at a wall full of store shelves of canned goods ... so he can know to do what every man and woman that ever seen her between thirteen and Old Man Hundred-and-One McCallum has been thinking about for twenty-nine days now' " (164). Ratliff is suggesting that Flem can experience sexual arousal only when he has reduced a woman to a piece of merchandise, when he has traded on her body as he would a coin or a can of sardines. The black girl's supine coopera-

tion, like Eula's trancelike acceptance of Flem, epitomizes the hamlet's submission to the clerk. Ratliff's fantasy is enriched by its
dramatic setting; even as he speaks, the gallery introduces him to
Ike's obscene performance in the barn stall. Flem's assault on the
girl and on the bovine Eula coincide with Ike's on the incomprehending cow, and they are connected by a buried pun that I.O.
finally says aloud much later. He refers to Ike's "stock-diddling,"
but Flem diddles a woman who has been turned into a commodity
kept in stock, a canned good rather than livestock. (Commercial
and sexual dishonesty are both suggested by "diddle.") This is a
moment of high anguish in *The Hamlet,* for it makes the reader
wonder whether the rites of love are truly privileged or whether
they depend on the structures of commerce and writing, in which
objects of arbitrary value are perpetually exchanged in systems of
usage.

Ratliff concentrates on defending the fabrics of sense in the hamlet from Flem's thrusts. Flem's very face tells Ratliff that he
threatens dangerous change and unfinished business:

> It was as though the original nose had been left off by the original
> designer or craftsman and the unfinished job taken over by someone
> of a radically different school or perhaps by some viciously maniacal
> humorist or perhaps by one who had had only time to clap into the
> center of the face a frantic and desperate warning.   [52]

Ratliff's tales aspire to finish that design; his trade, like his stories,
seeks to practice exchange as moral cohesion, to indulge extravagance as moral compensation, to champion imaginative largess
against petty usury. And Ratliff's charitable guardianship of the
hamlet's romantic life bespeaks faith in an economy above the
"dead power of money" (119).

iii

Readers may never settle what the precise nature of Flem's
menace to the hamlet is (nor would one wish them to). Because
Ratliff, as witness and narrator, tries to draw Flem's resemblances
to common forms of behavior so that he may understand his differences better, there are moments in which Flem seems a reflection

of the hamlet's evils, and others when he appears weirdly alien. We may account for both features by treating Flem as a representation (an imitation with a difference) of values and processes in the hamlet. The narrator describes Flem as a magnified version of the Varners in the following passage:

> In addition to the gray cloth cap and the gray trousers, he wore not only a clean white shirt but a necktie—a tiny machine-made black bow . . . a tiny viciously depthless cryptically balanced splash like an enigmatic punctuation symbol against the expanse of white shirt which gave him Jody Varner's look of ceremonial heterodoxy raised to its tenth power and which postulated to those who had been present on that day that quality of outrageous overstatement of physical displacement which the sound of his father's stiff foot made on the gallery. [58]

In discussing the "'normality' of Snopesism,"[10] critics have concentrated on what they view to be the perversities of the Varner/hamlet society and their parodic exposure in Snopesism. But I argue that Flem is an emphatic representation (an "overstatement") of the essential conditions of all social organization—a reflection of the speech, valuation, exchange, and prohibitions on which communal life has been founded. Flem embodies and practices the strict rules of usage, but without a sense of play, pride, self-consciousness, delight, or troubling scruple. My argument explicitly avoids a sociological or anthropological analysis of the hamlet's organization because the narrative has its own sense of what Flem overstates.

In the first place, the hamlet's social organization makes it a kind of text, a system of discourse. The passage above refers to Flem as an "overstatement," and he is virtually a walking form of writing—his white shirt bearing the "punctuation symbol" of his bow tie. Other elements in the novel have a similar, curiously syntactic status: Jody Varner is the "apotheosis of the masculine Singu-

10. Hyatt H. Waggoner writes that Flem "parodies the American dream, caricatures the American success myth" (*William Faulkner: From Jefferson to the World* [Lexington, Ky., 1959], p. 185). Vickery discusses Flem as a "parody" of Will Varner (*Novels of William Faulkner*, p. 169), and Joseph Gold ("The 'Normality' of Snopesism: Universal Themes in Faulkner's *The Hamlet*," *Wisconsin Studies in Contemporary Literature*, 3 [Winter 1962], 25–34) also argues that the Snopeses reflect the values of the hamlet.

lar" (7), Eula is a "word" (149), Ab is a "victim of libel and mis-statement" (9), Ratliff's partner is Bookwright, and even the sky is a "scroll and cryptogram" (183). As Derrida reminds us, writing (in all forms: speech, the alphabet, money, barter) is the condition of civilization, and the novel calls attention to the fact that the hamlet exists as a kind of discourse. Moreover, Flem's advent occurs within the inscribed rules or conventions of the hamlet's life (even if his ultimate course cannot be fully divined): he replaces his shirt weekly, "as though its wearer, entering though he had into a new life and milieu already channelled to compulsions and customs fixed long before his advent, had nevertheless established in it even on that first day his own particular soiling groove" (51). Flem's eyes, "the color of stagnant water" (52), seem to reflect dully the grammar of the civilization that surrounds him; he is a product of the hamlet's central economies. Flem's first appearance in the novel is the moment of his first business proposition; he "materialises" (with a suitable pun on his materialism) in the very act of arranging a deal with Jody. Later, once Flem's position is firm, the narrator remarks that "Varner and Snopes resembled the white trader and his native parrot-taught headman in an African outpost" and that "the headman was acquiring the virtues of civilization fast" (61).

What are the virtues of civilization that Flem "parrots"? Flem begins his reflection of economic discourse by learning that goods, people, information, and relationships seem to have extrinsic rather than intrinsic value. As if overstating Varner's belief in the worth-lessness of anything that cannot be sold, Flem finds no value in anything he cannot "use" or derive "benefit" from. He rejects Jody's bribe of a good farm and store credit because "aint no bene-fit in farming" (23). Read "big profit" for "benefit," of course; but it is Jody who first suggests to Flem in their preceding conversation that benefit is the foremost criterion of business, and Jody is the early aggressor in trying to turn a profit on Ab's incendiary reputa-tion. Later I. O. Snopes burlesques the benefits quotient as he negotiates with Eck about how to divide the costs of Ike's cow. (Under Ratliff's pressure, they intend to buy the cow, kill it, and feed it to Ike to purge him of his unnatural affection.) I.O. says that "the only way to figure it is to divide it according to who will get the most benefits from curing him" (207). The full travesty of the fact that everything has a designated price emerges only in the debate over moral value:

> "It aint the beef and the hide. That's just a circumstance. It's the moral value we are going to get out of it."
> "How do I need fifteen dollars worth of moral value when all you need is a dollar and eighty cents?"
> "The Snopes name. Cant you understand that?" [207]

In the tiniest detail, Flem recognizes only utilitarian reason; when Jody offers him a cigar, he refuses: "I dont use them" (24). The structure of economic discourse, as Snopesism reflects it, depends on unmotivated value and a grammar of appropriate exchange, much like a linguistic system. Inherent value, individual expression, delight, and idiosyncrasy seem out of place. Lump Snopes gives us another overstatement of the principle when he tries to persuade Mink to search Houston's body for cash: ". . . there aint nothing personal in this because it is a pure and simple business matter" (250). Mink reflects the system in his own way when he suggests they play checkers for money; Lump makes the mistake of thinking that the game is pointless ("The trouble with checkers is, he thought, it aint nothing but checkers") until he realizes that Mink is trying to lose his share of Houston's fifty dollars so that he won't have to look for it. The checkers game and the business matter are actually analogous systems, each played joylessly, with an "economy of moves" (250).

Flem magnificently exaggerates the condition of designated value by maniacally obeying The Books. Only what the books say counts because commerce wants "nothing personal," nothing unspoken, nothing variable. Flem exercises his power by controlling the hamlet's writing: he

> sat alone at the desk with the cash from the sold crops and the accountbooks before him and cast up the accounts and charged them off and apportioned to each tenant his share of the remaining money, one or two of them challenging his figures as they had when he first entered the store, on principle perhaps, the clerk not even listening, just waiting in his soiled white shirt and the minute tie . . . until they would finish, cease; then, without speaking a word, taking pencil and paper and proving to them that they were wrong. [90]

Flem's books make him invincible to error but also deaf to personal credit. Jody may make mistakes in his own favor, but he accepts the coin of a man's reputation when he extends long-term credit. The interest he charges not only represents actual profit to him, but suggests that a debtor's intention has real and appreciating value. Flem avoids such abstract currency. Ratliff fears this intent literalism and pictures Flem's assault on the Prince of the Underworld with "his mouth full of law" (152). Flem repeatedly refers to what the "law says" (151) in his argument: "He says he dont want no more and no less than his legal interest according to what the banking and the civil laws states in black and white is hisn" (151–152). What is written binds: a bargain is a bargain, a signature a signature, a contract a contract. Ratliff wants to see these beliefs as outrageous but finally impoverishing tautologies; nevertheless, Flem succeeds by following the rules because they do compose the essential structure of economic discourse. Flem's blind allegiance to the letter finds its travesty in Lump Snopes's diligent "study"; bespectacled, he pores over his books, except that Ratliff notices "the frames had no lenses in them" (203).

As his black and white clothes announce, Flem is a mere cipher in the hamlet's discourse; he is the law's letter. Without protest or imagination he simply accepts the job of manipulating the system to produce profits and to accumulate pointless wealth. I shall argue shortly that Ratliff's understanding of the economies of civilization is more humane because he can imagine ways to exercise such systems *as if* they were more than assemblages of arbitrary values and usage. The situation resembles the narrators' use of language in *Absalom*. Even as they recognize the written quality of memory and narrative, they experience moments of paradoxical recovery, articulated meaning, and intimacy. The same opportunities strike Ratliff, who believes that one should play the games of storytelling, trade, and love as if there were transcendent values; what is absent is made to seem present through the power of the supplement. That enlightened, creative gamesmanship produces a convincing, humane ethos is a view that Ratliff persistently champions. For example, Flem unthinkingly builds up a store of possessions—money, a wife, businesses, a child. The novel suggests, however, that he has title to such goods in name only, that he owns them without possessing them. Labove clearly distinguishes these two kinds of title; Flem fulfills his prediction of the man who will marry Eula:

> He would be a dwarf, a gnome, without glands or desire, who would be no more a physical factor in her life than the owner's name on the fly-leaf of a book. . . . the crippled Vulcan to that Venus, who would not possess her but merely own her by the single strength which power gave, the dead power of money, wealth, gewgaws, baubles, as he might own, not a picture, statue: a field, say. [119]

He is right, of course; the only preparation Flem makes for his wedding is to go to the bank first (148). Those who play games for their own sake and for their ability to enliven the playing imagination recognize that mere ownership counts little. Pat Stamper's perfect trade, after all, is to sell back what his victim already owns; and, as we have seen, Flem mechanically mirrors that principle when he sells Varner's own tobacco to him. When Ratliff sees Varner's mules being used by Ab, he realizes that Ab possesses what Varner owns: "Not *had* belonged, he thought. They still do" (49). A possession can be enjoyed, understood, used, and loved; but to claim ownership is to debase, diminish, exclude, and objectify—to withdraw the object from economic circulation. The distinction has a long history in American literature,[11] but it takes a deeply ambiguous form in Faulkner. Possession seems to move inexorably toward ownership, as the history of the wilderness in *Go Down, Moses* suggests; moreover, the distinction is difficult to make, since whether owned or possessed, an object has value, custody, and exchangeability.

Ratliff and his chums are proven wrong about the source of inspiration for Flem's mechanical assault on the hamlet. They cannot imagine that anyone would perform with Flem's singlemindedness unless he enjoyed deep pleasure and power as his profits. Ratliff persists in thinking of him as a Stamper-like artist, saluting his ability to pass off a garden hose as a snake if he chooses (283). But Flem actually bothers to disguise nothing; he is no artist, no magician, no sculptor. Flem succeeds paradoxically by giving you

11. The tension between the physical and imaginative possessions of America is the subject of Richard Poirier's *A World Elsewhere: The Place of Style in American Literature* (New York: Oxford University Press, 1966).

exactly what he offers: if he seems to be selling untamable horses, in fact he is; if he seems to be digging vainly in the lawn of a deserted mansion, if he seems to offer a garden full of holes, he is; and if you find bags full of recently minted coins, you had better read the dates that do not lie. Flem basely takes advantage of the menfolk's willingness to enrich their lives through dreams, vain imaginings, and foolishness.

I have been indicting Flem for his unimaginative, glandless exercise of the hamlet's economies. We have a formal expression of Flem's solipsistic, substanceless "use" of these systems in the metaphor of eating. Eating is part of the fallen, natural economy; eating the forbidden fruit enslaves humanity to sexual division, time, mortality, and moral knowledge. Jack Houston and Lucy Pate, even as sexually immature children, have already "eaten of the Tree with the will and capacity for assimilation but without the equipment" (212). The slightly fleshy Flem also belongs to the fallen world, but he does not eat out of temptation, gluttony, or weakness. Instead, he performs the role of omnivore by rote. The novel calls him an "omnivorous" spider (59); Ratliff marvels that "Flem has grazed up the store and he has grazed up the blacksmith shop and now he is starting in on the school" (71); and Flem is said to chew constantly although he uses no tobacco, as if he feeds on the very air of the hamlet. Flem has somehow learned to affect a purely internal economy: "The face looked at Ratliff again with no sign of life in it, not even breathing, as if the body which belonged to it had learned somehow to use over and over again its own suspirations" (86). When Jody questions him about his chewing, in fact, Flem mentions that "I chew up a nickel now and then until the suption is out of it" (24). He means a nickel plug, of course, but the metonymy is more accurate since Flem does literally suck the hamlet's money dry. F. J. Hoffman noticed the pun in Flem's name,[12] and we might say that the only residue of Flem's ingestion of the hamlet is the phlegm of his disease. Like most of Flem's traits, his eating is parodied by one of his "forgeries," St. Elmo; the lad staggers Will Varner, who complains, "He's worse than a goat. First thing I know, he'll graze on back and work through that lace leather and them hame-strings and lap-links and ring-bolts and eat

12. Frederick J. Hoffman, *William Faulkner* (New York, 1961), p. 89.

me and you and him all three clean out the back door. And then be damned if I wouldn't be afraid to turn my back for fear he would cross the road and start in on the gin and the blacksmith shop" (323–324). But St. Elmo gets no more pleasure from eating than Flem does; "Save for the jaw and the ears, he appeared to have gone to sleep chewing" (323).

Flem's mouth is too full of the law for him to enjoy what he eats, but others take varied pleasures in this simplest economy of the novel. Nothing is more touchingly presented than Ike's clumsily elaborate provisions for his cow's grain and for her subsequent need to relieve her udder. And during the barn fire, Ike, "lying beneath the struggling and bellowing cow, received the violent relaxing of her fear-constricted bowels" (176), yet he tries to tell her "how this violent violation of her maiden's delicacy is no shame" (176). These lovers know that eating, walking, and sleeping are the barest and best economies of a society of two, and that even shame may be forgotten in the company of love. Eula fancies cold potatoes, which she ingests with the same dull contentment as she does everything else, "tranquil and chewing" (117), like "one of the unchaste and perhaps even anonymously pregnant immortals eating bread of Paradise on a sunwise slope of Olympus" (124).[13] The last comparison occurs to the lovesick Labove, but Eula's diffident eating does set her apart both from the pointlessly ravenous Flem and the modestly satisfied appetites of Ratliff and his gallery mates. The meal of eggs, bread, side meat, and pie that they share is exuberant but simple—like their business deals, quiet chat, and work. Mink's mental poverty, his enslavement to a brutal, narrow code of revenge, is neatly suggested by his stubborn eating from the cold pot of peas, until he is finally forced to feed on crumbs stuck in his beard. Buck Hipps's food, like his wares, is much more exotic; he consumes boxes of ginger cakes as he gobbles up the menfolk's dollars, and as he satisfies their hunger for confections. (In mute disapproval, Mrs. Littlejohn rings the bell for dinner, summoning the men to more substantial, more mundane fare.)

Flem's fierce defense of the book of law overstates the rudimentary structure of arbitrary value, regulated exchange, and absolute

13. Eula's eating may remind us of the Persephone myth, which is discussed by Walter Brylowski in *Faulkner's Olympian Laugh: Myth in the Novels* (Detroit, 1968), pp. 139ff.

profit. By overstating the "virtues of civilization," Flem erases the subtler, more playful, more enlivening uses of civilized systems. Some of Flem's actions, however, overstate a different weakness of social organization. The hamlet's law controls violence, aggression, and willfulness by internalizing them; for example, Varner muscularly manages to postpone a murder when he arbitrates a quarrel between two explosive adversaries, Mink and Houston. Even Ab furiously agrees to execute the letter of the judgment after De-Spain's suit. Nevertheless, *The Hamlet* repeatedly notices the centrifugal inertia of an authority that is contractual rather than divine, of institutions that are fictitious rather than ordained. Flem reflects this state of affairs when he sponsors violently subversive behavior that the hamlet's institutions cannot control. For example, Flem's spotted ponies momentarily charge into the hamlet's central barn, but then its walls splinter before "the towering particolored wave full of feet and glaring eyes and wild teeth" (287). The barn's explosion is metaphoric; earlier, as he inveigles the horses to enter, Buck Hipps likens the barn to the hamlet's other institutions of established values: "What do you think that barn is—a law court maybe? Or maybe a church and somebody is going to take up a collection on you?" (285). After his brush with one of Flem's horses, Tull's face is actually disfigured, "as if an old Italian portrait of a child saint had been defaced by a vicious and idle boy" (329). Flem's defacing gestures at the novel's conclusion dramatize the terrifying potential for dissent in a consensual society. Before Flem's perfect indifference, the hamlet's law fades into inconsequence. The enfeebled judge incarnates obsolescence ("The Justice of the Peace was a neat, small, plump old man resembling a tender caricature of all grandfathers who ever breathed" [328]); his patient literalism ("within the definition of the law as provided" [335]) is withered by Flem's refusal to recognize the court's papers and by Lump's cheerful perjury. Snopesism reflects the dangerous properties of civilization, which depends on the condition of writing (through its spoken words, contracts, laws, and documents). The pony auction demonstrates that the conventions of trade may be manipulated to bring about their own near destruction, just as the law that a bargain is a bargain may jeopardize the very principle of law.

The Hamlet suggests the immanent violence of social transaction through the imagery of physical disfigurement. The violence, aggression, and injury that the conventions of trade and property are meant to solve erupt periodically in the very machinery of the society. Many of these who trade or attempt to take possession of something suffer injuries that mark the breakage and pain of usage. Ab carries a limp from one of his early misadventures in muletrading during the war; Armstid breaks his leg trying to possess the horse he owns; later, his abject defeat at Flem's hands sends him into mad excavation of the worthless Frenchman's Place garden: "Armstid [was] waistdeep in the ground as if he had been cut in two at the hips, the dead torso, not even knowing it was dead, laboring on" (360); and the runaway horses thoroughly bang up Tull and have given Hipps the scar he sports. Those who touch Eula sustain similar damage: Labove yearns for "her one time as a man with a gangrened hand or foot thirsts after the axe-stroke which will leave him comparatively whole again" (119); Hoake McCarron breaks his arm on the night he takes Eula's virginity (141); and Labove imagines that her husband will play a limping Vulcan to her Venus (119). In a curious way, Mink's murder of Houston erupts through an ambiguity in the law of possession and responsibility, and Mink nearly cripples himself when he tries to test the dangerous, spinning wheels of justice. Snopesism overstates the violence inherent in social transaction, but it illuminates the violation that is intrinsic to the laws of possession, exchange, and convention.

Ratliff's wise, mirthful exercise of the hamlet's economies structures a world in which there is no higher appeal; the values, standards, and meaning that he invokes in his opposition to Snopesism are the products of communal fabrication. As articulations, they embody the play of signifiers rather than the naming or recovery of a transcendent signified. At some moments, however, the novel approaches a nostalgia for natural significance, for the plenitude of an origin, and for a ranking of articulations that are closer or farther away from self-presence. Occasional remarks or pressures in *The Hamlet* may lead us to believe that Faulkner endorses a valorization of voice over writing, objects of barter over money, the immediacy of love over its expression—the thing itself over its representation. The novel refers to "the dead power of money" (119), and Ratliff makes fun of document-mad Northerners who start a goat farm not with goats, but with "a book of printed rules and a gold-filled diploma," "with a piece of paper and a pencil" (80–81).

Things precede words, the lesson seems to run, just as events precede their accounts: Mrs. Varner no longer reads and does not teach her daughters to read, "preferring now to be face to face with the living breath of event, fiction or news either, and being able to comment and moralise upon it" (97). And Ratliff wants to believe that Eula should transcend the rules of usage; he feels "outrage" at the waste of her marriage because it is "wrong by any economy" (161), and Labove senses "that quality in her which absolutely abrogated the exchange value of any single life's promise or capacity for devotion, the puny asking-price of any one man's reserve of so-called love" (119). Labove offers the most emphatic expression of Eula's presumed exception from the hamlet's self-confirming games.

Labove appears in *The Hamlet* as an obverse reflection of Flem; he is seen as such particularly by Ratliff, who understands Labove's mad career and suspicious disappearance as confessions of a sexual alliance with Eula. Late in the book, Ratliff thinks he can blackmail Flem by resurrecting what he takes to be the circumstances of Eula's first seduction: " 'That fellow, that teacher you had three-four years ago. Labove. Did anybody ever hear what become of him?' " (360). The early stages of Labove's story duplicate Flem's: both step on escalators of social advancement that will carry them out of anonymous rural poverty. Like Flem, Labove rejects his father's farm, deciding simply that he would rather be governor (105). The deadly, oppressive necessity of his ambition hollows out all of his activities, and he becomes a man who lives by rote. Labove shares Flem's faith in the letter of the law and plans for legal training: Labove's "was a forensic face, the face of invincible conviction in the power of words as a principle worth dying for if necessary" (106).

> At night passers would see the fierce dead glare of the patent lamp beyond the lean-to window where he would be sitting over the books which he did not love so much as he believed that he must read, compass and absorb and wring dry with something of that same contemptuous intensity with which he chopped firewood. [111]

The knowledge that he stores up, part of which he sells to his students, he treats like commercial goods: "He carried the key to the [school] building in his pocket as a merchant carries the key to his store" (111). Moreover, like Flem, Labove earns money (his tuition) playing a game he neither understands nor enjoys. When the university's football coach explains a scholarship, Labove doubts that " 'anybody will give me all that just for playing a game' " (108); he never quite learns the distinction between "actual fighting" and the "rules for violence" in football (admittedly a nice distinction); and the only scale he has to evaluate the purpose of the game is monetary (" 'I knew what the shoes cost. I tried to get the coach to say what a pair was worth. To the University. What a touchdown was worth. Winning was worth' " [110]).

Labove's dull literalism—a life composed of "turning pages of dead verbiage" (113)—mimics Flem's. But the novel goes on to present him as a grotesque monument to Eula's transforming power. Labove's mechanical ambition shuts down in her presence, and he discovers the exhilaration of extravagance in a realm beyond ordinary worth. Eula's inert eroticism makes Labove love's fool; her sublime richness—symbolized by her lavish body—engulfs his beggarly life of letters. She "abrogated . . . the puny asking-price of any one man's reserve of so-called love" (119); she is like "fine land rich and fecund and foul and eternal . . ., producing a thousandfold the harvest he could ever hope to gather and save" (119). His niggardly fidelity to a written life becomes the very mark of disease and he craves just one sexual possession as "a man with a gangrened hand or foot thirsts after the axe-stroke which will leave him comparatively whole again" (119). (Even Eula recognizes that touching her will dismember Labove; he "paws" her as an "old headless horseman Ichabod Crane.") Labove's dusty books are blown away by Eula's "moist blast of spring's liquorish corruption" (115); a future of mechanical game playing vanishes before "the supreme primal uterus" (115), "the queen, the matrix" (116). The metamorphosis of Labove depends on the illusion (at any rate) that Eula is some original, innocent, powerful presence that may be possessed and lost. In Labove's eyes, Eula makes a shambles of every human economy. He has thrown away "the price of three years of sacrifice" in buying the privilege of eternal dedication to her (122); he is willing "to buy" with his very life the ratification of his "success" in touching Eula; and later Labove's puny successors in the courtship of Eula are described as "dispossessed" (131) and "bankrupts"

(134), as if they too must fail to meet her superhuman asking price. Labove's prostration before the apparent fullness of Eula's presence suggests that she is a source of natural significance, love, and immediacy before loss or dead words. Yet the novel steadily presents her as a sign, a word, an embodiment—already a component in the hamlet's economy of articulation.

Quoting and paraphrasing Rousseau, Derrida notices that currency and writing are seen by a metaphysics of presence as representations that pose distance from their originals: "If 'the sign has led to the neglect of the thing signified,' as *Emile* says speaking of money, then the forgetfulness of things is greatest in the usage of those perfectly abstract and arbitrary signs that are money and phonetic writing."[14] *The Hamlet* persuades us of its remarkable modernity as it repeatedly suggests that the "thing signified" cannot be distinguished from the sign that signifies, that money and writing are no more arbitrary or abstract than other exchangeable forms of wealth or speech, and that all human discourse is nothing more or less than the perpetual play of signifiers beclouded by "forgetfulness" and deathliness. Ratliff, the consummate tradesman, recognizes that no social organization can exist without the mediacy of signs: he refers to "the first time anywhere where breath inhaled and suspired and men established the foundations of their existences on the currency of coin" (202), and Will Varner remarks wryly that "breathing is a sight-draft dated yesterday" (313), as if the very terms of human mortality conform to the provisions of a cosmic contract, an economy that makes sense of life and death.

Nothing escapes its place in an economy in *The Hamlet;* everything derives meaning from its participation in a structure. One manifestation of this condition is that all signs tend to act like dead coins. For example, names can be assessed dollar values, as I.O. and Eck's debate over cow costs demonstrates. Messages become forms of money, too; Mink gives Ratliff one note "collectible by law" and another oral note that threatens barn burning and stands up quite as well as cash. Ratliff uses information as money regularly, and I.O. burlesques the connection between coins and words by his capacity to "forge" either: he is like a machine "into which you could insert the copper coin or lead slug of impulse to action, and

14. Derrida, *Of Grammatology,* p. 300.

you would get something back in return, you would not know what, except that it would not be worth quite as much as the copper or the slug" (202); this is what he does to words as well. *The Hamlet* suggests that speech, phonetic writing, bartered objects, money, and even human bodies circulate through analogous systems of articulation, and that such articulation is the very hinge (the articulation at the 'origin') of the "foundations of existences."

Rousseau complains that money has led "to the neglect of the thing signified," according to Derrida, but *The Hamlet* understands money as a sign that is both signifier and signified. Cash counts as much as painted horses or worn-out harnesses; arbitrary convention agrees on their value as items of exchange. Ratliff, for example, even suggests that money is a more personal possession ("your things") than goods:

> "When a man swaps horse for horse, that's one thing and let the devil protect him if the devil can. But when cash money starts changing hands, that's something else. And for a stranger to come in and start that cash money to changing and jumping from one fellow to another, it's like when a burglar breaks into your house and flings your things ever which way even if he dont take nothing." [34–5]

Money is plainly valuable neither intrinsically as metal nor for what it can buy, but as a personal, symbolic possession: it signifies itself. When the pony auction is about to begin, the men prepare to listen to Hipps's pitch; the following sentence suggests that their money is an intimate possession: "Along the fence below him the men stood with, buttoned close in their overalls, the tobacco-sacks and worn purses, the sparse silver and frayed bills hoarded a coin at a time in the cracks of chimneys or chinked into the logs of walls" (290). This cash becomes part of their very clothes and houses (stuffed into overalls, chimneys, and walls). (The syntax of the sentence enacts the intimate concealment as it suspends the object of the preposition "with"; the reader must pass grammatically through those pockets, then the sacks, before he discovers the private valuables.) Money has value precisely because it stands for itself, and not because it represents something that is in danger of being forgotten. There are rather touching examples of money's endearment to the hamlet. Mrs. Armstid, for instance, tells the justice that she could

195

identify the very money that she accuses Flem of stealing: " 'I would know them five dollars. I earned them myself... ' " (331). The bill carries its own meaning for her. Earlier, when Armstid takes her money to buy the horse, it is as if he extracts it from her body: "He reached out his hand. The woman held the banknote in her folded hands across her stomach. For a while the husband's shaking hand merely fumbled at it. Then he drew the banknote free" (301). Similarly, Mink sees his wife's ten-dollar gift not as an abstract denotation of purchasing power, but as a message in their private conversation. She was a whore before their marriage, and now Mink recognizes the profit of an old trade. The bill he throws away is "still warm with body-heat" (244) as much because of how it was earned as where it was hidden. Unwittingly he makes a play on words about the prostitute's ethics: " 'Did you sell something for it, or did you just take it out of his pants while he was asleep?' " (245). That "it" might refer to Will's sex as easily as to the cash suggests Mink's symbolic association of them.

Just as the novel refuses to value things over money, so it will not see spoken language as any truer, purer, or more personal than written language. The rural simplicity of the hamlet does not guarantee that face-to-face words may be trusted, or that personal presence purifies ambiguity or deceit, or that a man is as good as his word. The justice who tries to arbitrate the suits at the end of the novel points out that in "the law, ownership cant be conferred or invested by word-of-mouth. It must be established either by recorded or authentic document, or by possession or occupation" (336). Buck Hipps's verbal assignment of title is unenforceable, just as his promise to Mrs. Armstid, Lump's sworn oath, and even Eck's confession of ownership prove false. If what is spoken may be duplicitous, what is written also evaporates before the whims of interpretation or denial. The justice has faith in the power of "authentic documents," but the Snopeses make careers out of exploiting the fact that both the strength and the weakness of writing inhere in the mutual respect of its users. Flem's slavish literalism does not compel him to recognize the court's books, as we have seen. The justice cannot take his authority for granted merely because he surrounds himself with impressive texts like the "thick Bible which has the appearance of loving and constant use [as?] of a piece of old and perfectly-kept machinery" (328), or because "he spoke exactly as if he were reading from a paper" (333). Jody congratulates himself on Ab's failure to sign a contract before "I could put a fire-clause in it" (22), but of course contracts and signatures mean nothing to Ab if they are inconvenient. When De-Spain tries to stop him from moving by invoking their contract, Ab responds simply, " 'I done cancelled it' " (18). Later, when Houston asks what has happened to the blacksmith, I.O. explains, " 'His lease has done been cancelled' " (64). The worth of any document arises only from consent; what has been 'reduced' to writing is no more binding or permanent than what passes in speech: "Do you think that any Snopes is going to put all of anything on one piece of paper that can be destroyed by one match?" Ratliff asks in angry frustration.

The Hamlet presents a world in which there are no values or authority that precede their appearance in a system of articulation or an economy. At every origin, at every approach to a precivilized or suprahuman ground for existence, one encounters the marks of "visibility, spacing, death." We can see this clearly in Ratliff's grotesque fantasy of the underworld; heaven and hell appear indistinguishable because they share vocabularies, laws, histories, and models of authority. The difference between the fallen and unfallen realms is unknowable. Moreover, Flem arrives mouthing the very terms of heavenly discourse. His talk of "redeeming" his "soul" reminds us that Jesus' divine message depends on economic metaphors to enlighten humanity: the King James New Testament makes God's kingdom a world of "saved" souls, "redemption," life "bought with a price," and the "gift" of the Messiah to fallen mankind. Such a vocabulary embodies the very sacrifice of Christ's incarnation, for to become man is to become what one wishes to transform. (It is the appearance of Flem that is referred to as an "advent.") In the beginning is always the word, the contaminated articulation at the origin which denies the full presence of God at the same time that it tries to speak it. We shall see a corresponding situation in *The Hamlet*'s version of a divine incarnation, but for the moment we might also notice that the novel opens with a formal recognition that every beginning is an architrace and not an original presence. *The Hamlet* begins literally with a trace, "the skeleton of the tremendous house," all that remains from the time that "had almost obliterated all trace" of the foreigner's "sojourn" (3). As is almost paradigmatic in Faulkner's fiction, the Frenchman's vast dream, the "original" "site" of such splendor, can be spoken of only in its loss. The original boundaries exist only as "faded records," just as "his dream and his pride" survive in a word, "the stubborn tale of the money he buried somewhere" (4). The plot of the novel begins by duplicating the condition of language—it shows speech arising as the site of loss.

Eula's fate in *The Hamlet* seems to epitomize the process of dispossession that Flem initiates and sustains. Varner's daughter superficially represents a kind of heavy, natural, innocent divinity that is stolen and defiled by Flem's dead wealth. But Eula's status is more complicated than that; she is no mere exaggeration of the unspeakable pleasures of the erotic virgin, the "fecund field," or Olympian leisure. Rather, she embodies the paradox that what seems an immediate, full presence has already been marked as 'lost' by its articulation. Every incarnation of divinity is already a word. Eula's paradoxes unfold simply at first; her prematurely adult body makes her seem like Homer's goddesses, "at once corrupt and immaculate, at once virgins and the mothers of warriors and of grown men" (114), and she looks, "in the rich deshabille of her loose hair and the sloven and not always clean garments she had groped into between bed and breakfast table, as if she had just been surprised from a couch of illicit love by a police raid" (148). This virgin-whore is somehow always already lost; when she leaves on her honeymoon the beautiful face is already disappearing: "the lost calm face vanished. It went fast; it was as if the moving glass were in retrograde . . . " (151). Even the magnificent opening description of Eula in Book 2 is plagued by the paradox. Though she is "the baby," she possesses an innocence almost indistinguishable from experience. The narrator repeatedly uses the phrase "not quite" or "not yet" to suggest her imminent maturity, and he fills the opening paragraph with gerundives that capture the urgency of her changes ("bursting," "trampling," "teeming," "enlarging" [95]). Her virginal eroticism blends exquisite purity with its own deflowering: "her entire appearance suggested some symbology out of the old Dionysic times—honey in sunlight and bursting grapes, the writhen bleeding of the crushed fecundated vine beneath the hard rapacious trampling goat-hoof" (95). As soon as Eula finds her way into the world (and the narrative), her purity becomes a kind of foulness, her virginity a sexual violation, her fullness a bursting.

Eula Varner Snopes is a heavy, grotesque parody of Caddy Compson; the characters and narratives of both novels associate the two adolescents with perfect virginity, natural innocence, and transcendent significance. But as in *The Sound and the Fury* memory became a kind of speech, marking its object with "visibility, spacing, death," so *The Hamlet* produces an incarnated divinity who is part of the common speech of human economies. Flem does not strictly overreach himself in plucking this "Rhinemaiden" from her prospect; his purchase of Eula merely confirms that he exploits, without inventing, the virtues of civilization. Before Flem, Eula is already a coin. Will treats her sexual escapades practically: "'All we want anyway is to keep her out of trouble until she gets old enough to sleep with a man without getting me and him both arrested. Then you can marry her off. Maybe you can even find a husband that will keep Jody out of the poorhouse too'" (98). The entire community senses that Eula has negotiable worth: the narrator refers to her sexuality as an "abundance which has *invested* her cradle" (128; emphasis added); the rejected suitors of last summer are "foreclosed bankrupts" (134); and when several of them flee the news of Eula's pregnancy, it is as if "they put in a final and despairing bid for the guilt they had not compassed" (141). Even Ratliff and Labove, who want to except Eula from the ordinary, nevertheless rely on the language of money to describe her uniqueness, as we have seen. When Ratliff later rages at Flem's merchandising of passion, he must sense that Snopes merely reflects the awful fact that Eula is a part of the human economy.

Eula has been articulated in the hamlet; she becomes one of its words. I shall return to the long passage that most richly describes this state (p. 149), but on one level Eula's conception is likened to the speaking of an Olympian word (the narrator puns on "ejaculation"). In another effort to describe Eula's highly charged immobility, the narrator remarks, "It was as if her muscles and flesh too were even impervious to fatigue and boredom or as if, the drowsing maidenhead symbol's self, she possessed life but not sentience" (115). The language here is precise in calling Eula a "symbol's self"; it is not that she seems to be a 'transparent' sign or representation of a concept, but that she constitutes within herself both signifier and signified, maidenhead and maiden. Even Eula unwittingly confesses her complicity in a verbal world when she calls Labove an "Ichabod Crane," a rather urbane analysis of her plight. Confined to the hamlet's discourse, Eula also grows up within the games of the menfolk. Even though she is dead to sport (she has no playmates), she is nevertheless part of it. Eula is "the nucleus, the center, the centrice" (129) of adolescent sexual play; she stands untouched at school dances, but "she would be assaulted simultaneously beneath a dozen simultaneous gingham or calico dresses in a dozen simultaneous shadowy nooks and corners" (115). Being a "matrix" does not lift her out of the game, it makes her its object. Eula's extravagant body reminds us that she is, like all other articulations, limited by visibility and spatial form. Her body signifies no higher good than itself, "emanating that outrageous quality of being, existing, actually on the outside of the garments she wore" (102). The overstatement of her body reminds us that Eula is a figure of speech.

It is not Flem Snopes that puts the "damned" (but not "tragic") expression on Eula's face; Eula is not stolen by Flem from the hamlet's pantheon; instead, she is doomed by the very fact of her incarnation. Her existence for the hamlet is indistinguishable from her loss to it. The following sentence complexly unfolds the paradoxes of her status:

> If he [Ratliff] had lived in Frenchman's Bend itself during that spring and summer, he would have known no more—a little lost village, nameless, without grace, forsaken, yet which wombed once by chance and accident one blind seed of the spendthrift Olympian ejaculation and did not even know it, without tumescence conceived, and bore— one bright brief summer, concentric, during which three fairly well-horsed buggies stood in steady rotation along a picket fence or spun along adjacent roads between the homes and the crossroads stores and the schoolhouses and churches where people gathered for pleasure or at least for escape, and then overnight and simultaneously were seen no more; then eccentric: buggies gone, vanished—a lean, loose-jointed, cotton-socked, shrewd, ruthless old man, the splendid girl with her beautiful masklike face, the froglike creature which barely reached her shoulder, cashing a check, buying a license, taking a train—a word, a single will to believe born of envy and old deathless regret, murmured from cabin to cabin above the washing pots and the sewing, from wagon to horseman in roads and lanes or from rider to halted plow in field furrows; the word, the dream and wish of all male under sun capable of harm—the young who only dreamed yet of the ruins they were still incapable of; the sick and the maimed sweating in

sleepless beds, impotent for the harm they willed to do; the old, now-glandless earth-creeping, the very buds and blossoms, the garlands of whose yellowed triumphs had long fallen into the profitless dust, embalmed now and no more dead to the living world if they were sealed in buried vaults, behind the impregnable matronly calico of others' grandchildren's grandmothers—the word, with its implications of lost triumphs and defeats of unimaginable splendor—and which best: to have that word, that dream and hope for future, or to have had need to flee that word and dream, for past.   [149]

The syntax of this sentence is tortured by its own success in circumscribing the hamlet's possession of Eula. The sentence proceeds as an extended apposition to Ratliff's knowledge about her marriage to Flem. The clause that follows the first dash ("a little lost village . . . ") seems to provide a metaphor for Eula's special life. Earlier likened to "the very goddesses" in Homer, Eula seems to be a divine incarnation; the hyperbole has it that the hamlet is fertilized by an "Olympian ejaculation." But the second syntactic disruption ("one bright brief summer . . . ") abandons this apparent mythical history to concentrate on the summer of Eula's marriage, and after another intrusion to describe Varner, Eula, and Flem the sentence finally allows "bore" to find its direct object, "a word." That word, as an even later apposition makes clear ("a word, the dream and wish of all male . . . "), is not "Eula" herself, but the statement of her lost virginity, of her sexual possession. That is, the sentence seems to give us a metaphor for Eula (a divine ejaculation—a seed, a word, an incarnation of the ideal), but concludes by describing the process of her loss to the hamlet. The lengthy modulation of the syntax enacts the very condition it names, for every articulation becomes an utterance of loss. Eula never becomes a presence in the sentence until she is already lost. (I also think that the syntax is deliberately suspended on "bore" so that the birth/loss of Eula may be deferred, as if the sentence seeks to put off the consequences of incarnation.) During the moment of syntactic suspension, moreover, when it seems that Eula is the offspring of the Olympian ejaculation and the hamlet's womb, the reader entertains an important cluster of ideas about Eula. If she is a "spendthrift . . . ejaculation," she becomes through the play on the latter word, as we have seen, both an utterance and an insemination. As either, however, Eula is a substitute, an other, something

The Play of Faulkner's Language

apart from her original. The ejaculation is an expression, but also only a representative of its parentage. (Eula never seems maternal, but we vividly remember Mrs. Varner lying exposed to the moon during Eula's gestation.) By being "spendthrift," Eula's conception also seems a magnificent extravagance to local economies. Yet extravagance may be measured only within an economy, and Eula—despite her enormous value—takes her place in a system. Eula's fall is not from innocence to experience, or from virginity to marriage, but 'from' Olympus into mortality. The fall is a dissemination of the seed; articulation is the origin.

The Hamlet presents another version of the same paradox in its treatment of Ike's love for the cow. The grotesque pastoral in Book 3 which celebrates their attachment seems to place the lovers in a sanctuary, as if only idiocy and bestiality may occupy a world free of profit and property. We have come to read the lyrical extravagance of such passages as Faulkner's melancholic, angry elegy for the death of romantic, selfless love in the novel. The splendid moments of Ike's mornings with the cow seem to pay tribute to the final forms of chivalry, romance, and an ideal of unconsummated desire, before they collapse into the debasement symbolized by Ike's barnyard spectacle. Yet the novel, as it persistently recognizes its own complicity in the economies of literary discourse, subtly marks Ike's innocence and bliss as already somehow polluted. Kinds of speech already fill in the breaking of immediacy—both between the lovers and between the narrative's 'subject' and voice. The novel evokes the lovers' bliss, immediacy, and mutual self-presence only through mists of separation, deathliness, and speech. The career of this narrative episode conforms to the flight of Icarus, a rising toward the unreachable sun of presence. Ike's rites of courtship are already inscriptions of loss.

The love that passes between Ike and Houston's cow takes the form of frustrated desire. Section 2 of Chapter 1 in "The Long Summer" (Book 3) describes their 'courtship,' and it insists that the full immediacy and intimacy of love cannot coexist with either Ike's expression of his devotion or the novel's articulation of it. The episode must begin with a state of separation and can only follow the movement toward (re)union; nor does the narrative ever find the lovers within a state of blissful self-possession. Their passion originates in the novel with its frustration; Ike, as he lies waiting for

202

the cow, makes a "hoarse moaning sound" because "he cannot make one with her through the day's morning and noon and evening" (168). The cow forbids Ike's touch because of her fear, and Ike at first finds himself in a grotesque travesty of a courtship's first stage. She eludes his bid for intimacy: "It is because he can go no further. He tried it" (168). Eventually the cow accepts his touch, but what distinguishes the exaltation of their love is that Ike unwittingly renounces the sexual possession that so often speaks the death of love in Faulkner's fiction. Instead, his speech—his voice and touch—enables him to worship before the cow's udder, in mute prostration before what Labove calls the "supreme primal uterus" (115):

> He touched her again, his hand, his voice, thin and hungry with promise. Then he was lying on his back, her heels were still thudding against the plank wall beside his head. [169]

The survival of their passion is assured by Houston's interruption of them at this moment; and even later, when Ike 'elopes' with the cow, their intimacy does not involve sexual consummation.

Such frustration does not appear as a kind of innocence, however; it appears as a painful constraint. Ike's courtship is plagued by falls and marked by the "visibility, spacing, death" of a speech that seeks to supplement the lovers' absences from each other. Ike can pursue the cow only through a series of literal falls; to leave the second floor of Mrs. Littlejohn's house he learns to drop from step to step:

> He would know he was going to fall; he would step blindly and already moaning onto nothing and plunge, topple, sprawling and bumping, terrified not by pain but by amazement, to lie at last on the floor of the lower hall, bellowing, his blasted eyes staring aghast and incredulous at nothing. [172]

The passage suggests that Ike's love begins with a fall, and Faulkner's frequent association of the Edenic fall with temporality, the loss of sexual innocence, and the division into sexes may remind us to look for sexual nuance in Ike's falls, too. Indeed, his "moaning" echoes sexual ecstasy (as does Benjy's), and his "plunge, topple, sprawling and bumping" may parody the movements of intercourse. Faulkner plays with this idea elsewhere in the descriptions of Ike's love: when he falls into the branch (consider Caddy) with the cow, "they lay inextricable and struggling on the floor of the ravine, he once more underneath, until, bellowing and never ceasing her mad threshing, the cow scrambled up" (177). And when fire erupts around the cow's barn stall, Ike charges to the rescue: "Each time his feet touched the earth now he gave a short shriek like an ejaculation, trying to snatch his foot back before it could have taken his weight" (175). But Ike cannot pull back; his innocent desire is already clouded with separation, loss, and a travesty of sexuality.

The very incarnations of the lovers to each other both allow and forbid intimacy. Ike seeks union with the cow, but the two never become lost in one. The frustration of their passion—its oddly perfect incompleteness—prompts division to beset the very image of union; looking into his lover's eyes, Ike sees himself doubled and reflected: "Within the mild enormous moist and pupilless globes he sees himself in twin miniature mirrored . . . " (184). The specters of separation and alienation haunt the very moments of presumed intimacy. Later, "they lean and interrupt the green reflections and with their own drinking faces break each's mirroring, each face to its own shattered image wedded and annealed" (185–186). These qualities are facets of the visibility and spacing that characterize both a fallen love and the novel's description of it.

The narration of Ike's love for the cow worries constantly and extravagantly that every effort to speak of their affection will disfigure it. Section 2 begins cautiously, describing not a specific but a typical episode: "Then he would hear her, coming down the creekside in the mist" (167). Only after several paragraphs (on p. 168) does the narrative attempt to render a particular incident ("It was the third time . . . "). It is as if the narrative voice at first wants to restrain the impulse to name and dispatch events with the usual confidence (and violence) of realistic fiction. The style of *The Hamlet* labors to celebrate the grotesque beauty of an idiot's love through language that is also extravagantly contorted. The style holds itself away from the awesome grandeur of this idiotic love, magnifying it through circumscription. The love itself, like Eula's presence in the hamlet, nearly supersedes local economies. It occurs during "summer's spendthrift beginning" and is accompanied by prodigies of nature: a stormcloud drenches them "from a sky already breaking as if of its own rich over-fertile weight" (187); Ike picks a "diadem" of flowers that are "more than enough" (186) and bathes his hands in the cow's milk, "the strong inexhaustible life ichor itself" (188). As even these phrases suggest, of course, the extravagance is not only natural but also stylistic. The extreme prolixity, hyperbole, and polysyllabism become an extravagance within the novel's own literary economy: "The trunks and the massy foliage were the harps and strings of afternoon; the barred inconstant shadow of the day's retrograde flowed steadily over them as they crossed the ridge and descended into shadow, into the azure bowl of evening, the windless well of night; the portcullis of sunset fell behind them" (182).

The narrative also suggests that it cannot follow Ike and the cow into their deepest intimacies. The narrative uneasily assumes the responsibility for bringing their love into the visibility and spacing of the novel's speech. Like daylight, the narrative coerces appearance: Ike "stands in sun, visible . . . already cohered and fixed in visibility" (172); like dawn, the novel 'finds' the cow in the morning, already "backing upward out of invisibility" (182). But nightly moments of fullness and presence remain *illusory* states beyond the novel's speech. At night, the lovers fall asleep to the world of travel, separation, self-consciousness, and speech and—formally—to the novel: "The rapid twilight effaces them from the day's tedious recording" (188). Effacement is the narrative's greatest charity to the lovers as it endows the illusion of a realm beyond language, an original plenitude of immediacy. The way of Icarus is to rise toward self-presence; the sentence that precedes the blank space on the page that ends section 2 ushers the lovers to that threshold: "They lie down together" (189).

The implication of lost or future splendors is the narrative's trick, a derivation of immediacy, as Derrida might put it. And the power of such derivation in *The Hamlet* arises from the discourse's own certainty that there is no life, no presence, no origin apart from the articulation. Ike's idiocy might seem to be a refuge from the contamination of civilized discourse, and the narrator remarks that Ike "had been given the wordless passions but not the specious words" (199). Words are specious because they are false to the things they denote, we might infer; and the etymological pun on specie suggests the novel's habitual association of words and coins. Ike appears innocent of words and coins, which "forget" the things they stand for. But a second play on "specious" wrongly distorts Ike's idiocy, as if his muteness disqualifies him from using his species' words. The punning reminds us that Ike's lack of words does not deprive him of speech; his gestures (like Benjy's) are a kind of writing, expressions of frustration, loss, and sense. And although Ike Snopes cannot pronounce his surname, he succeeds in naming himself: he declares himself to be "Ike H-mope" (170, 198), a garbling that may suggest "Ike, who mope(s)" or "Ike, he mope(s)" and which evokes the air of grief over Ike's several dispossessions. As he nearly speaks, so Ike nearly trades. Houston forces a fifty-cent piece on him, but he loses it, and "who to know what motion, infinitesimal and convulsive, of supreme repudiation there might have been" (180). Yet he looks for the coin reflexively, even though, watching him, "you would have said, known, that he did not intend to find it" (181). That is, as he and the cow wander witlessly through a wilderness of "forgotten ... sites ... monuments of a people's heedless greed," Ike himself enacts a dumb parody of commercial transaction, 'buying' Houston's cow, taking ownership of her, and finally debasing her in his barn-stall "engagements." To buy is always the first step toward killing. Like everything else that seems at first to embody purity, prelapsarian innocence, or original plenitude, Ike's love can be represented only in its loss: already initiated into civilization, Ike is one "who is learning fast now, who has learned success and then precaution and secrecy and how to steal and even providence; who has only lust and greed and blood-thirst and a moral conscience to keep him awake at night, yet to acquire" (185).

Flem reflects the arbitrary, deathly foundation of writing as he manipulates the various systems of meaning in the hamlet meaninglessly. Against him, Ratliff promotes an ethics of joy, a playfulness that values improvisation, fantasy, and extravagance in the absence of a revealed and binding morality. Flem's subversively conformist path is littered with those who, unlike both Flem and Ratliff, allow the systems of articulation to tyrannize them. Ab Snopes, for example, performs early in the novel as a bad forgery of Thomas Sutpen. He tracks manure onto DeSpain's hundred-dollar rug after the plantation owner insults him; but the act is so blunt a statement, so crude a marking, that it betrays an enfeebled imagination. Ab's pathetically impoverished vocabulary of responses condemns him to farm a little, burn a barn, and move on, as if in echo of the original exertions of settling the wilderness:

> "So that there wont come a time some day when he will look around and find out he has run out of new country to move to." Varner ceased. "There's a right smart of country," [Flem counters]. [23]

The narrator comments in another context: "Geography: that paucity of invention . . . " (215). Ab obeys an obsolete pattern, and his son, who has a knack for discovering how the centers of a social discourse change periodically, simply turns his back on him.

Jack Houston's anguish may be seen as even more directly the result of a failure to write his own life. Houston's father poses the first threat to the son's self-articulation: "up to this time, with all that [Houston] had done and failed to do, he had never once done anything which he could not imagine his father also doing, or at least condoning" (216). Lucy Pate, Houston's childhood sweetheart, senses this poverty and eventually succeeds altogether in usurping his authority to express himself. In childhood Lucy exercises her control by putting her thoughts into Houston's handwriting: she forges his school papers so skillfully that "if he had not known he had submitted a blank one and if it had not been that he could neither pronounce nor recognise some of the words and could not understand all of what the ones he did know were talking about, he could not have sworn himself he had not written" (214). The blank page of Houston's life is ready to accept another's writing, and Lucy chooses Houston because he was the "one possessing the possibilities on which she would be content to establish the structure of her life" (210). The tragedy of Houston's forged life is that at his ghostwriter's death his identity fades away. Houston has renounced the rights of speech, and Lucy's death surprises him in his willed muteness. (Nearly the same thing happens to Rider in "Pantaloon in Black," as we shall see.) Houston "grieved for her for four years in black, savage, indomitable fidelity" (208), paralyzed by his inability to transform his sense of victimization ("he was boiling with that helpless rage . . . which . . . has no object to retaliate upon" [191]). This is the kind of failure of invention, of course, which originally leads him to try to escape the future by going to Texas and becoming a professional timekeeper. With miserable fascination, Houston remembers his nights of intimacy with Lucy, but he can only imagine the restoration of his blankness as a solution to her loss: "There would be nights which were almost blank ones" (220).

Houston finds permanent blankness in death; that he is "wedded and twinned forever" to his murderer, Mink Snopes, suggests that his crisis of articulation is doubled in the novel. Words fail Mink, too, but not because he renounces them. One source of Mink's unceasing frustration in *The Hamlet* lies in his being barely literate, both literally and metaphorically. The vocabulary (of words and actions) at his disposal seems too small for a declaration of himself. When Ratliff first sees his shack, he is struck by the singular good repair of Mink's mailbox sign:

> ... the crude lettering of the name might have been painted on it yesterday. It seemed to shout at him, all capitals, MINKSNOPES, sprawling, without any spacing between the two words, trailing off and uphill and over the curve of the top to include the final letters. [73]

Mink's fierce effort to shout himself climaxes in Houston's homicide, for Mink considers his act an almost successful statement of his rage. He wants to "finish" the utterance of murder with a word—Mink wants a complete statement: "What he would have liked to do would be to leave a printed placard on the breast itself: *This is what happens to the men who impound Mink Snope's cattle*, with his name signed to it" (222). That he cannot issue such a message above his signature Mink counts as yet another frustration of "his rights as a man." Words even fail him when he finally breaks his courtroom silence to tell off Flem only to find that he has nothing to say: " 'Tell that son of a bitch—' " (340). For all his awesome strength of will, Mink's life is pitifully confined to speaking the single word "revenge"; his terrifying return in *The Mansion* to blast Flem out of his study manages only to repeat the murder of Houston. Mink's primitive, incomplete statements parody any conviction that making meaning is a simple matter. Mink is perpetually surprised that every gesture requires a successive one and that game playing is endless: "I thought that when you killed a man, that finished it, he told himself. But it dont. It just starts then" (247).

Flem's "advent" and success in the hamlet, and his setting out for Jefferson at the novel's conclusion, intimate that the sterile commercialism of Snopesism will prove the order of the day. I have argued that Flem originates nothing as he joylessly, witlessly exploits the arbitrary conventions of economy. Ratliff, after practicing a fine resistance to Flem's renegotiation of custom, finally suffers a humiliating defeat when he buys the worthless Frenchman place. He is victimized by two mistakes: on the one hand, Ratliff acts on a desperate faith that value has a fixed (or at least traditional) standard; on the other, he is seduced into opposing Flem on Snopes's ground, in Snopes's terms. Ratliff's allegiance to the past involves unswerving respect for Varnerism; he never believes Will's assessment of the Frenchman place as worthless because Varner would never commit such a misjudgment, and because Ratliff shares Varner's pleasure in misrepresentation as a part of trade. That Flem accepts the property as part of Eula's 'dowry' confirms Ratliff's opinion that Varner and his 'headman' value it highly. Moreover, Ratliff signals his confidence in the hamlet's mythology by subscribing to the rumors of antebellum wealth. Ratliff's conviction is an act of faith in the community—in its conventions, customs, values, and fictions. These are attributes that he has defended throughout the novel, of course, but they are travestied in their final form. Uncle Dick Bolivar becomes the voice of the past: "he antedated everyone" and has in his cabin "a tremendous Bible [another avatar of the hamlet's scriptures] and a faded daguerreotype of a young man in a Confederate uniform which was believed by those who had seen it to be his son" (350). Comically, he coerces faith from the skeptical: "'Tech the peach fork,' the old man panted. 'You that didn't believe.' When Bookwright touched it, it was arched into a rigid downpointing curve, the string taut as wire" (351). Bolivar parodies Ratliff's humane faith in the historical and the sacred.

In his desperation to impede Flem's acquisition of power and wealth, Ratliff abandons the very values he wishes to protect. His aims in the deal are indistinguishable from those generally governing a Snopes maneuver: ownership, "gross profit," and revenge. Surely Ratliff's fate is sealed by his partnership with Armstid, for Henry burlesques the burlesque that is Snopesism. As soon as the trio agrees that the old garden hides buried treasure, they move to exclude the rest of the community.

> "There was somebody in the ditch, watching us," [Ratliff] said. "We got to buy it."
>
> "We got to buy it quick," Bookwright said.   [354]

Their plan exemplifies a lamentable collapse of possession into ownership; Armstid believes that they already possess the coins they have found ("'Mine's mine,' Armstid said. 'I found it. I worked for it. I'm going to do any God damn thing I want to with it'" [354]), but they cannot rest until they have established sole title to the property. Once they buy it, Henry exults madly, "'It's mine now. I can dig all day if I want'" (363). Ratliff's customary pleasure in shrewd dealing likewise fades before Flem's power. Though less inflamed, he shares Armstid's avarice and vengefulness: "they lay among the quilts and slept fitfully, too tired to sleep completely also, dreaming of gold" (364). Armstid and Ratliff crave the money precisely because they can double its worth by taking it out of Flem's pocket before putting it in their own:

> "... But then we cant do anything here until after midnight, after Flem has done got through hunting it."
>
> "And finding it tomorrow night," Armstid said. "By God, I aint—."
> [347]

Ratliff's management of the transaction is embarrassingly unimaginative. He deals with unexpected bluntness:

> "Where you headed?" Varner said. "Town?" Ratliff told no lie; he attempted none. . . .
>
> "I come out to meet you. I want to speak to Flem a minute."   [359]

He announces his object with urgency ("That Old Frenchman place"), rejects Flem's price immediately, and plays his presumed ace without delay when he brandishes Labove and Eula. Ratliff never wonders why, if Flem actually believes there is money on the grounds, he would sell it for less than its gossip-determined worth, and Ratliff plays with none of the style, patience, and fun of his earlier matches. He is betrayed by a lapse from his understanding of the community's rules of usage, and the novel expresses his failure as a series of misreadings. First he neglects the dates on the coins, then he misses a sign that might have reminded him how Flem has transformed the hamlet: as the three approach the lawn they do "not know that the fallen pediment in the middle of the slope had been a sundial" (344). The obsolete clock might have warned them that " 'it's already tomorrow now' " (354).

Recovering his humor and dignity after he realizes Flem's victory, Ratliff revives the vocabulary of play as he and Bookwright check the coins: " 'Bet you one of them I beat you,' Ratliff said. . . . Each of them took up a coin, examined it briefly, then set them one upon the other like a crowned king in checkers, close to the lantern" (367). But this game is only a humiliating miniature of the ones that count, and Flem's impersonal triumph remains undiminished. Ratliff realizes that Flem has nothing personal in mind during his charade: " 'But how did he know it would be us?' Bookwright said. 'He didn't,' Ratliff said. 'He didn't care' " (367). Flem, having seized the reins of the hamlet's speech, takes the last words of the novel as he looks toward Jefferson: " 'Come up' " (373). The sentence casts a long shadow across the rest of the trilogy, but it also echoes Ratliff's earlier " 'Come up, rabbits. . . . Let's hit for town' " (51) when he anticipates the pleasure of skirmishes with Ab and others. The faint repetition persuades us of Flem's powers of usurpation.

CHAPTER 5

The Ritual of Mourning
in *Go Down, Moses*

i

As *Go Down, Moses* (1942) mournfully broods on the shrinkage of the Mississippi wilderness and remorsefully chronicles the eradication of the McCaslin lineage, it presents us with a fresh configuration of the crisis of loss. The novel repeatedly seeks to conduct its readers to the very sites at which the breakup of immediacy or possession occurs. Unlike *The Sound and the Fury* and *Absalom, Absalom!,* which concentrate on strategies for recovering what seems to have been lost in the past, or *The Hamlet,* which deals with changes threatened by the future, *Go Down, Moses* collects a series of moments in which objects vanish almost in front of our eyes. From the comic collapse of antebellum splendor in "Was," through the executions of Old Ben and the wilderness around him, to the pathetic exits of the last McCaslin in "Delta Autumn" and the last Beauchamp in "Go Down, Moses," the novel dwells on the process of loss. Each of the stories, as it stages its losses, simultaneously discovers the urge to speak, to articulate grief. The characters in *Go Down, Moses* speak as they manipulate the rituals of the hunt, practice the forms of courtship or marriage, play games, or calculate gestures. As we have seen before, articulation and loss coincide, and in *Go Down, Moses* we encounter another version of language as, doubly, loss and gain: the impulse to speak confirms the breakup of possession and immediacy even as it seeks to overcome it. Speech, in all its guises, proves itself an inscription of deathliness, forgetfulness, and separation. In this sense, all language is the language of grief for Faulkner. Those who perform the rituals of the hunt in *Go Down, Moses,* for example, understand that they are speaking their grief over the loss of the wilderness, or big game, or a simpler, more heroic past; myths and rituals are not practiced as witcheries that can recover sacred origins. Instead, like all forms of language, they mark the object of their mourning celebration as always already lost, and offer themselves as utterances that seem to fill up the voids.

The repeated impulse in *Go Down, Moses* is not only to manipulate common rituals so as to get them to speak one's will, but also to ornament those rituals with talk. Lucas Beauchamp and Sam Fathers, for example, conduct versions of the hunter's pursuit and conquest with, respectively, comic and magical effects. But in both cases they perform such rites as statements, utterances that create significance, history, and authority. In this respect, the ceremonies of the hunt and the rituals associated with marriage function as speech; but an equally important trait of such performances of ritual is that they regularly climax in actual word or conversation, from Tomey's Turl's understanding that he needs "the word" to consummate his hunt for Tennie, through Sam Fathers' stories about the ur-wilderness, to Mollie Beauchamp's insistence that her grandson's death receive proper public notice in the newspaper.

It goes without saying that the disappearance of the Mississippi wilderness stands at the center of the three stories that follow Isaac McCaslin's hunting career. Arthur Kinney used the term "wilderness trilogy" to emphasize their common subject,[1] and the annual visits of Ike and his fellow hunters from the late 1870s to the late 1940s mark the retreat of unspoiled land. By the time of "Delta Autumn," of course, the "primeval" forest "was drawing inward" and is at the moment of its extinction; but throughout the other stories of the novel the wilderness is also perpetually running down. The McCaslin and Beauchamp farms in "Was" have already supplanted forests, leaving their occupants to play with comically domesticated versions of the hunt and ritual initiation. Lucas kicks aside the small game on the plantation because it is unworthy of the notice of one who remembers the primitive dangers and pleasures of the big hunts. And Rider, obsessed with Mannie's death, scarcely

1. Arthur F. Kinney, "Faulkner and the Possibilities for Heroism," *Southern Review,* 6 (Autumn 1970), 1110–1125.

sees that the exhaustion of his wife is somehow related to his furious logging career, which wastes a wilderness in exchange for a "bright cascade of silver" coins. The wilderness is always receding in *Go Down, Moses,* and the certainty of its disappearance is emphasized by the very rituals that honor its dwindling presence and mourn its passing. Ike realizes that the yearly hunt imitates ceremonially the exhaustion of the wilderness; killing old Ben becomes a ritual execution, an artistic transmutation of decay.

As if doubling the disappearance of the wilderness in *Go Down, Moses,* each story also stages the loss or endangerment of a wife. "Was," though it charges immediately into a high-spirited account of two 'successful' courtships, begins almost imperceptibly with a reference to the death of Ike's wife, whose disappointment, treachery, and willfulness are explained only in section 4 of "The Bear." There Alice McCaslin's demand that Ike occupy the family plantation provokes him to think of her as morally "lost" long before her love dies to him. Lucas Beauchamp twice must respond to Molly's disappearance, once when she is installed by Zack Edmonds as the master's woman and again when she wanders off in search of a divorce from her gold-crazed husband. Rider's grief over the death of his six months' wife is the starkest crisis of loss in the novel, but we should not forget that it is succeeded by the sheriff's own dead marriage, by Old Ben's "lover-like" embrace of death, by Boon's loss of his wilderness spouse, Lion, and by Roth Edmonds' renunciation of his Negro mistress.

Go Down, Moses specifies the analogy between the wilderness and a wife several times; in "The Bear" Ike comes to his new wife as if her virginal promise may be understood in terms of the pristine fullness of the forest: "and they were married, they were married and it was the new country, his heritage too as it was the heritage of all, out of the earth..." [2] The wilderness, like a wife, is desired, possessed, and exhausted by the men who father plantations and families upon her. Men dwell in deep intimacy with the new land and then watch, sadly and guiltily, as the body of their partner withers at the delta of exhausted loins. America as receptive virgin is an icon that has been ably elucidated by Henry Nash Smith and

2. William Faulkner, *Go Down, Moses* (New York: Modern Library, 1955), p. 301. I shall quote throughout from this edition.

Leslie Fiedler,[3] and most brilliantly exploited by F. Scott Fitzgerald (as he makes Daisy into the emanation of the "vast republic") and Hart Crane (as Pocahontas becomes America's mythic body in "The Dance" of *The Bridge*). With these historical and psychological explanations for the coalescence of the loss of the wilderness and the loss of wives, I also wish to recall the equation of speech and desire that we have noticed in Faulkner's other novels. The urge to speak originates at the site of dispossession and the desire to recover, and *Go Down, Moses* offers several facets of the crisis through which the word must come to supplement the absence of the object of love. On the one hand, the mourners of *Go Down, Moses* yearn for the actual return of what has been lost— patrimonial splendor, the unaxed timber, Mannie's full presence. On the other, the stories dramatize recognitions that the expressions of grief may represent what never existed in the first place.

That the stories of *Go Down, Moses* repeat the jeopardization of the wife suggests that the breakup of erotic love stimulates the language of loss; but the other face of deprivation in the novel is paternal. The weakness or absence of fathers challenges their sons to speak paternal strength or presence into existence, to create fathers so as to rebel strongly against them. Paternal voids plague all of the protagonists in *Go Down, Moses*; it is another kind of dispossession that bonds the crises of the stories. Isaac McCaslin knows of his own father only through the anecdotes of his surrogate father, Cass Edmonds, an older cousin. When Ike reaches his majority, he realizes that he must contest Cass's version of the past in order to father himself. Lucas Beauchamp, Rider, Sam Fathers, Samuel Worsham Beauchamp, and even Cass Edmonds (who is called the "woman-made" McCaslin) suffer from darkened paternal origins. How the imagination articulates such a loss becomes one of *Go Down, Moses*'s persistent questions, a dilemma in perfect antistrophe to the erotic losses of the wife and the wilderness.

What I have been calling forms of articulation in *Go Down, Moses*—the rituals of the hunt, the initiation, marriage, the rehear-

---

3. Henry Nash Smith, *Virgin Land: The American West as Symbol and Myth* (New York, 1950), and Leslie Fiedler, *Love and Death in the American Novel* (New York, 1960).

sal of local legend—correspond to similar systems of discourse in the earlier novels. Traditionally in the criticism of *Go Down, Moses* ritual and myth have been studied from the perspective of their primitive practice. Based on the speculation of Mircea Eliade, Ernst Cassirer, or Suzanne Langer, essays have examined how Ike's initiation by Sam Fathers conforms to ethnological fact, or how "The Bear" depends on evoking the time of sacred origins through the myths and rituals of the hunt.[4] I argue, however, that *Go Down, Moses* demystifies such behavior by presenting it as a kind of writing rather than as magic. In the first place, the time of origins, Eliade's *in illo tempore,* never emerges in *Go Down Moses*; every attempt to recover the unaxed wilderness or to celebrate Old Ben's mythic immortality reveals itself as a self-conscious representation of their loss. The time of the "old people" and the space of the wilderness' communal ownership are created in the novel only under the auspices of Sam Fathers' fictions, and not through any wilderness mystery cult. The current rites of the hunt, like the hunting talk, proclaim their difference from whatever the original practices might have been; they are time-bound substitutions that need periodic revision and disfigurement. Moreover, the hunt as language (rather than as magic) respects the irreversibility of loss; the ritual that articulates grief manages only to utter the loss, it cannot annul it. The 'speakers' of the hunt see it as a doubling of death, not as its mythic solution: "perhaps only a country-bred [man] could comprehend loving the life he spills" (181), Ike concludes after killing his first buck.

The rites of courtship and marriage, too, become expressions in *Go Down, Moses.* Uncle Buck uses his parodic courtship of Sophonsiba Beauchamp to articulate a fundamental ambivalence toward his lineage and sexuality. Lucas understands the management of his marriage as a series of public statements, what he "says" to his community in the language they all share. And Ike views his initiation into the intimacies of the wilderness as his acquisition of the rights of "man-talking."

As the disposition of marriages produces intimacies, identity, self-assertion, and order, so does play in the novel. *Go Down,*

4. A typical example of simply applying Eliade's model of ritual initiation to "The Bear" is Gorman Beauchamp's "The Rite of Initiation in Faulkner's *The Bear,*" *Arizona Quarterly,* 28 (1972), 319–325.

Moses stages several crucial games: the Beauchamp-McCaslin poker game and Rider's dice game are most memorable. Like the games in *The Hamlet,* these matches embody larger issues. The acute racial tension between Negro, Indian, and white is mirrored in the nightmarish repetition of black, red, and white in the novel's favorite games: cards, dice, checkers. And those who play the novel's cracked games despite obvious distortions and cheating express a commitment to the conventions of arbitrary sense, while those (like Rider) who demand absolute justice violate the games with plaintive violence.

Go Down, Moses haunts incessantly the sites at which loving intimacy has already just become the longing of speech. Two words that punctuate each of the seven stories are "wait" and "grief," and the novel rocks beautifully between protesting loss by pleading for it to stop and initiating the rites of mourning.[5] The act of speaking grief, which occupies all of the stories, constitutes one of the unifying features of the novel; I want to suggest that *Go Down, Moses* provides several metaphors drawn from its rhetoric of grief for its problematic kind of unity. Objections to calling *Go Down, Moses* a novel abound,[6] and depreciations of its structure point to the casual ties between protagonists, the varied settings, and its apparent thematic looseness (are slavery, race, family, or freedom engaged by all of the stories?). Faulkner deliberately disfigures the structure of *Go Down, Moses,* however, to show it buckling under the grief of the losses it sustains. One way to understand its arrangement is through a phrase taken from the title story; the narrator describes Samuel Beauchamp's funeral procession through town, the spectators and cars "in formal component complement to the Negro murderer's catafalque" (382). As it displays the moribund self-delusion of the Old South, as it stumbles across Indian burial

5. In an unpublished essay, Laurence B. Holland considers *Go Down, Moses* as an extended elegy.

6. The most pernicious argument against the unity of *Go Down, Moses* rests on the view that Faulkner hurriedly and carelessly tailored the stories for joint publication. See, for example, a particularly odious version of this theory in Marvin Klotz, "Procrustean Revision in Faulkner's *Go Down, Moses,*" *American Literature,* 37 (March 1965), 1–16. Though neither is very imaginative, two other studies at least testify to the serious attention Faulkner paid to the revision of *Go Down, Moses*'s earlier stories: James Early, *The Making of "Go Down, Moses"* (Dallas, 1972), and Joanne V. Creighton, "Revision and Craftsmanship in the Hunting Trilogy of *Go Down, Moses,*" *Texas Studies in Language and Literature,* 15 (Fall 1973), 577–592.

mounds or the corpses of Old Ben and Lion, as it hoists Sam Fathers onto his platform and discovers Ike in a deathly attitude on his camp cot, the entire novel becomes the bearer of bodies, a catafalque.

The two parties of mourners in "Go Down, Moses" separate at the boundary of the town. I suggest that the stories of *Go Down, Moses* divide similarly, to display a structure of opposition. Complements harmonize by opposing, and the novel embodies the many paradoxes of mourning through its formal complementarity. For example, one tension for Faulkner is between the convention of chronological time (and its literary ally, narrative) and his view that there is "no such thing as time," that the future and the past are part of a present that is "shaped quite a bit by the artist."[7] The temporal structure of the novel confirms the opposition: on the one hand, a rough chronology takes us from the antebellum South in "Was" to the mid-1940s of Chicago racketeers in "Go Down, Moses." But the shaping of time, on the other hand, disfigures that innocent chronology; for example, "Was" is an anecdote told by Cass to Ike decades after it has occurred. The novel everywhere reminds us that the telling of the past is a perpetual act of shaping. As *Go Down, Moses* leaps from Ike at eighty to the circumstances of his parents' courtship in "Was," as it dramatizes moments of fantasy and memory about old Carothers' time, of the youth of the wilderness, as it filters moments through several temporal and narrative biases, it compels chronology and narrative into a tense antagonism.

The structure of *Go Down, Moses* also opposes comic behavior in domestic settings to the solemn retreats into the wilderness. The first three stories introduce all of the important rituals of the novel—courtship and marriage, the ceremonies of pursuit and initiation, the conventions of conversation. But they appear as fox hunts through kitchens, bear hunts through beds, initiations into the folklore of women, and conversations that seek to rob one of the past rather than to evoke it magically. This parodic prelude performs several functions. It deliberately contaminates the rituals of the wilderness so as to demystify their content and emphasize

7. Loïc Bouvard, "Notes and Discussion: Conversation with William Faulkner," trans. Henry Dan Piper, *Modern Fiction Studies*, 5 (Winter 1959–1960), 362.

their structure as statements. It also constructs a passage of actual withdrawal from domestic to primitive conditions, as the parlors, pantries, and plantation fields become the points of departure for the first words of "The Old People": "at first there was nothing." The stories that precede these words compromise their innocence and also, paradoxically, augment their achievement. For the illusion of the return to sacred origins is all the more grandly sustained against the novel's introduction of profaned myth and ritual. The first three stories also enact a dumbshow of grief since their protagonists rarely succeed in voicing the depth of their loss; the stifled or feeble efforts to speak prefigure the elaborate artifice of mourning arranged by Sam Fathers and Ike. Finally, parody also discharges embarrassment; the religious solemnity that attends both the ritual pursuit of Old Ben and the scriptural aspirations of Ike's address to Cass grows more human in the presence of antic imitation.

The complementary structure of *Go Down, Moses* also rests on a correspondence between the subjects of the first three stories and those of the wilderness trilogy. Both "Was" and "The Old People" focus on a child's initiation into the fraternal brotherhood of hunters, and each contains the effort to enfranchise Ike with an account of his paternity and legacy. "The Bear" and "The Fire and the Hearth" share the chronicle of a hunt, the taking possession of one's patrimony, the sense of a better past drawing to its end, and the dilemma of choosing between the wilderness ethic and one's wife—a dilemma that demands some kind of renunciation. The pain of undeniable loss, the yearning for forgetfulness and release from consciousness, and the horror of endless grief draw "Pantaloon in Black" and "Delta Autumn" together; each imprisons its cot-bound mourner in a shower of tears, of grieving rain. The themes of *Go Down, Moses* suggest reasons and metaphors for such a bicameral structure. The first three stories involve black protagonists (Tomey's Turl, Lucas Beauchamp, and Rider), while the wilderness trilogy concentrates on Ike's career. Blackness (as "Pantaloon in Black" suggests) is not simply racial, of course; blackness represents social disenfranchisement, inarticulateness, and a tragic crisis that dissolves into comic treatment. These qualities permeate all three of the opening stories, and, as all of their crucial events seem to occur at night, darkness covers the first half of *Go Down, Moses.* The novel's form duplicates old Carothers McCaslin's divided lineage as it explores the paradoxes and conflicts generated by a patriarch whose will and testament is written in black and white. The paradox of mixed or divided blood sustains the paradox of the novel's structure. (Paradox as form governs the oppositions of narrative episode, tone, gender, and time in *The Wild Palms,* too.) But *Go Down, Moses* also *disfigures* the lineal relations of its characters; Rider, for example, only rents land from a McCaslin, and the last story mentions Gavin Stevens' surprise at the discovery that Mollie Beauchamp and Hank Worsham are sister and brother. It is as if the symmetry of the novel's biracial 'family' is under the pressure of erasure or confusion, posing a deliberate indictment of old Carothers' untroubled, shortsighted segregation. The biological relationship of the novel's characters recedes before a centrifugal force; for instance, the reader scarcely realizes that Tennie and Tomey's Turl are Lucas Beauchamp's parents as he moves from the first story to the second. The genealogy of the characters may be traced to old Carothers' efforts to mark, to enslave, to own, and to create a dynasty; but the novel turns his heirs into a "communal anonymous brotherhood," the phrase Ike uses to describe the possession (without ownership) of the wilderness. The novel itself stands as a formal rebuke to the offenses it records.

ii

"Was" is indisputably one of Faulkner's funniest short stories. Its central comic convention involves the incongruity of humans being treated as animals: Uncle Buck tries to hunt Tomey's Turl as if he were a fox; Sophonsiba Beauchamp becomes Uncle Buck's "bear," unwittingly brought to bay; and she turns hunter into hunted, making Buck her buck, her dear a deer. We are free to enjoy this tomfoolery because there seem to be no serious consequences. The McCaslin twins may be annoyed by their having "won" Tennie from Hubert Beauchamp since they are ostensibly abolitionists, but they consider it a small price to pay to extricate Buck from Hubert's and Sophonsiba's matrimonial toils. For all their gruffness and mutual suspiciousness, the participants accept their predicaments as games to be enjoyed, as forms of recreation. The slapstick foxhunt that precedes Turl's escape sounds the story's comic grace note; the hounds chase a pet fox through the house until they finally tear through the kitchen where Buddy is making breakfast:

> ... Uncle Buddy was bellowing like a steamboat blowing and this time the fox and the dogs and five or six sticks of firewood all came out of the kitchen together with Uncle Buddy in the middle of them hitting at everything in sight with another stick. It was a good race. [5]

The fun of good sport carries over into Buck's pursuit of Turl. The chase has become a semiannual event: everybody has an assigned part, Buddy in the kitchen, Cass as the scout for "'anything [that] begins to look wrong'" (8), Uncle Buck running toward his horse as he ties his ceremonial necktie, and the Beauchamps' slave blowing a fox horn to announce Buck's arrival. Cass registers the resemblance of their pursuit to a hunt: he remembers Uncle Buck telling him to "'stay back where he [Turl] wont see you and flush. I'll circle him through the woods and we will bay him at the creek ford'" (8). But Cass "closed in too fast; maybe he was afraid he wouldn't be there in time to see him when he treed. It was the best race he had ever seen" (8). Buck's pause to eat breakfast and his scrupulous care to put his tie on whenever he may encounter a lady suggest that he may not dread his visits to Warwick as much as he says, and he at least submits politely to the customs of dinner, toddies, and Sophonsiba's daunting conversation—the rituals of this domesticated hunt.

Turl's periodic escapes seek more than to provide everyone with high-spirited exercise, a little more challenging game, or occasions for neighborliness, however. Turl is seriously, if sporadically, wooing Tennie; his flights protest a master's control over the slave's body and emotions. The sinister edge of Buck's hunt appears early in one of Cass's naive observations: noticing Turl's ability to elude them, he remarks, "Maybe Turl had been running off from Uncle Buck for so long that he had even got used to running away like a white man would do it" (9). The irony, of course, is not only that Turl's foxiness should impress Cass as being nearly human (i.e., white), or even that the pursuit of Turl should expose slavery's assumption of Negro bestiality, but that Turl is in fact part white.

Hubert is said to refer offhandedly to "that damn white half-McCaslin" (6), and later, when Turl's hands emerge to deal the cards in the poker game, the narrator describes "Tomey's Turl's arms that were supposed to be black but were not quite white" (29). Tomey's Turl is the McCaslin twins' half brother; old Carothers has fathered them all. The narrative, imitating Buck's and Buddy's minds, tries to suppress this fact, but the consequence is that the hunt for Turl turns out to be a fox hunt through the McCaslins' genealogical house. Turl is the offspring of old Carothers' miscegenation and incest, and Turl's participation in "the best race he had ever seen" suddenly becomes a poignant pun.[8] At several points in *Go Down, Moses* we notice Buck's and Buddy's efforts to free or compensate the slaves they have inherited from their father; at the least, perhaps the consequences of old Carothers' sexual and racial crimes within his own family will be halted if the brothers can prevent Turl from marrying, and if they remain true to their own sterile bachelorhood. A childless Turl would mean that McCaslin blood would no longer flow in the veins of slaves, and, remaining heirless themselves, the twins may atone for old Carothers' unbridled sexuality. The line's sole male heir would then become Cass Edmonds, who has descended from old Carother's daughter and been freed of the McCaslin surname. Buck's determination to recapture Turl and to defend his own celibacy functions as a disguised statement of guilt and rectification.

Serious statements or gestures that masquerade as insignificant fun comprise the fundamental mode of discourse in "Was." Buck and Buddy repeatedly hope to discharge their ambivalence about slavery, sexuality, and their lineage in deliberately duplicitous behavior. Perhaps the emblem of "Was," though it is not spelled out in detail until later, is the charade of bondage and emancipation that Buck and Buddy play with their slaves. The twins intuit one paradox of slavery: to become masters is to enslave themselves to ownership, to possess is somehow to be dispossessed. Uncle Buck complains that "he and Uncle Buddy had so many niggers already that they could hardly walk around on their own land for them . . ." (5). Yet the two McCaslins cannot renounce their own paternity or

8. The pun on "race" is noticed by Marie-Helene Mathiex, "Les négations et le problème racial dans *Go Down, Moses*," in Viola Sachs, ed., *Le blanc et le noir chez Melville et Faulkner* (The Hague: Mouton, 1974).

their society to free the slaves outright (and when they once try, the slave insists on staying and purchasing his liberty); nor can they put aside their guilt. Instead, they contrive a manner of supporting slavery that actually subverts it: they begin their administration of the plantation by transferring all of the slaves into old Carothers' unfinished mansion and moving into a slave cabin themselves, expressing their own bondage to the institution of bondage. They also arrange an

> unspoken gentlemen's agreement between the two white men and the two dozen black ones that, after the white man had counted them and driven the home-made nail into the front door at sundown, neither of the white men would go around behind the house and look at the back door, provided that all the negroes were behind the front one when the brother who drove it drew out the nail again at daybreak. [262–263]

The twins calculate this ritual to suspend the contradictory demands of enslavement and liberation; it typifies their troubled efforts simultaneously to act and not to act, to speak and remain silent.[9]

Buck makes his ritual hunt of Turl express a similar ambivalence. If he is as adamant about avoiding Sibbey as he says, we may wonder why he stops to eat breakfast (thereby just missing Turl before he finds sanctuary in Warwick), or why he puts on his tie in the middle of the night when Hubert once tries to improve his sister's marital chances by dumping her on the McCaslins' porch at midnight. Hubert jokes with Buddy that one thing that makes Buck more human than his twin is that he is "woman-weak" (26), and he probably draws his conclusion from the fact that it is always Theophilus who chases Turl, "even though they all knew that Uncle Buddy could have risked it ten times as much as Uncle Buck could have dared" (6). Buck's attraction to Sophonsiba is smothered under the constraint of his moral conviction and cowardice. He finds his bachelorhood both necessary and dispensible, and his solution is to enact a travesty of courtship that both affirms and denies his desire. Ostensibly, Buck is resolute and cautious around

9. I shall consider Buck and Buddy's 'conversation' in the commissary ledgers as another example of this desire.

Sophonsiba, but he doesn't mind flirting with danger. He signals his polite entrance into Warwick's hospitality by bowing to Sophonsiba: "He and Uncle Buck dragged their foot" (11), Cass remembers. But Buck is also dragging his feet metaphorically, gesturing his reluctance or inability to act on his desire. Compounding his risks, Buck tiptoes into the dark house after giving up the chase and surprisingly heads toward the bedrooms. Buck makes the apparent mistake of reading an unlocked door as a sign of vacancy instead of as Sophonsiba's invitation, but at least subconsciously he must entertain the possibility of accidentally ending up in her bed. How else can we explain his persistent hushing of Cass or the alertness with which he "ease[s] himself carefully down onto the edge" (20) of the bed? Dining, drinking, exchanging innuendo, creeping up the dark stairs and hallway, "rolling" into bed, and listening to Sophonsiba utter "the first scream," Buck enacts a parody of courtship and consummation. Like all of his speech, however, this statement of desire wants to deny itself; it seeks evasion, suspension, and incompletion.

Hubert's and the McCaslins' poker game aims at the same kind of safe irresolution as the playful rites of slave ownership and courtship. The hands dealt and the stakes raised are so fiercely calculated by the players that we might fail to notice several important violations of the game's law. For example, when Buck gets into immediate trouble, losing to Hubert and evidently "winning" Sibbey, he simply runs off into the woods. Hubert permits Buddy's substitution and complies with the continuation of a game that has already taken his sister off his hands. ("'By God, Buck McCaslin, you have met your match at last,'" he unwittingly puns [25].) When he realizes that Turl is the dealer, Hubert consents to end the game with an uncalled hand and settle for the resolution he had earlier rejected, the sale of Tennie. That Hubert and the McCaslins accept these disfigurements of the game—'tag teams,' revised stakes, Turl's probable cheating—suggests their playing conspires to reestablish an equilibrium rather than to generate any resolution of their dilemmas. The game flees consequence; Hubert expects that they "will be right back where all this foolishness started from" (28), with the trifling exception of Tennie's transfer. Their play is a kind of forgetfulness, a kind of silence: "Then [Hubert] stopped talking. For about a minute it was like he and Uncle Buddy had both gone to sleep" (28); and the game ends when Hubert decides to leave Buddy's hand "not called." The irony of games that only seem to resolve matters has been introduced by Hubert's initial bet that Buck would catch Turl (a bet, incidentally, that Hubert is surprised to be held to). Hubert and Buck repeatedly complete their deal:

> "Five hundred dollars," Mr. Hubert said. "Done."
> "Done," Uncle Buck said.
> "Done," Mr. Hubert said.
> "Done," Uncle Buck said [17]

Buck and Buddy McCaslin hope that their endless play will afford them a refuge from change, time, and moral choice. They recoil with infantile horror from the pain of guilt; Ike notices that their ledger entries are identical because "both looked as though they had been written by the same perfectly normal ten-year-old boy, even to the spelling, except that the spelling did not improve" (263). Puzzled, voluntarily silenced, they can manage only "to fumbleheed that truth" (282) or to make "a formal acknowledgment" of it, "even though only by inference" (105). The twins prefer the illusion that they can hide forever in their rituals of evasion. When they return home, they hasten to assert that things are once again as they have always been: Buck charges Buddy to get breakfast started, virtually repeating his words on the morning of Turl's escape (30, 5); and he sets the pet fox loose again, though it "trees" to the roof too quickly. The best races last the longest; in the first fox hunt, the "fox had treed behind the clock on the mantel" (5), as if pointing to a shelter from time. Buck's flirtation with the disaster of resolution makes time seem to speed up: " 'It seems to me I've been away from home a whole damn month' " (30). What dooms the McCaslins' evasions is that the future they hope to ward off already exists. Formally, the story establishes the fact of Isaac McCaslin's life before it tells the story of his parents' courtship; thus Buck's 'escape' is a comic self-delusion. Similarly, the air of relief at the conclusion ought to be clouded by the next story, since Lucas Beauchamp is the racially troubled offspring of the poker game. Even the comedy of Buck's pursuit of Turl looks sinister under the eye of history; the story is set in 1859, and the imminent Civil War will transform that chase into the spectacle of brother fighting brother, master stalking slave. Faulkner summarizes the insistence of time by changing the title of the story from "Almost" to "Was."[10] Buck and Buddy would be happy to make their races, rituals, and writing speak a perpetually suspended innocence, to play roles in a comedy of inconsequence. But the duplicity of their performances shows through everywhere, and Hubert tries to remind Buck, "'This is the most serious foolishness you ever took part in in you life'" (24).

Buck's partner in all this foolishness is Cass Edmonds, his nine-year-old nephew. Cass's role in "Was" has commonly been unappreciated, but he is not only a significant character in the story, he is also its author. The memories that survive from his childhood comprise his version of the McCaslin past—of his abolitionist uncles, plantations, and slavery. And the particular moments he associates with the winning of Tennie—Sophonsiba's seductiveness, Buck's sexual transgression, and Turl's insistent desire—compose the portrait of a child's discovery of the adult world. I suggest that Cass experiences his night on Warwick as an initiation; in "The Old People," which formally complements "Was," Isaac McCaslin undergoes a solemn version of the ritual that is for Cass comic and domesticated. Cass will grow up to accept his distaff patrimony from old Carothers, to occupy the morally encumbered plantation that Isaac renounces. Later, General Compson scornfully refers to him as "'having one foot straddled into a farm and the other foot straddled into a bank'" because "'all you damnd Sartorises and Edmondses invented farms and banks to keep yourselves from having to find out what this boy [Ike] was born knowing and fearing'" (250). Cass's adult commitment to the virtues of commerce, civilization, and compromised morality arises from the kind of world into which he has been initiated. He notices, for example, that Sophonsiba's claim of aristocratic title to Warwick is merely a spinster's word game (as he tells Ike later, one owns whatever land one takes): "it would sound as if she and Mr Hubert owned two separate plantations covering the same area of ground, one on top of the other" (9). And Tomey's Turl, who is Cass's comic equivalent of Ike's Sam Fathers, teaches him an ethic of domestic practical-

10. Early, *Making of "Go Down, Moses,"* p. 16.

ity rather than wilderness idealism: " 'I gonter tell you something to remember: anytime you wants to git something done, from hoeing out a crop to getting married, just get the womenfolks to working at it. Then all you needs to do is set down and wait' " (13). Accommodation governs all of the Edmondses' affairs.

For Isaac McCaslin the lessons taught by the wilderness will require him to renounce both the domesticated land of his plantation and the free sexual possession of his wife, who makes acceptance of the plantation a condition for her love. Isaac understands that his marriage to the wilderness subordinates his human sexuality, and he frequently experiences moments in the forest that substitute for sexual intimacies; even after imagining his marriage, he insists that "still the woods would be his mistress and his wife" (326). Cass, on the other hand, is initiated into the seductive charms of "womenfolks," who view "hoeing out a crop" and "getting married" as harmonious rituals of domestic occupation. Sophonsiba, after she marries Buck McCaslin, forces him to drive the slaves out of the mansion and to reestablish his authority over the land. Sophonsiba's power over Buck appears in "Was" to Cass's childlike eyes; he senses that she can cloak her language, like her very body, in erotically suggestive promise. Buck, who seems partial to monosyllables, is perfectly stunned by Sophonsiba's elaborate performance of desire. Her highly suggestive fable of Uncle Buck as "a bee sipping from flower to flower" (11) only barely conceals her invitation "to show him her garden" (14), just as her clashing jewelry and excessive perfume try to force the issue. Sophonsiba's speech is always a sexual costume, and she emphasizes the fact by sending the ribbon around her neck as a message to Buck on the field of battle. Every word promises a disrobing. When Buck crawls into her bed, as I have suggested, their mutual scream parodies, at least, the cry of sexual ecstasy. Cass incomprehendingly notices the connection of language and sexuality when he glimpses Sophonsiba's roan tooth flashing whenever she smiles; the "flick and glint between her lips" (11) fascinates Cass during her sexual allegory, and it seems an image produced by a boy's curiosity about female cavities. Cass clearly remembers moments that contribute to the atmosphere of sexual initiation, though he cannot understand them as a nine-year-old. With Buck he passes through Warwick's gateless posts (in Faulkner's iconography an image of sexual invitation, too) and into Sophonsiba's bedroom, where he looks on with a son's surprise as the two adults meet in bed.

If Cass is marked by a kind of initiation into the world of womenfolks, wiles, and plantations, it is as the culmination of the several parodic hunts in "Was." The "fox" hunt after Turl is one such pursuit, but another is Buck's inadvertent capture of Sophonsiba. Hubert makes the analogy for Buck's misadventures in the domestic wilderness specific:

> "You come into bear-country of your own free will and accord. All right; you were a grown man and you knew it was bear-country and you knew the way back out like you knew the way in and you had your chance to take it. But no. You had to crawl into the den and lay down by the bear. And whether you did or didn't know the bear was in it don't make any difference. So if you got back out of that den without even a claw-mark on you, I would not only be unreasonable, I'd be a damned fool." [22–23]

This is our introduction to the bear hunt in *Go Down, Moses,* and its parodic, comic status complicates any claim the ritual might make to antique majesty. Many details of the pursuit appear first in disarray: when Turl turns to bay at Tennie's cabin, he charges Buck, knocking him over; but instead of a hunter's bloody wound, Buck only soaks in whisky from his crushed hip flask. Old Ben clutches Lion in a "lover-like" embrace of death, but Turl actually wins over his pursuers: "it looked like they were trying to jump up and lick him in the face" (14). Even the model for Isaac's Moses-like leadership turns into a small joke when we learn that the twin's pet fox is "old Moses" (30). "Was" inverts behavior that we are later asked to take seriously, subjecting it to parodic distortion.

Cass's other role in the story may help to explain the parodic effects. When Buck runs into poker problems, he sends Cass to tell the story to Buddy. This is not Cass's only performance of the narrative, however, for he also passes the story to his cousin Ike— Buck and Sophonsiba McCaslin's son. Born into his father's old age, Isaac suffers historical vertigo; he stands in distant isolation from the time and sense of his own origins. What he knows about Buck and Buddy, the Beauchamps, and the younger South has "come to him through and from his cousin McCaslin . . . out of the old time, the old days" (4). Isaac depends on Cass for his very paternity; through his authorship of the past, Cass becomes "rather his brother than cousin and rather his father than either" (4). The syntax of the passage that introduces Ike reflects his need for patriation; the first paragraph consists of a series of noun phrases in apposition to "Isaac McCaslin," as if the sentence vainly seeks the source of its own animation. The cryptic history of Ike's career which follows only distorts his acts of renunciation and his love of the wilderness, and section 1 ends amid the recognition that only the generous tellings of the seven stories to follow can chronicle Ike suitably, can connect "is" to "was."[11]

No telling can serve its story innocently; Ike gets his past both "through and from" Cass, who is both medium and origin. Cass's interests in the story account for its parodic featues, for his narrative is duplicitous, attempting to enfranchise Ike with an unadmirable heritage. As Cass gives, he takes away; Buck and Buddy's fumble-heeding of the truth, Sophonsiba's grotesque enticement, the absurd rituals of evasion, the bizarre perversions of hunting and courtship all rob Ike of a past worth honoring. Even as a young man, Cass repudiates a consequential past and makes fun of the wilderness rituals. His version of the past dramatizes the paralysis of Old Carothers' sons before their conflict of patrimony and conscience; it warns Isaac against any similarly foolish equivocation; and it presses implicitly the Edmondses' course of compromise and accommodation. Cass's parodic comedy is a kind of dispossession of Ike, then, even though it subtly reveals the dimensions of the moral crisis. Buck and Buddy are victimized by their inability to articulate their ambivalence, but Cass's story testifies to the power of language, its ability to (re)write the past in one's own words. And Cass's narrative—as parody—embodies his own uneasiness about ridiculing Ike's origins; Leslie Fiedler remarks that parody is "only a reluctant and shamefaced way of honoring what one is ashamed to acknowledge."[12] Surely Cass must address the guilt and shame of his distaff legacy and its apparent peace with miscegenation, incest, and slavery. In revising "The Old People" for *Go Down, Moses* Faulkner changes the characters in section 3 from

---

11. Section 1 of "Was" was written for the story's inclusion in the novel (ibid.).
12. Fiedler, *Love and Death*, p. 56.

Quentin and his father to Ike and Cass. Discussing the Spirit of the Buck that appears to Ike, Cass discourages morbid preoccupation with death: "there is only one thing worse than not being alive, and that's shame" (186). Originally, Mr. Compson had told the suicidal Quentin that there is nothing worse than death; Cass's added exception signals a troubled resolve.[13]

For the moment of the story, Ike is enslaved by Cass's narrative; he cannot contest its assumptions until he is given an alternative legacy by Sam Fathers' stories in "The Old People," and until he speaks his version of history in "The Bear." His dependence and Cass's temporary mastery are felt in the odd way the story notes the presence of Cass; never "Cass," always "he." Nine-year-old Bayard Sartoris was the original first-person narrator of "Was";[14] Faulkner revises by giving the story to Cass and making it nearly third person. That is, Cass becomes responsible for the configurations of the tale, but he does not actually perform it for us or Ike. I suggest that the voice calling Cass "he" is Isaac's; he has been forced to accept Cass's account and tells it as his own. Having no alternative, Ike unwillingly speaks Cass's story as it has come to him out of the old days; moreover, Ike's inability simply to use Cass's name may suggest that he cannot achieve the detachment necessary to understand the story as a fiction. It is Ike's own story, yet not his own: before him still lies the challenge of speaking his origin.

iii

"The Fire and the Hearth" occupies the same corner of outwardly comic highjinx as "Was" in *Go Down, Moses*: its precursors are two short stories, published separately, which present Lucas Beauchamp's amusing efforts to rid himself of a moonshine competitor ("A Point of Law") and to scare up buried gold ("Gold Is Not Always").[15] The larger structures of the novel, however, will not let us see Lucas' schemes simply as rural diversions. As he "hunts" for local treasure, recalls an initiatory struggle with his

13. William Faulkner, "The Old People," *Harper's*, 181 (September 1940), 418–425.

14. Ibid.

15. William Faulkner, "Gold Is Not Always," *Atlantic*, 166 (November 1940), 563–570, and "A Point of Law," *Collier's*, June 22, 1940.

white cousin, defends the dignity of his marriage, and repeatedly attends to his stature in the community and the responsibilities of his name, Lucas articulates a sense of loss. His race, family, and epoch conspire to deprive him of the right to speak, but Lucas will not be silent. With greater courage than Buck and Buddy, who faint before the trials of language, but without the verbal guile of Cass, Lucas Beauchamp fashions a statement of identity, paternity, and history out of the few words he possesses.

Lucas shares with many of Faulkner's other characters a conviction that there was a better, now irrevocable past. As he notices electricity and garages invade the Edmonds plantation, Lucas shakes his head over what "were the old days, the old time, and better men than these" (44). Lucas' *ubi sunt* state of mind pays its foremost tribute to the original McCaslin, old Carothers, even though his crimes have fathered Lucas' disenfranchisement. Lucas respects old Carothers' strength and will, concluding that old Cass had "enough of old Carothers McCaslin in his veins to take the land from the true heir simply because he wanted it" (44). The narrator concurs that "back in that dark time in Mississippi . . . a man had to be hard and ruthless to get a patrimony to leave behind himself and strong and hard to keep it until he could bequeath it" (106), and Roth Edmonds marvels that Lucas is "more like old Carothers than all the rest of us put together" (118; italics omitted). Despite the resemblance, and despite being "the oldest McCaslin descendant" (36) except for Isaac, Lucas cannot proclaim his genealogical rights because "in the world's eye he descended not from McCaslins but from McCaslin slaves" (36). His loss strikes him first when he risks his life to fetch a doctor for Zack's dying wife only to find that his cousin has stolen his own Molly to replace her. At the moment of recognition, he seems to have recrossed "a kind of Lethe" to find "a world outwardly the same yet subtly and irrevocably altered" (46). In the subsequent argument with Zack, Lucas realizes that old Carothers will never be more than a private father: "'All I got to give up is McCaslin blood that rightfully aint even mine or at least aint worth much since old Carothers never seemed to miss much what he give to Tomey that night that made my father'" (57). Naturally, Isaac's repudiation of the patrimony Lucas desires makes him seem to have "turned apostate to his name" (39), to have had the land stolen from him by Cass. Lucas grows old in a world "altered" by the losses of his paternity, patrimony, and stature.

Lucas' opening gambit in "The Fire and the Hearth" is calculated to dispose of George Wilkins, who runs a rival moonshine still and who has an eye on Lucas' daughter, Nat. George Wilkins insults Lucas by encroaching on patrimonial land; he is "an interloper without forbears," "a jimberjawed clown" "whose very name was unknown in the country twenty-five years ago" (40). A name with a past is Lucas' most valuable possession, and he does not take Wilkins' presumption lightly. George's confident courting of Nat also ignores Lucas' sense of propriety and social standing; he muses that his plot to expose Wilkins' illegal moonshining "will be a lesson to him about whose daughter to fool with next time" (62; italics omitted).

Though his motives may be vengeance and self-defense, Lucas also expects to enjoy his success as a private celebration of his capacity to manipulate communal mechanisms. Disenfranchised and subordinated, Lucas persistently looks for ways to express dignity and defiance, to appropriate the full rights of citizenship. He views his plan to deceive Roth Edmonds and finger George Wilkins as a gratifying triumph for his language: "Then he could approach Edmonds and speak his word and it would be like dropping the nickel into the slot machine and pulling the lever: all he would have to do then would be just to watch it" (36). Lucas takes pleasure in being able to get his schemes to "say" what he wants them to; "he had even planned the very phrases, dialogue, in which . . . he would inform Edmonds" (42–43). Lucas is also document-shrewd; when he learns that a marriage certificate will protect him and George when his plot goes wrong, he finds someone to forge and backdate the papers; and he invents a map of buried treasure (claiming that at first "I misread the paper" [91]) to trick the metal-detector salesman. Intuiting the intimacy between paper and money, words and coins, Lucas similarly strives to make the bank hold and return his money, " 'for a black man same as for a white' " (109); he writes a check to test the arrangement as he seeks to establish communal authority through the rights (and rites) of exchange. Lucas also subtly designs his speech to assert his dignity and protest his dispossession: Roth remembers that Lucas always "referred to his father as Mr Edmonds, never as Mister Zack; he watched him avoid having to address the white man directly by any name at all with a calculation so coldly and constantly alert, a finesse so deliberate and unflagging, that for a time he could not tell if even his father knew that the negro was refusing to call him mister" (114).[16] The gesture of self-nomination summarizes Lucas' desire to originate an identity while also acknowledging his lineage; he makes the disfigurement of his name both the greatest honor and the most profound challenge to the first McCaslin:

> ... not refusing to be called Lucius, because he simply eliminated that word from the name; not denying, declining the name itself, because he used three quarters of it; but simply taking the name and changing, altering it, making it no longer the white man's but his own, by himself composed, himself selfprogenitive and nominate, by himself ancestored, as, for all the old ledgers recorded to the contrary, old Carothers himself was. [281]

Despite the constraints on his speech, Lucas Beauchamp manages to have his say. In two central episodes of "The Fire and the Hearth," Lucas uses the ritual of the hunt to state the paradoxes of his troubled race and history. Wilkins' new threat leads Lucas to remember his first experience with dispossession, Zack's theft of Molly. That crisis breaks when Lucas discovers the contradiction of his past: he performs his heroic journey for the doctor in honor of "old Carothers McCaslin who had sired him and Zack Edmonds both" (46). But Lucas' affirmation of brotherhood gives way to Zack's assumption of racial superiority and will—the very marks of old Carothers' legacy. To protest Zack's action is both to imitate Carothers' courage and to defy it, since taking a slave's woman for one's own is what has fathered Lucas. Like the other protagonists in *Go Down, Moses*, Lucas suffers his dilemma as a crisis of articulation: what does one say in the circumstance of loss? He summarizes the situation: " 'How to God ... can a black man ask a white man to please not lay down with his black wife? And even if he could ask it, how to God can the white man promise he wont?' " (59). As he considers alternative reactions, Lucas rejects killing Zack as soon as he sends Molly back because "it would be like I had done said

16. Richard Wright remembers in *Black Boy* (New York, 1937) how racial deference was epitomized in terms of address.

aloud to the whole world that he never sent her back because I told him to but he give her back to me because he was tired of her" (48–49; italics omitted). Lucas makes the conflict a question of speech: "'I went to Zack Edmonds' house and asked him for my wife. Let him come to my house and ask me for his son!'" (50). Lucas realizes that what Zack has done challenges him to voice a protest, or commence grieving, or initiate a conversation with the past so as to understand it.

Only Molly's loss provokes Lucas to speak and, in speaking, to confront the house of McCaslin. Lucas' anger sends him into the false dawn after Zack, like a hunter stalking a wild foe; silently surprising Zack in his bed, Lucas stays his razor over "the undefended and defenseless throat" (52), a moment that resonates with Rider's slitting Birdsong's throat and Ike's creasing his first buck's neck. The ritual elements of the hunt help to formalize Lucas' inquiry into the conditions of his dispossession. His violent hatred and love for old McCaslin find a perfect expression in his wrestling with Zack, Lucas "facing across the bed and the pistol the man whom he had known from infancy, with whom he had lived until they were both grown almost as brothers lived" (55). A bed—old Carothers' couch of incest and miscegenation—is precisely the site at which Lucas gains, as he loses, his paternity. Clasping Zack, Lucas holds "his left arm almost like an embrace" (57) and fires the pistol into his cousin's ribs. "Embrace" is the word used to describe Old Ben's deathly grasp of Lion, too; Lucas is trying to understand his own version of the hunter's paradox of loving the life one spills. But old Carothers hates the life he spills into his slave, and Lucas realizes that his actual antagonist in this contest is his grandfather: "'Because all you got to beat is me. I got to beat old Carothers'" (54). In his passion, as recognition bursts on recognition, Lucas even entertains suicide momentarily, as if in putative imitation of his great-grandmother Eunice. But Lucas chooses speech rather than the silence of suicide, and he tries to murder Zack. Instead, "the incredibly loud click of the miss-fire" seals his frustration. Lucas' effort to confront the conditions of his identity succeeds: his racial and familial disenfranchisement is embodied in his challenges to the "white man" and to the "woman-made" cousin; old Carothers' careless, dangerous phallicism is represented by the pistol wrestled over in the bed, just as the "miss-fire" reminds Lucas of the purely insignificant accident of his birth. So violent a statement of his bondage converts Lucas from hunter to quarry: Zack "saw the whites of the negro's eyes rush suddenly with red like the eyes of a bayed animal—a bear, a fox" (55). Nevertheless, Lucas' ability to fashion the plentiful contradictions of his legacy satisfies him in an important respect. The bullet that has misfired is a souvenir of Lucas' statement of defiance and dignity; he notices that the shell is "not much larger than a pencil, not much heavier, yet large enough to contain two lives" (58). And what he has written with the bullet, Lucas has also spoken; by both imitating and also challenging old Carothers, Lucas feels that he has mastered him. Momentarily, he appropriates his grandfather's own voice: "*Old Carothers,* he thought. *I needed him and he come and spoke for me*" (58).

That Lucas needs old Carothers' voice to break its hundred years of silence to say, almost inaudibly, "my son" dictates that the contest with Zack must be a speaking ritual. The gestures and imagery of their struggle suggest that Lucas roughly follows the sequence of the hunt—from early morning tracking through the discovery of the quarry's bed and the threat of the knife to the climactic baying and shot. Lucas' comic gold hunt is a similar attempt to get the past to speak through a ritual. When a $1,000 gold piece falls on his head as he hides his still beneath an Indian burial mound, Lucas concludes that he is about to hit a jackpot. He does not abandon his crops, wife, and leisure in the lunacy of simple greed, however; the money for which he hunts is a tangible version of the patrimony his grandfather has denied him. Legend insists that there is McCaslin wealth buried locally, and Lucas assumes that he has discovered "the money which old Buck and Buddy had buried almost a hundred years ago" (40). The narrator suggests that the coin's thump is "a sort of admonitory pat from the spirit of darkness and solitude, the old earth, perhaps the old ancestors themselves" (38). Those dark ancestors may be the Indians (and Lucas' search in the burial mound allies his dispossession with Sam Fathers'), but the money also represents the darkened legacy of old Carothers. The denomination itself—$1,000—duplicates the sum left to their unacknowledged heirs by Carothers, Buck, and Buddy. On his twenty-first birthday, Lucas arrives at Isaac's to claim his share and to demand custody of his missing brother's amount. Ike impresses on Lucas that the money "was your father's" (108), and Lucas agrees that it is the money that "Old Marster left for pappy" (108). Lucas' legacy is metaphorically buried in darkness—in his grandfather's silence, and in his own blackness—and his excavation of the mound is a formal expression of his sense of loss and his desire to claim family riches. It seems particularly noteworthy to him that "them two white men" have reportedly made off with $22,000; their theft repeats Lucas' racial dispossession.

To recover the full remnant of the McCaslin fortune would be to supplement original losses for Lucas; he could coerce old Carothers' voice to speak a recognition against its will. Consequently, Lucas takes his hunt quite seriously. The metal detector is a "divining machine before him as if it were some object symbolical and sanctified for a ceremony, a ritual" (87). Since he is trying to get old Carothers to come and speak for him again, it is not surprising that Lucas considers the machine a " 'talking box . . . that dont seem to know how to say nothing but No' " (92); and he makes the occasion one of inventing maps, papers, readings, and misreadings. One of Lucas' most highly valued possessions is "a small metal dispatch box which his white grandfather, Carothers McCaslin himself, had owned almost a hundred years ago" (51); Lucas perpetually awaits McCaslin's message.

Lucas' zeal and the public's incomprehension of his dream turn his pursuit into a comedy; the mood cast by the gold hunt is parodic, but the parody does not rob Lucas of his dignity. The rhetoric of the story absorbs all that is ludicrous about Lucas; it prevents the reader from dismissing Lucas because it discharges the absurd and preserves the pathetic. For example, when Lucas finds the gold piece, he may attach excessive symbolic importance to it; but the style of the passages is rhetorically oversized and seeks to annul our laughter by anticipating it. Lucas' brain was "boiling with all the images of buried money he had ever listened to or heard of" (38); the "dry insensate dust . . . had yawned for an instant and vouchsafed him one blinding glimpse of the absolute" (39); and he spares Wilkins as a "libation to Chance and Fortune" (39). The narrator exaggerates Lucas' enterprise, administering an "admonitory pat," but in so doing he suggests that the extremities are sadly the product of Lucas' grotesque contortions to express himself against extreme constraint. The comic reversals in his hunt function similarly, as if to suggest that Lucas may choose only forms of speech that are partially inappropriate or demeaning. As soon as he begins his hunt for a patrimony, he notices that he has been followed to the mound by his daughter. Nat—jeopardized by Lucas' gold hunting—becomes its rival: he breaks "out of the jungle in time to see, in the wan light of the accelerating dawn, the quarry fleeing like a deer across a field and into the still nightbound woods beyond" (41). To dramatize that she believes the hunt will destroy their marriage, Molly turns herself into a quarry, too: she forces Lucas to join Roth and the others in her pursuit; " 'We been hunting her all night. We found where she went down to the creek and we been tracking her' " (124).

In his effort to proclaim his kinship with old Carothers, Lucas Beauchamp threatens to repeat his crime against marriage. Old Carothers' violations of Eunice, and then Thomasina, like Zack's appropriation of Molly, resemble too closely Lucas' unfeeling dismissal of his wife when she endangers his ambition. When he first accepts old Carothers' bequest, Ike warns him that it is " 'too much to keep hidden under a break in a hearth' " (109); the statement's metaphor explains the inherent conflict between dynastic dreams and domestic virtues. Lucas and Molly have made their marriage express the tranquil order of diminished opportunities. To racial, familial, and temporal losses, Lucas has opposed a marriage that symbolizes permanence and personal pride: the hearth possesses "a slow, deep solidity of heat, a condensation of the two years during which the fire had burned constantly above it, a condensation not of fire but of time" (51). Inverting Ike's career, Lucas has given up his youthful hunting to the consolation of his marriage. Molly's second disappearance provokes him to confirm that renunciation.

Lucas' renunciation of his gold hunting is made to seem costly and somewhat pathetic. Throughout the story his energy and ingenuity create the impression of youthful strength, while Molly inevitably appears "gnarled," "tiny, like a doll," "a bundle of dried and lifeless sticks" (127), her arm "dry and light and brittle and frail as a rotted stick" (126). Roth sees that though Molly is "actually younger than Lucas [she] ... looked much older, incredibly old" (100). Molly has sacrificed her own voice to the serenity of scriptural promise, and she demands that Lucas do the same. But Lucas protests momentarily. He accepts the prospect of a divorce because Molly jeopardizes what he is trying to say through his gold hunting: he explains to Roth, "'I'm a man.... I'm the man here. I'm the one to say in my house, like you and your paw and his paw were the ones to say in his'" (120). He tempts the court to "pronounce" the dissolution of their marriage, only backing down at the last instant: "'We dont want no voce'" (128). "Voce" may play on voice (as it would etymologically, too), and the formal sign of Lucas' repudiation of his voice is his quotation of Molly's text. He charges Roth to give his divining machine away because Lucas is out of time: "'Man has got three score and ten years on this earth, the Book says'" (131). Challenging the figures of his dispossession with his voice, Lucas manages to utter words of protest, defiance, paternity, and selfhood. Though they never reverse his losses, they temporarily substitute for them until Lucas discovers the inevitable silence.

iv

"Pantaloon in Black" draws the parodic trilogy of *Go Down, Moses* to a harsh and disquieting conclusion. A crisis of grief stands at the heart of this story, as in the others: Rider desires to speak to the death of Mannie, his wife, but he can find no words for his agony, just as he can neither deny her loss nor calm his memory. Subjecting Rider's private rites of mourning to grotesque simplification and to parodic distortion, *Go Down, Moses* tightens its concentration on the problem of dispossession as it moves through "Pantaloon" and looks ahead to the wilderness trilogy. Rider's inability to phrase his loss urges the performances of ritual and conversation that follow; his vain expectation that Mannie might actually return in his memory prepares for the hunters' wiser acceptance of loss as they mourn; and the comic, savage misunderstanding that Rider's privacy provokes contrasts with the intimacies that corporate grief produces in the succeeding four stories.

With a familiar gesture, the narrator begins "Pantaloon" at the site of the beloved's loss, at Mannie's graveside. His wife's death after six months of marriage puts Rider in a situation that resembles Lucas Beauchamp's during Molly's six-month absence. A tenant on Roth Edmonds' land, Rider even "built a fire on the hearth on their wedding night as the tale told how Uncle Lucas Beauchamp, Edmonds' oldest tenant, had done on his forty-five years ago and

which had burned ever since" (138). Such psychic kinship is what
makes Rider part of the novel's grieving family; his first act in the
story is to fashion Mannie's burial "mound" (135). Faulkner resists
unifying the stories of *Go Down, Moses* superficially; he does not
make Rider another cast-off McCaslin, nor does he emphasize
Rider's bondage to Roth Edmonds' plantation or to the exploitation of the wilderness. By suppressing such obvious unifying features as race, family, the use of the land, and the disappearance of
unaxed timber, Faulkner throws a monstrous light onto Rider's
black grief. The blackness of Rider's mourning engulfs the story,
and it is an image for the blankness, silence, and peace that he
craves when he realizes that his anguish is inconsolable. A sentence
that describes Jack Houston's grief nearly summarizes Rider's too:
"And they were married and six months later she died and he
grieved for her for four years in black, savage, indomitable fidelity,
and that was all" (*H,* 208).

As his tribute to Lucas Beauchamp's hearth fire suggests, Rider's
marriage to Mannie similarly allows him to express passion, devotion, pride, and a sense of permanence. Mannie's gentle domestic
rituals—from sweeping to scrubbing to shopping—impress a design
on their lives; they are the barest assertions of dignity and self-
sufficiency in a community that has deprived Rider and Mannie of
racial, class, and familial privilege. Mannie becomes an emanation
of the poor man's American dream as she encourages Rider's rise
through the logging company's ranks, as she makes a ceremony out
of Rider's payday (accepting the "bright cascade of silver dollars"
he offers [138]), and as she helps Rider rebuild their cabin (137).
Rider also values Mannie because she has replaced the vanities of
his youth; Rider's decision to marry Mannie and to give up gambl-
ing and whoring to become a man is a single gesture. He said,
"'Ah'm thu wid all dat,' and they married" (138), as if Mannie
must supplement what Rider chooses to lose. Rider makes his wife
an exalted symbol of renunciation, sharpening his resemblance to
Lucas, whose last action in "The Fire and the Hearth" is to preserve
his marriage by renouncing a young man's pursuit.

Mannie's death deprives Rider's world of coherence, intimacy,
and warmth; its consequences resemble those that throw Quentin
Compson's mind into disequilibrium. Like *The Sound and the
Fury,* "Pantaloon in Black" begins at the hinge of lost plenitude, the

words of the fiction, like the images of memory, already inscribing the loss of the "thing itself." Rider's efforts to remember Mannie's presence, like the story's attempt to recount her importance, succeed only in creating a simulacrum of her, a derived presence that is stained by death and ghostly transparency. The plot echoes this condition by making Rider one who loses whatever he loves, who kills what he possesses. He seems to wear out Mannie, his oversized body endangering her from the outset: he explains to her that he needs a big dog because " 'you's de onliest least thing whut ever kep up wid me one day, leff alone for weeks' " (139). As he wears away Mannie by possessing her, so Rider enacts the fatal depletion of the wilderness. His most celebrated logging feat is to ride "the log down the incline, balanced erect upon it in short rapid backward-running steps above the headlong thunder" (144), as if in epitome of the human presence in the forest. His nickname justly points to his prodigious capacity to use and waste; the night watchman recognizes him as the "one who was called Rider and was Rider" (152), and we learn that Rider's name occurs simultaneously to those who witness what he does to women and to the wilderness: "the men he worked with and the bright dark nameless women he had taken in course and forgotten... began to call him Rider" (151). Riding becomes the story's metaphor for the coincidence of possession and loss; Rider's precarious descent figures the loving exhaustion of both Mannie and the wilderness. It is a beautiful dance performed over the thunder of imminent destruction.

I have argued that Quentin Compson's anguish arises with the recognition that "was" and "again" are the "saddest" words of all because the past cannot be recovered. Despite making a shrine of his memory, Quentin manages to recall only a Caddy whose corruption and 'death' have already been written over the recollections of childhood. Rider's nostalgia for Mannie's original presence compels him to seek a similar reappropriation; the book of memory similarly conjures up only a ghostly beloved; and, like Quentin, Rider rejects the consolation of speech. Rider furiously hurries Mannie's corpse into the ground because he wants to deny her death; acting on the folklore that " 'she be wawkin yet' " (136), Rider returns to their cabin hopeful that they may reunite. His expectant memory distills the past in "the dusk-filled single room where all those six months were now crammed and crowded into one instant of time" (139–140). But memory is already the articulation of loss, and the ghost's presence only confirms Mannie's absence. Rider's step toward reunion already measures separation; his voice, like any other, widens the gap it hopes to fill:

> But this time as soon as he moved she began to fade. He stopped at once, not breathing again, motionless, willing his eyes to see that she had stopped too. But she had not stopped. She was fading, going. "Wait," he said, talking as sweet as he had ever heard his voice speak to a woman. [140–141]

Neither the coaxings of his voice nor the devotion of his memory will enable Rider to make Mannie "wait." The disquieting directness of "Pantaloon" forces this theme to the surface of the plot; Rider literally pursues a course in which Mannie appears as a trace. The dirt road retains, "vanished but not gone, fixed and held in the annealing dust, the narrow, splay-toed prints of his wife's bare feet" (137). Rider will not settle for traces and prints; he is imprisoned by the need for recovered presence, his body "breasting the air her body had vacated, his eyes touching the objects . . . her eyes had lost" (137). Walking home, Rider is said to be "setting the period now as he strode on," and that phrase may suggest that his effort to retrace Mannie's steps is already a kind of silent sentence, fashioned out of the periods of memory. Near the story's conclusion, Rider resigns himself to death because he has crossed "the junctureless backloop of time's trepan" (152). As we have seen repeatedly, time's trepan, its snare, is that it is junctureless; no backloop ever intersects with the past, and Rider fails to recover the fullness of "was."

Rider's pathetic bondage to Mannie's presence depends on his innocence of language. Social and racial disenfranchisements conspire against Rider's voice, as they do against Lucas Beauchamp's; but Rider lacks the resourcefulness to speak his word in the common language. He confronts the opportunity to name himself, for example, since he "could not remember his parents at all" (136); yet instead of imitating Lucas' self-nomination, Rider accepts first his aunt's nickname (Spoot) and then one decided by his fellow loggers. Rider's voice is constantly failing him ("The faint frail voice was already lost in the night's infinitude" [148]); he never joins the loggers in their joyful singing (144); and when he does speak, others silence him ("'Hush!' the old man said" [145]). Choked with contradictions ("'Ah just misread de sign wrong'" [149]) and platitudes ("'Ah'm snakebit now and pizen cant hawm me'" [148]), Rider's sentences carry off none of his grief. The deputy remembers that in prison Rider was "'yelling, though there wasn't no words in it'" (158). In his wordless mourning Rider may remind us of Benjy Compson; both are infants (literally, without speech). Rider handles a shovel that "resembled the toy shovel a child plays with at the shore" (135); he holds his cot "over his head like it was a baby's cradle" (158) and throws the other prisoners across the room "like they was rag dolls" (159). "Pantaloon in Black" rushes the novel toward an agony of silence; loss cries out for words that will console and substitute. Rider's plight grotesquely figures the imprisonment of the inarticulate as he escapes into the sleep of self-forgetfulness, his snoring sounding "not like groans of pain but like someone engaged without arms in prolonged single combat" (142).

Combating loss without arms, Rider becomes a prisoner of grief. He speeds through the night's blackness, exhausting the consolations and transmutations of death. When he arrives at the logging camp, Rider tries to drown his agony in work: "Then he could stop needing to invent to himself reasons for his breathing" (145). Rider can only flee a crisis of invention. His last gesture in camp intuits a connection between the loss of Mannie and the loss of the wilderness; he heaves the largest log ever from the truck and then hurls it down the incline, but as it is poised above his head, "the log seemed to leap suddenly backward... of its own volition" (146). Rider initiates Mannie's loss by possessing her, but he cannot make her "wait" once she has begun to fade; Rider's effort to create a moment of motionless movement—his equivalent for the retention of Mannie's memory—fails because disappearance is always already under way.

Rider instinctively tests other methods of evading the rites of mourning. He tries to outrun grief, but geography, as *The Hamlet* puts it, is a "paucity of invention"; his careening over the countryside allows him only to circle back to the site of his loss. Demanding a jug of "bust-skull white-mule whisky" (156), Rider tries to extinguish his consciousness, which is wholly absorbed by grief's memories. Uttering his crude version of an ode to an urn, Rider apostrophizes, "speaking to the jug: 'Come on now. You always claim you's a better man den me. Come on now. Prove it'" (148). And in his fear that words will supplement his loss and naturalize his grief, Rider also shuns the repentance advocated by his aunt: God had no reason to "come messin wid me" (145) and prayer avails nothing because "'Efn He God, Ah dont need to tole Him'" (150). Rider cannot apprehend that language might compose him, substitute reminiscence for recovery, and invite the intimacies of shared mourning.

Rider's murder of Birdsong protests his loss; it is a vain effort to say no to Mannie's death. The violent stroke is a nascent word of defiance as Rider discovers a suitable analogy for his victimization. The nightwatchman incarnates privilege (he is white) and authority (the "boss-man"); his cheating resembles God's inscrutable "messin"; and his name even evokes the felicities of speech forbidden Rider. By slicing the throat of Birdsong, Rider unwittingly laments his own stifled voice. But Rider's eloquence—as he pivots gracefully to avoid Birdsong's carnage—is confined to this one suicidal gesture. The only alternative to grieving is nothing—as Harry Wilbourne summarizes in *The Wild Palms*—and Rider, like Quentin Compson, prefers the peace of blankness, blackness, and death. Antically, Rider predicts his 'suicide' by dancing on his shadow, as Quentin had done: "He stood in the middle now of the unimpeded shadow which he was treading again as he had trod it last night" (151). Frustrated in his desire to annihilate memory, Rider wails, "'Hit look lack Ah just cant quit thinking. Look lack Ah just cant quit'" (159). Rider refuses the prison of grief ("'Jest dont lock me up'" [157]), unlike Wilbourne, and eventually receives death's pardon.

The sheriff's deputy makes a travesty of Rider's story as he recites the facts of the case to his wife. Rider's repudiation of the forms and conventions of mourning threatens his loss with inconsequence. As he leads his wife's burial, returns immediately to work, and then murders the man who has been cheating him for years, Rider's misery turns opaque. It is concealed by the blackness of silence, and the deputy's misreading confirms the prophecy of the story's opening: "the grave, save for its rawness, resembled any other marked off without order about the barren plot by shards of pottery and broken bottles and old brick and other objects insignificant to sight but actually of a profound meaning and fatal to touch, which no white man could have read" (135). The deputy turns the story of Mannie's death into a "barren plot," a comedy in which "pantaloon" is unknowingly cuckolded by death. The deputy intuits, however, that there is an unexplained pathos in Rider's story; he directs his narrative at his wife, the partner in a soured marriage, who nevertheless remains deaf to the deputy's hints of marital violence and to the coincidence that she has been cheated in a game of chance that day, too. The deputy even discovers a simple eloquence as he describes the tears of Rider's hysterical laughter and grief "making a kind of popping sound on the floor like somebody dropping bird eggs" (159); but the story collapses into puzzlement and inattention. Rider refuses and the deputy fails to phrase grief suitably; the wordless agony of "Pantaloon in Black" demands the rites of speech that the subsequent stories perform.

v

"The Old People" is founded on a duplicity akin to that of "Was," its complement in the bicameral structure of *Go Down, Moses.* The story records Isaac McCaslin's initiation into the society of hunting and stages a ritual reappropriation of mythic origins, the sacred place and time of the pristine wilderness. A substantial body of criticism discusses the ceremonies of initiation and the myths of the hunt in the wilderness trilogy. Isaac's career in the forest also teaches him, however, that the practice of these rites by civilized men is a kind of speech or writing; they are art rather than magic, substitution rather than repossession, translation rather than annulment. In this second respect, Isaac is initiated by Sam Fathers into a society of authors, whose words create a past that never was, whose articulations are the nearest approach to original plenitude, and whose language is dedicated to the rites of mourning.

"The Old People" feigns innocence. The narrator describes Isaac's first kill and Sam's ceremonial induction of the boy into manhood: "Sam stooped and dipped his hands in the hot smoking blood and wiped them back and forth across the boy's face" (164). Isaac believes that he has been "marked forever" (165), and he expects his memory to retain perfectly the image of his first buck: "the buck still and forever leaped . . . forever immortal" (178). Isaac's identity begins to cohere around this moment; initiation into the family of hunters gives Ike a set of values, a history, and a vocabulary to compose himself. The story refers to him simply as "he," in the same way Cass is referred to in "Was," as if to suggest that this is Ike's complementary story of self-definition. Ike looks back on his first trip to the wilderness as the moment of his birth; the wagon was "progressing not by its own volition but by attrition of their intact yet fluid circumambience, drowsing, earless, almost lightless. It seemed to him that at the age of ten he was witnessing his own birth" (195).

The sense that Sam Fathers is bequeathing him a new self and a new family is prominent is Isaac's mind because he has already begun to reject the genealogy and legacy he knows through Cass's stories. Isaac wants to be an Ishmael, proclaiming his allegiance to the dispossessed heirs of McCaslin's ruthless dynasty: "They were the white boy, marked forever, and the old dark man sired on both sides by savage kings, who had marked him, whose bloody hands had merely formally consecrated him to that which, under the man's tutelage, he had already accepted" (165). Sam's stories about his forebears invoke a purer occupation of the land; instead of McCaslin's claims of title, the Indians appear to possess the land without owning it, holding it in common trust: Isaac's family's "hold upon it actually was as trivial and without reality as the now faded and archaic script in the chancery book in Jefferson which allocated it to them and . . . it was he, the boy, who was the guest here and Sam Father's voice the mouthpiece of the host" (171). To host the land rather than to buy it is the sacred tradition that Sam's ancestry seems to house.

The narrative tends to endorse Ike's faith that he has celebrated a mythic recovery of the pristine forest and its original occupants. Mircea Eliade's description of ritual explains one aspect of the story's effects:

> Through the paradox of rite, every consecrated space coincides with the center of the world, just as the time of any ritual coincides with the mythical time of the "beginning." Through repetition of the cosmogonic act, concrete time, in which the construction takes place, is projected into mythical time, *in illo tempore,* when the foundation of the world occurred.[17]

17. Mircea Eliade, *The Myth of the Eternal Return: Or, Cosmos and History* (Princeton, 1954), p. 20.

At the moment of Ike's initiation, the story sweeps away history, along with the reader's memories of the first three stories, to create "the mythical time of the 'beginning' ": "At first there was nothing" (163). The style stages an *ex nihilo* creation of the wilderness, repeating "the cosmogonic act." The syntax of the opening sentences is simple, as if at ease in bringing the objects it names into existence: at first nothing, then water, then light, then Sam and Ike, and then the buck. As Ike believes his initiation has conducted him into the brotherhood of sacred possession, so the narrator momentarily indulges his innocence. Ike believes that he can successfully blend the legacies of his own grandfather McCaslin and Sam Fathers, purifying the lines of ownership; the narrator (falsely) concurs: "the child, not yet a man, whose grandfather had lived in the same country and in almost the same manner as the boy himself would grow up to live, leaving his descendants in the land in his turn as his grandfather had done" (165). (Isaac, of course, leaves no descendants in the land and rejects his grandfather's plantation.)

Because it simulates the process of mythical return, "The Old People" is permeated by figures of cyclical repetition. As Ike becomes one with his ancestors, as the present wilderness becomes the center of the world and the present moment becomes *in illo tempore,* the hunters experience repetition palpably. He and Sam move toward the buck, which "must have completed his circle now and was heading back toward them" (180). Ike's expectant cycle of inhalation and exhalation is repeated by the wilderness: "He stopped breathing then; there was only his heart, his blood, and in the following silence the wilderness ceased to breathe also" (182). And the very sentences of the story begin to repeat themselves in apparent tribute to the myth of eternal return:

> Then once more he and Sam stood motionless together against a tremendous pin oak in a little thicket, and again there was nothing. There was only the soaring and sombre solitude in the dim light, there was the thin murmur of the faint cold rain which had not ceased all day. [181]

Practiced naively, such a ritual reappropriates the very presence of the mythical origin. I have argued, however, that the plenitude of the origin never returns in Faulkner's fiction; Sam Fathers' supervision of Ike's initiation and his rehearsal of the pertinent myths support this argument. Sam understands that the rite of initiation remains something of an illusion, that it is more the statement of a sentiment than an act of metamorphosis. Immediately, the initiate seems to regress to boyhood: the appearance of a second buck provokes Ike into "thinking with the old despair of two and three years ago: *I'll never get a shot*"; and he turns on Sam "in the truculence of a boy's grief over the missed opportunity" (183).

In his innocence, Isaac concentrates excessively on the magic of the hunt, but Sam Fathers tries to demonstrate that the conventions of wilderness behavior are primarily conventions of speech. Sam intuits that the sacred time and place of the origin are knowable only in their absence and 'recoverable' only through language. In the first place, the full presence of the wilderness is deceptive. One critic has referred to the "numen-engendering style" of "The Old People,"[18] but things appear in the forest only as they begin to disappear. For example, Ike sees the buck "as you always see the deer, in that split second after he has already seen you, already slanting away in that first soaring bound" (163). And the looming majesty of the forest most intensely impresses Ike only as he begins to part from it, "the wall of the wilderness behind them now, tremendous and still and seemingly impenetrable in the gray and fading light, the very tiny orifice through which they had emerged apparently swallowed up" (177). These effects prefigure Ike's discovery in "The Bear" that the rituals of the hunt must be celebrated as rites of mourning, articulations of what has already begun to be lost.

All of Sam's customs in the woods point to his preoccupation with the language of grief. Sam tells his stories about the lost past not to provide Ike with a counterlegacy, but to supplement the voids of his own paternity. Sam gets his name because he is "Had-Two-Fathers"—fathered by Doom (Ikkemotubbe) but passed off on a slave. Too many fathers is the same as none, and Sam accepts the challenge of fathering himself through narrative:

> The boy would just wait and then listen and Sam would begin, talking about the old days and the People whom he had not had time ever to

18. Glauco Gambon, "Faulkner's 'The Old People': The Numen-Engendering Style," *Southern Review*, 1 (January 1965), 94–107.

> know and so could not remember (he did not remember ever having
> seen his father's face), and in place of whom the other race into which
> his blood had run supplied him with no substitute. [171]

Sam's stories do not relate or remember the past, they create it; like
Derrida's supplement, these narratives "substitute" for a loss at the
origin and invent what they have never known. Sam's fiction is
bound by the understanding that it can never pretend to recover
uncontaminated origins: the unfallen possession of the wilderness is
known only in its loss. Ikkemotubbe, the first ancestor, is already
a red impersonation of old Carothers, entangled in deception, mur-
derous greed, and crimes against his sons. The wilderness has always been disappearing "because on the instant when Ikkemotubbe
discovered, realised, that he could sell it for money, on that instant
it ceased ever to have been his forever" (257). The very act of pronouncing the past establishes its contamination of the present, converts "the old people" into lost people, the brotherhood of Indian
hunters into the soldiery of dynastic warfare, "The Man" into fate,
Du Homme into Doom.

Sam initiates Ike into the rites of speech as much as into the rites
of the kill; in a passage added when "The Old People" was revised
for inclusion in *Go Down, Moses,* the narrator remarks that soon
Ike "too would make one before the winter fire, talking of the old
hunts and the hunts to come as hunters talked" (175). And Sam
recognizes that Cass Edmonds' stories—an example of which we
have heard in "Was"—provide Ike's chief paternity: "Sam always
referred to the boy's cousin as his father, establishing even before
the boy's orphanhood did that relation between them ... of the
child to the man who sired his flesh and his thinking too" (174).
When Ike turns twenty-one and tries to narrate a personal and
cultural history, he is strictly fulfilling Sam Fathers' deepest design
for his spiritual heir—the destiny of speech. In "The Bear" the
narrator suggests that the possession of the wilderness is "completed" only by Ike's capacity to describe it in his own words and
images: "the surrey itself seemed to have ceased to move (this too
to be completed later, years later, after he had grown to a man and
had seen the sea) as a solitary small boat hangs in lonely immobility"
(195). Much earlier, Sam forecasts the connection between writing

and maturity: "'You will write your age in two numbers and you will be ready to become a man,'" he tells Ike (174).

Sam's climactic gesture in "The Old People" is to salute the spirit of the Great Buck, which appears after Ike's initiation. As Sam and Ike pursue the deer, the horns sound to signal a kill. In the apparent statement of its absence, however, the buck seems to grow present: "It was coming down the ridge, as if it were walking out of the very sound of the horn which related its death" (184). The animal is neither a ghost nor just another buck; its mystery arises because it is a related presence, the product of speech. Sam designates it as "Oleh, Chief, Grandfather," turning it into a word that fills up the voids of racial, social, and familial dispossession. Even though he denies its claims, Cass Edmonds later admits that it had "substance" and "cast[s] a shadow" (187), and as such it corresponds to the fictional figures of Sam's other stories, which seem to be "casting an actual shadow on the earth they had not quitted" (171). Sam seeks to initiate Ike into the special tongue of those who have discovered how to read and write the wilderness, a tongue indecipherable to others, such as Walter Ewell, who could "swear there was another buck here that I never even saw" (185).

That Ike's initiation is centrally a matter of conversation is dramatized by the last section of "The Old People." As in "Was," Cass attempts to dictate Ike's sense of the past. He subjects his cousin's initiation to a reinterpretation, a willful misreading. Cass wants to dispossess Isaac of the Great Buck because he, too, has seen Sam designate it as the word of loss and crime. Sensing Ike's eventual indictment of his McCaslin/Edmonds heritage, Cass argues that "suffering and grieving" are offenses against the plentiful opportunities life offers, and that shame is worse than death:

> And even suffering and grieving is better than nothing; there is only one thing worse than not being alive, and that's shame. But you can't be alive forever, and you always wear out life long before you have exhausted the possibilities of living. [186]

There need be no regret about loss since there are "plenty of places still unchanged" (187). Ike's dissent will govern his performance of the hunt as a rite of grief and will inspire his act of renunciation as the expression of shame. We want the ghosts, Isaac insists.

vi

No work of American literature is shadowed by a larger body of criticism than "The Bear," but most essays treat it either in isolation or as part of the trilogy of stories about Isaac McCaslin in the wilderness. Readers have grown used to disregarding Faulkner's distinction between the two rival forms he gives "The Bear"—a distinction that urges the reader to consider the work either as an independent short story or as one chapter of a novel. As a solitary story "The Bear" concentrates on the narrative of Old Ben's death; the conversation between Isaac and Cass in the commissary (section 4 of the novel's chapter) has no place in the short story, according to Faulkner. A publisher's misjudgment accounts for the presence of that section in some separate versions of "The Bear," but Faulkner advises us to "skip that when you come to it,"[19] and he reprints "The Bear" in *The Big Woods* as he had done originally, [20] without the cousins' debate. I think there are good reasons for Faulkner's fastidious double writing. Obviously, Ike's discourse on Southern history provides a frame of generalization for the centrifugal themes of slavery, race, family, time, and freedom that the seven stories of *Go Down, Moses* share. But section 4 belongs to the novel precisely because it is talk; beyond its content (much of which directly addresses the problems of textuality, inspiration, interpretation, and eloquence) the conversation consummates a central impulse of all the stories. By having traced the crises of loss and articulation through the novel, we may be able to appreciate how Isaac's utterance—the performance itself—completes his career in the wilderness. It translates the loss of the wilderness into an eloquent renunciation of the tamed land; it provokes Isaac to create an identity through the voice of dissent; and it allows him to name and recreate his family's sins—he must retrace them even as he hopes to erase them. Faulkner provides a suitably linguistic metaphor for the two halves of Isaac's experience (the hunt and the conversation): "It was—the pursuit of the bear was simply what you might call a

19. Frederick L. Gwynn and Joseph L. Blotner, eds., *Faulkner in the University: Class Conferences at the University of Virginia, 1957–1958* (New York, 1959), p. 273.
20. William Faulkner, "The Bear," *Saturday Evening Post*, May 9, 1942, pp. 30–31, 74, 76–77.

dangling clause in the description of that man when he was a young boy."[21] The rituals of the hunt are used by Sam Fathers and Isaac to speak their grief over the perpetually vanishing wilderness, and Ike's explanation to Cass of his renunciation completes the statement of mourning.

At first, the ritual of the hunt in "The Bear" simply seems to celebrate the mythic timelessness of the wilderness. The hunters participate in "the ancient and unremitting contest according to the ancient and immitigable rules" (192). The wilderness looms "tremendous and still and seemingly impenetrable" (177), and even though there are signs of its exploitation, the "wilderness soared, musing, inattentive, myriad, eternal, green; older than any mill-shed, longer than any spur-line" (322); the woods "did not change, and, timeless, would not" (323). Old Ben incarnates the paradox of a used yet timeless wilderness:

> Old Ben was not even a mortal beast but an anachronism indomitable and invincible out of an old dead time, a phantom, epitome and apotheosis of the old wild life which the little puny humans swarmed and hacked at in a fury of abhorrence and fear like pygmies about the ankles of a drowsing elephant;—the old bear, solitary, indomitable and alone; widowered childless and absolved of mortality. [193–194].

The hunt for Ike is "a yearly rendezvous with the bear which they did not even intend to kill" (194), "the yearly pageantrite of the old bear's furious immortality" (194). Major DeSpain and General Compson even choose to celebrate their birthdays during the December retreat, as if through the ritual to subject chronology to their will. As it creates the sense that "there would be a next time, after and after" (204), the hunting ritual seems to conjure up a refuge from time. Eliade comments on the effect: "The primitive, by conferring a cyclic direction upon time, annuls its irreversibility. Everything begins over again at its commencement every instant. . . . This eternal return reveals an ontology uncontaminated by time and becoming."[22] I am not suggesting that the hunters practice primitive rites of immortality or transport themselves to

21. Gwynn and Blotner, eds., *Faulkner in the University*, p. 273.
22. Eliade, *Myth of the Eternal Return*, p. 89.

the sacred site of origin. Their casual, unreflective sport, however, harmonizes with ritual's faith in mythic timelessness. Sam Fathers and Isaac McCaslin see instead that the wilderness, like Old Ben, is already disappearing, already lost. Rather than expecting eternal return, they discover deeper consolation in voicing the change that has already begun, mourning the loss that has already made itself felt.

All of the hunters, of course, recognize the possibility that this particular bear might die; despite the legend of Old Ben's invincibility, Major DeSpain announces that General Compson "'drew blood'" and "'we have never done that before.... Next year ... we'll get him'" (226). Sam and Ike share this recognition, but they are alone in designating Old Ben the representation of the vanishing wilderness. Critics of "The Bear" have informed us fully how the simple practice of the hunters' ritual resists the cultural and natural facts of the disappearance of the wilderness in *Go Down, Moses*. I want to concentrate on the performance of the ritual as an act of mourning, as a willed execution of Old Ben, and as a formal expression of the forest's loss.

The early portions of "The Bear" present Isaac's discovery that the hunt is an aesthetic imitation of death and loss rather than a mythic celebration of their transcendence. The shadow of paradox slides across Old Ben, who seems at first "absolved of mortality," an "apotheosis" and an "anachronism" (193–194); but when Ike is ten "he could see them, the two of them [himself and Old Ben] shadowy in the limbo from which time emerged and became time" (204). Old Ben seems to originate in the limbo of timelessness, yet, in accordance with a condition I think central to *Go Down, Moses*, Old Ben materializes for Ike only at the hinge of his emergence into time. Soon, "for the first time he realised that the bear ... was a mortal animal" (200–201). Sam and Ike contrive a version of the hunt that imitates the process of death and incorporates the rites of grief: Sam knows that "somebody" is going to catch and hold Ben "someday," and Ike urges, "'That's why it must be one of us. So it wont be until the last day. When even he dont want it to last any longer'" (212). The narrator summarizes Ike's sense of how the pursuit of Ben may transform decay and death into an artifact: "It seemed to him that there was a fatality in it.... It was like the last act on a set stage.... He would be humble and proud that he had been found worthy to be a part of it too or even just to see it too" (226). Their ritual will enact loss.

To fulfill his image of a set stage, Ike considers the other participants in the hunt as the actors and audience of death's pageant. Local farmers hear of Lion's prowess and arrive to witness his contest with Ben: "'We figgered we'd come up and watch, if you dont mind. We wont do no shooting, lessen he runs over us'" (223). Choosing Lion and Boon as the medium by which Old Ben is executed, Sam and Ike arrange to watch the spectacle. The aesthetic qualities of the moment of Ben's death have been noted by several readers, who customarily argue that the moment arrests motion, creating a timeless artifact.[23] Yet the moment does not impress Ike's memory with a tableau of arrested motion or dynamic stasis. Rather, it resonates with the pounding rhythms of violent blows and presents Old Ben as already running between life and death. Isaac arrives at the 'privileged' moment too late, after Old Ben has already turned and begun to die. Here one of the novel's chief figures is repeated; appearance is the onset of disappearance. The gestures of the scene are all risings and fallings: Old Ben "rising and rising," then tumbling to the ground, only to surge "erect" again before crashing down (241). Boon's arm "rose and fell," as if in echo. Such movements describe what they perform, for the killing of Ben represents (and constitutes) the possession and loss of the wilderness, its erection and collapse, embrace and death. Sam and Ike write a version of the history of the wilderness in the rite of the hunt: Boon's "loverlike" clasp—as he "probes" Ben's heart—symbolizes the necessary deflowering of the virgin land. They fell "of a piece, as a tree falls." So beautiful a transfiguration makes the performers "almost" resemble "a piece of statuary" (241). Sam's own collapse comments ironically on the fact that Ben's death is a "desperate emulation" of the very processes it mourns: he suffers, the doctor decides, from "shock" and "exhaustion" (246)—shock at the exhaustion of the wilderness. To use the hunt as an emulation or duplication of death is to use it as language, for the ritual then becomes a representation of loss. The hounds, as they pursue Old Ben, leave "in the air that echo of thin and almost human hysteria, abject, almost humanly grieving" (197); the cry of the hunt is al-

23. For example, Blanche H. Gelfant, "Faulkner and Keats: The Ideality of Art in 'The Bear,'" *Southern Literary Journal*, 2 (Fall 1969), 43–65.

ready the sound of grief. In describing Ike's realization of Ben's doom, the narrator corrects himself significantly: "It seemed to him that something, he didn't know what, was beginning; had already begun" (226). *Go Down, Moses* insists throughout that "was beginning" must always be pronounced "had already begun."

Old Ben's status throughout "The Bear" prepares for these effects: curiously, the bear becomes another of the absent centers that occupy Faulkner's texts. Old Ben's climactic appearance to Isaac after the young hunter's patient search is one of the novel's most memorable scenes, but it is preceded by a series of episodes that establish Old Ben more strictly as an absence than a presence. All of Ike's encounters with the bear impress him as being either a reappearance or a disappearance of the sought object. From the outset of Ike's wilderness career, Old Ben is already a word, a name: "He had already inherited then, without ever having seen it, the big old bear . . . that . . . had earned for himself a name, a definite designation" (192–193), "the bear which had run in his listening and loomed in his dreams since before he could remember" (200), the "foreknown" (196), even a literary figure—"old Priam reft of his old wife and outlived all his sons" (194). This condition is crucial in the novel since it runs closely with the grain of the other stories: there is always a writing at the origin; and what seems 'present' to Ike's eyes later, when Old Ben coalesces out of the wilderness, is actually a derived presence, created by language. Ike "had experienced it all before, and not merely in dreams" (195–196).

As Old Ben appears only in reappearing, so he seems present only as an absence. Ike marks Old Ben as a "nothing" the first time he approaches:

[The hounds were] leaving even then in the air that echo of thin and almost human hysteria, abject, almost humanly grieving, with *this time nothing ahead of it, no sense of a fleeing unseen* smoke-colored shape. He could hear Sam breathing at his shoulder. He saw the arched curve of the old man's inhaling nostrils.
"It's Old Ben!" he cried, whispering. [197; emphasis added]

This passage nearly epitomizes Faulkner's language, as it names and describes a "shape" that is not there and yet which becomes the antecedent of "it" in Isaac's identification. Words cannot efface the absence they seek to overcome. Versions of this scene recur in "The Bear"; Old Ben seems near as Ike "knew that the bear was looking at him. He never saw it. . . . Then it was gone" (203). I suggest that Old Ben's absence permeates even the moment of his materialization before Isaac's eyes. Isaac must surrender the tokens of civilization and conceptual order—the gun, watch, and compass—before Old Ben will reveal himself in a realm free of time and space. Ike's forfeiture seems to permit the magical manifestations of the timeless Old Ben and the fullness of the wilderness. Yet the episode is more complicated than it seems to be. It is true that Ike "relinquishes" himself completely to the forest, becoming "a child" "lost" in the uncontaminated woods. But the wilderness does not coalesce, or Ben appear, until Ike has begun to find his way again by reading and tracking the bear's prints. Ike begins to follow the chain of traces, as each "print began to dissolve away" (209), "merely keeping pace with them as they appeared before him as though they were being shaped out of thin air just one constant pace short of where he would lose them forever" (209). It is the tracing that causes the wilderness to coalesce; and it is not until Ike *rediscovers* the watch and compass that Ben appears,

> . . . emerging suddenly into a little glade and the wilderness coalesced. It rushed, soundless, and solidified—the tree, the bush, the compass and the watch glinting where a ray of sunlight touched them. Then he saw the bear. [209]

Ben is derived from the traces of his ever receding presence. Such an appearance reminds us that Old Ben is a representation. And when the trace creates the presence of Old Ben, it is as if the bear is only a simulacrum of the 'original': "not as big as he had dreamed it but as big as he had expected" (209). In the moment that Ben stares at Ike he is "fixed" and "immobile," but Ben's appearance is already the beginning of his disappearance: the bear does not emerge, "it was just there," and then it "faded, sank back into the wilderness without motion" (209). The prerequisite reunion with watch and compass reminds us that the simulacrum is the very product of the time of loss and the space of separation. Ike's conduct in the hunt follows a rough version of the rites of speech: it gives up the hope of fully reappropriating the thing itself; it depends on the articulation at the origin, the necessary authority of language; and it creates an inscription of difference that acknowledges the deathliness and lostness of its subject. (Old Ben represents the status of the wilderness, too, which the story presents as always already lost; the narrator remarks that when Ikkemotubbe first realizes that he can sell the land, "on that instant *it ceased ever to have been* his forever" [257; emphasis added].)

The first three sections of "The Bear" comprise the "dangling clause" of Ike's description as a young man, and the clause will find completion when Ike makes the renunciation of the plantation the predicate of his childhood. But the ritual of the hunt also directly celebrates the custom of talk, as we remember from "The Old People." The words of the hunt both precede and succeed the actual pursuit of the quarry. "The Bear" begins with a salute to the vast wilderness and to "the best of all breathing and forever the best of all listening, the voices quiet and weighty and deliberate for retrospection and recollection and exactitude among the concrete trophies . . . in the libraries of town houses or the offices of plantation houses or (and best of all) in the camps themselves where the intact and still-warm meat yet hung . . ." (192). This remarkable passage nearly makes us see the pursuit as a pre-text for talk. It suggests that speaking and hearing are the essential cycle of the body's life ("breathing and . . . listening"), as if to exhale is always to broach a word. The retrospective and recollective powers of language appropriately occupy the narrator here, as he offers a description of the novel's language of lamentation. The slain game provides an apt image for the situation of language, always arising at the hinge of cooling vitality and presence. Whiskey is the suitable meed of the hunters because it seems not "the blood they spilled but some condensation of the wild immortal spirit" (192); "condensation" perfectly captures the sense that talk both distills and diminishes the original as it differs from it. The best game of all concludes the wilderness contests, too. The deaths of Ben, Lion, and Sam occasion rites of interment; Ben's corpse is the center of a spontaneous commemorative ceremony—"almost a hundred of them squatting and standing in the warm and drowsing sunlight, talking quietly of hunting, of the game and the dogs which ran it, of hounds and bear and deer and men of yesterday vanished from the earth" (248). And when Lion follows Ben, General Compson "spoke as he would have spoken over a man" (249) at the funeral.

Isaac's conversation with his cousin, Cass Edmonds, resolves the "dangling clause" of his wilderness childhood. I have argued that Ike and Sam Fathers manipulate the hunt as a form of speech, and I wish to explore how Ike's renunciation of the patrimonial plantation completes a statement. The opening words of section 4 act as if to finish a sentence: "then he was twenty-one. He could say it . . ." (254); and the rejection of the McCaslin title is Ike's declaration of rebuke, remorse, and correction. This gesture and the long dissertation to Cass that accompanies it solve a primary dilemma for Isaac, a dilemma that he shares with the other protagonists of *Go Down, Moses*. How can Ike "translate" or "transcribe" (his words for the situation) the lost past into the present? How may his hand write and his voice speak the lessons of pride and humility and the ideal of unowned land that the hunt has articulated? And how might Isaac rewrite the chronicle of violence and violation that the McCaslin ledgers record?

Critics of "The Bear" have vigorously debated the historical and moral implications of Ike's decision to refuse the plantation. In our intent evaluation of the effects and effectiveness of Ike's renunciation, however, we may neglect the fact that Isaac's gesture is an utterance rather than a regional policy. Ike's first concern on his twenty-first birthday is to fashion a statement of his adult selfhood, to "say it." His renunciation is, first of all, an enunciation. As Sam did through his stories, as the two of them did through their execution of the ritual hunt, Ike seeks to articulate his dispossession. Killing his first buck, like participating in Old Ben's death, is governed by the paradox of "loving the life he spills" (181); the rite of the hunt passes the process of loss into one's own loving control. Ike, as he grows older, envisions a life faithful to the rituals of the wilderness:

> . . . the boy of twelve had been unable to phrase it then: I slew you; my bearing must not shame your quitting life. My conduct forever onward must become your death; marking him for . . . that day and himself and McCaslin juxtaposed not against the wilderness but against the tamed land, the old wrong and shame itself, in repudiation and denial at least of the land and the wrong and shame even if he couldn't cure the wrong and eradicate the shame. [351; italics omitted]

Isaac's act of repudiation is one way to "phrase" the meaning of the wilderness. It is a gesture that says no to taming and ordering the land: "He could say it, himself and his cousin juxtaposed not against the wilderness but against the tamed land . . . not in pursuit and lust but in relinquishment" (254–255). Old Carothers' lustful "translation" of the wilderness into money (254) is an utterance that Ike seeks to rewrite, as I shall argue shortly. Disowning the plantation also serves Isaac as a statement of grief. Cass's quotation of Keats's "Ode on a Grecian Urn" doesn't convince Ike that it is a suitable analogy for his state of loss; the poem is about "a young man and a girl he would never need to grieve over" (297; italics omitted), while Isaac must contend with his grief for "the dark and ravaged fatherland," the corpses of Old Ben and the wilderness. As it speaks of ravage, so Ike's public repudiation prefigures, without expecting to accomplish, the cleansing of the land from the sins of title: "the Book" tells Ike that the land was created to be held "mutual and intact in the communal anonymity of brotherhood" (257), and Ike believes that his denial restates the ideal of brotherly possession and the corresponding ideal of racial fraternity. I am not urging a reassessment of Isaac's politics or morality, but I think we might more fully appreciate the eloquence of his gesture. Isaac wants to emulate John Brown, whose action is more potent as a word than as a work: "out of all that empty sound and bootless fury one silence, among that loud and moiling all of them . . . illiterate and had no words for talking or perhaps was just busy and had no time to" (284). Brown's "simple act" is not a dumb silence, however; it voices a spare and graceful affirmation of equality: "I am just against the weak because they are niggers being held in bondage by the strong just because they are white" (285; italics omitted). Isaac performs his act of renunciation as a kindred expression; in his community Isaac's decision is a silence amid the confident conversation of dynasty. Its stillness subversively withholds consent. To his cousin, Ike's renunciation becomes a pronouncing of his heart's truth.

Isaac's wife provides the clearest measure of how desperately Ike wants to speak to his tainted legacy by renouncing it. When she offers her naked body and sexual pleasure in exchange for Isaac's promise to accept the plantation, she realizes that she is asking Isaac to forfeit the voice of dissent. Isaac sees that her body is a double of the wilderness (when they marry "it was the new country," 311), and her "immeasurable promise" echoes that of the new land to its domesticators. His wife wants to silence his voice; she presses her promise even as "the hot fierce palm clapped over his mouth, crushing his lips into his teeth" (312).

The problem of restating truth, of repeating the rites of the wilderness among the books of the commissary, raises the issue of "transcription." Since Isaac's central crisis is one of speaking, he explores the nature of original truth, textuality, and the possibilities of fallen language. Isaac argues that his act of renunciation conforms to biblical eschatology, and he also detects in the difficulties of the Bible's authors an analogy for his own efforts to translate his wilderness insights. His opinions about language, for all their contortions and inconsistencies, reflect Faulkner's own and are worth attending to. Isaac's most memorable statement about language has also come to be the most misleading since its difficult context is often neglected: the authors of the Bible "were trying to write down the heart's truth out of the heart's driving complexity, for all the complex and troubled hearts which would beat after them" (260). When Ike adds that we "have nothing else to read with but the heart," one might infer a substantially naive model of language. Might a perfect text actually immolate itself to allow the full communion of reader and writer? Can the Bible turn its "complex" pages into transparent views of God's full, "simple" truth? Ike offers a more problematic analysis. The origin of biblical truth is not the plenitude of divine truth, but God's words. Scripture cannot aspire to reveal the fullness of God's presence, or incarnate the complete truth of His heart; rather, it wants to "transcribe" God's words, "what He wanted said" (260). The origin of even the sacred text is the word in the mouth of God—concealing as it reveals, underlining the difference it wants to erase. That word, the unrecoverable source of authority, has been lost in the effort to deliver it. The Bible's authors "were trying to write down," "to transcribe and relay His words . . . through the complexity of passion and lust and hate and fear which drives the heart" (260). The heart's complexity is a medium in which the original writing is to be inscribed. In a fallen world, language moves strictly through indirection and paradox; in order to transcribe simplicity, the word must be made complex; in order to circumscribe truth, it must bear falsehoods

(" 'So these men who transcribed His Book for Him were sometime liars' . . . 'Yes. Because they were human men' " 260). Ike apprehends that all truth becomes the play of complexities in a text; if his memories of the hunt, his renunciation of the farm, and his debate with Cass are not "somebody talking in a book" (297), they are nothing.

Isaac's statements about the paradoxical nature of truth endorse the positions we have noticed in other works: truth emerges from the play of differing; it requires intimate opposition, inconclusiveness, and inconsistency. Ike suggests this situation as he offers a tautological solution to an anticipated objection: " 'And I know what you will say now: That if truth is one thing to me and another thing to you, how will we choose which is truth? You dont need to choose. The heart already knows' " (260). At best this is a mystery, but not one whose content matters. Despite his disagreement with Cass, Ike does not seek to invalidate his cousin's position; and despite his fastidious, ironic questions, Cass does not dismiss Isaac. The cousins concur in their difference; Isaac actually is quoting his cousin when he argues that "there is only one truth and it covers all things that touch the heart" (260). That truth is one without being single allows them to differ; seven years earlier Cass had supported his own argument for accommodation with "what the heart holds to becomes truth, as far as we know truth" (297; italics omitted).

The moment of awkward, fierce, and tender intimacy between the cousins might remind us of Quentin and Shreve's narrative flight, and Isaac uses his conversation for similar purposes. In dissenting from Cass's understanding of the South and their common lineage, Isaac attempts to fashion a distinct identity. Ike's disagreement with Cass duplicates his disagreement with old Carothers; in each case he must converse with another person (literally, turn his words back) in order to compose himself. Like Lucas, Isaac feels himself an orphan to old Carothers' outrage and his father's moral cowardice; he can call himself

"an Isaac born into a later life than Abraham's and repudiating immolation: fatherless and therefore safe declining the altar because maybe this time the exasperated Hand might not supply the kid." [283]

Isaac names himself as Lucas had done, owning up to his name but also willfully reinterpreting it; he may be the heir of the McCaslin dynasty, but he refuses to risk martyrdom on the altar of his fathers' faith. Ike's talk also responds to a childhood of Cass's paternal narratives. Be contradicting his cousin, Ike attempts to gain mastery over the stories that have fathered him: "'Let me talk now.... I knew a long time ago that I would never have to miss my father, even if you are just finding out that you have missed your son'" (288). Ike knows that he is imprisoned by Cass's accounts of what Ike never had time to remember; the Civil War, for instance, Ike "had inherited ... as Noah's grandchildren had inherited the Flood although they had not been there to see the deluge" (289). Isaac cannot dispel the words of Cass which represent his origins; he can only differ with them, introducing the edge of dissent into their desperate intimacy: "McCaslin, his kinsman, his father almost yet no kin now as, at the last, even fathers and sons are no kin" (308).

The rituals and language of the hunt comprise a legacy that Ike hopes to honor by renouncing the McCaslin plantation; the same gesture also seeks to answer the corrupt legacy of old Carothers McCaslin, his grandfather. Isaac's task is to remember and to re-read his family's chronicle so that he may begin to write his words of correction. The past survives for Ike only in the form of language—whether it is the "harsher book" (289) of Cass's accounts or the cryptic traces of the ledger entries. Before he can declare his renunciation, Isaac must create a narrative of the past, imagining its characters and their actions. Even as he challenges old Carothers' voice Ike must reanimate it, as we have seen Lucas do, and as the narrators of *Absalom* have done for Sutpen. Ike's conversation with Cass, like his youthful meditations on the ledgers, rescues the past from an apocalypse of forgetting:

> To him it was as though the ledgers in their scarred cracked leather bindings were being lifted down one by one in their fading sequence and spread open on the desk or perhaps upon some apocryphal Bench or even Altar or perhaps before the Throne Itself for a last perusal and contemplation and refreshment of the Allknowledgeable before the yellowed pages and the brown thin ink in which was recorded the injustice and a little at least of its amelioration and restitution faded back forever into the anonymous communal original dust. [261]

To judge the past—as the imagery of the Last Judgment suggests—paradoxically demands retracing and rewriting the very passages one seeks to erase. By reciting old Carothers' crimes Isaac can begin to interpret, contradict, and redress them.

The commissary ledgers rehearse a litany of the sins of the fathers. Old Carothers' offenses are clear, but Isaac emphasizes that they all may be seen as perversions of the common language, as violent statements to which Isaac must reply. Carothers McCaslin's initial act is to "fragment" the wilderness, breaking the communal circulation of the land and converting it into his private idiom. This appears to Ike as an evil translation; Carothers' only goal in farming is "to grow something out of it which had not been there before and which could be translated back into the money" (254). Cass, on the other hand, salutes his grandfather, who, "when it was a wilderness of wild beasts and wilder men, . . . cleared it, translated it into something to bequeath to his children, worthy of bequeathment for his descendants' ease and security and pride and to perpetuate his name and accomplishments" (256). Isaac discovers that Carothers' handwriting in the oldest ledgers describes its author: "old Carothers' bold cramped hand far less legible than his sons' even and not much better in spelling, who while capitalising almost every noun and verb, made no effort to punctuate or construct whatever, just as he made no effort either to explain or obfuscate the thousand-dollar legacy to the son of an unmarried slavegirl" (269). That Carothers should be a bold capitalizer one might expect, but his "cramped hand" also reminds Ike that the original design is impeded by its overreaching. Carothers' inattention to punctuation and construction displays a mind ignorant of the tasks of shaping and interpreting, tasks left to sons and grandsons. Buck's and Buddy's inferior spelling may signal their longing for illiteracy, as if their moral agony might die into unintelligibility; but it also betrays old Carothers' determination to keep his sons under the tyrannical rule of the letter of his law. The passage also suggests that old Carothers' bequest to Tomey's Turl is a kind of sentence—one that offhandedly dismisses paternal responsibility. Isaac concludes that his grandfather had rejected the moral expense of acknowledging his own son, just as Sutpen had done: "*So I reckon that was cheaper than saying My son to a nigger*" he thought" (269–270). McCaslin's monstrous language also produces one "concrete indication," the plantation mansion, which testifies to "his own vanity's boundless conceiving" (262). The last phrase—"boundless conceiving"—puns on Carothers' incest, since in disregarding the sexual boundary between father and daughter, he seeks to conceive his own grandson and reach toward immortality. Isaac will come to insist that old Carothers' obscenities be inscribed and pronounced in the book of memory, bound by the same lines of accounting with which he has bound his slaves, "frail as truth and impalpable as equators yet cable-strong to bind for life them who made the cotton to the land" (294).

As Ike reads the family's records, he discovers that to remember is to repeat; in unearthing and making restitution for his grandfather's crimes, Isaac has both to imitate his gestures and to impersonate his speech. The air of "desperate emulation" inspires Isaac to undertake these tasks, and he understands that "even in escaping [his legacy] he was taking with him more of that evil and unregenerate old man" (294). Isaac extends his grandfather's will by trying to deliver the McCaslin bequests to Turl's children; he describes, for example, his pursuit of James Beauchamp: "Traced by Isaac McCaslin to Jackson Tenn. and there lost" (273). When Fonsiba disappears, Ike proves "an experienced bloodhound too and a successful one this time" (277). The diction of these statements evokes the hunt, and Ike's tracking of old Carothers' heirs involves him in a sober version of the genealogical hunts performed by his father in "Was." To "trace" the perpetually vanishing outcasts of old Carothers' "boundless conceiving" is to underline the paradox of Ike's moral position: on the one hand, he acknowledges those whom his grandfather dismisses; on the other, he can only pass along the bequests through which old Carothers means to say nothing.

After executing his grandfather's will, Ike should not be surprised that his handwriting signals kinship: "his own hand now, queerly enough resembling neither his father's nor his uncle's nor even McCaslin's, but like that of his grandfather's save for the spelling" (273). Isaac's writing and speech implicate him in recreating what he wants to redeem. At first the ledgers strike Isaac as being safely dead documents; before opening them at age sixteen, Isaac assumes that "what the old books contained would be after all these years fixed immutably, finished, unalterable, harmless" (268). Like

Quentin Compson, Isaac doubts the power or pertinence of the "tedious record"—until the ledger entries erupt with notations of miscegenation, incest, and suicide. Isaac, too, accepts the challenge of recreating the past, constructing a narrative to connect the facts, inventing what he does not know, altering what does not fit, breathing simulated life into the words, hunting reasons and causes in the wilderness of the cryptic entries. Isaac's creative reading makes the characters take "substance and even a sort of shadowy life with their passions and complexities too as page followed page" (265). At several points, Isaac's meditative narrative translates old Carothers' offensive actions into verbal equivalents, as if a stylistic imitation can bring them under the control and censure of the speaker. For example, Carothers' violent breakage of the wilderness into fragments sends repercussions into the opening passages of section 4 of "The Bear," where an extended pattern of sentence fragments chronicles the parceling of the land. Later, as Isaac recites the history of dispossession, he watches his syntax ritually repeat the cycles of occupation and exile: "Dispossessed of Eden. Dispossessed of Canaan, and those who dispossessed him dispossessed him dispossessed . . ." (258).

Isaac's reading and writing in the ledgers seek to confront and to contradict his grandfather; Ike explains what old Carothers obfuscates, blames what he ignores, repudiates what he bequeathes, and makes bequests to what he repudiates. Ike replies to old Carothers' malicious legacy in the words that fail his uncle and father. As the McCaslin twins cower behind nonsensical hunts and poker games, so they build barricades with their ledger entries. Faced with the enormity of Eunice's apparent suicide (when her master and lover fathers a child on their own daughter), Buck and Buddy deaden their language into mere fact:

> *June 21th 1833 Drownd herself*

and the first:

> *23 Jun 1833 who in hell ever heard of a niger drownding him self*

and the second, unhurried, with a complete finality; the two identical entries might have been made with a rubber stamp save for the date:

> *Aug 13th 1833 Drownd herself* [267]

The twins' agony of ambivalence about slavery turns them toward an indirect conversation, "as if, long since past any oral intercourse, they had used the diurnally advancing pages to conduct the un-avoidable business of the compulsion which had traversed all the waste wilderness of North Mississippi in 1830 and '40 ..." (263). Their entries long to die into meaninglessness; they become "almost indecipherable," as if events "had convinced Buck not only of the vanity of faith and hope but of orthography too" (273). The follow-ing entry intends to announce Fonsiba's birth, but as it does so it also erases the names of Beauchamp, Tomey's Turl, and Tennie, suppressing the advent of another black McCaslin: "*Miss sophon-siba b dtr t t @ t 1869*" (273). Old Carothers' potent words have unmanned his sons, and they yearn, childlike, for his authority. Confronted by an unmanageable slave, they wish, "He hasnt gone yet Father should be here" and wonder, "What would father done" (265). Isaac notices that their entries "both looked as though they had been written by the same perfectly normal ten-year-old boy, even to the spelling, except that the spelling did not improve" (263).

The process by which Old Carothers' monstrous legacy changes into Isaac's meditative language is parodied by the fate of Uncle Hubert's bequest. Like Carothers' translation of the wilderness into "something to bequeath to his children" (256), Uncle Hubert plans to leave Isaac something tangible: it is "no pale sentence or para-graph scrawled in cringing fear of death by a weak and trembling hand as a last desperate sop flung backward at retribution, but a Legacy, a Thing, possessing weight to the hand and bulk to the eye and even audible, a silver cup filled with gold pieces ..." (301). Pressed financially, however, Hubert watches with amazement as he turns the gold coins into IOUs written on scraps of paper, in-cluding "raggedly-torn ledger-pages" (306), and as the cup itself is mysteriously transformed into a coffee pot, "standing amid the col-lapse" (306). In Faulkner's fiction, things are perpetually mas-querading as tangible and present. But beneath the wraps, they are already turning into slips of paper and penciled messages. Hubert's naive bequest underlines a genuine one; Isaac accepts the burden of the debt that the McCaslin past has accumulated in his name.

vii

"Delta Autumn" follows the career of Isaac McCaslin's utter-ances nearly to its conclusion. By renouncing the plantation and by performing that gesture as a counterstatement to established versions of history and meaning, Isaac successfully emulates John Brown, who makes "out of all that empty sound and bootless fury one silence" (284). But a life dedicated to *not* possessing the farm is at best only a speaking silence; it does not manage to translate, repeat, disfigure, and speak again. Isaac seems to have sacrificed his voice to the single reversal of old Carothers' enormity; he is unable to revise the rites of grief or freshen the urgency of speech. This last story of the wilderness trilogy presents a variation of the poison of silence, akin to the silence that Quentin Compson wants to steal from another sound and fury.

Isaac's voice has been ravaged by a career of eloquent silence. His opinions in "Delta Autumn" appear sententious and brittle: "'There are good men everywhere, at all times. Most men are. Some are just unlucky'" (345). Ike's words are only husks of the probing, supple speculations of his commissary performance. Flaccidness replaces the spontaneity, puzzled discovery, airy expansion, and ingenious improvisation of his conversation with Cass. Perhaps the state of his language resembles that of the fatherland; the vital possession of the wilderness by the original communal brotherhood survives only as an encrusted nomenclature: "and all that remained of that old time were the Indian names on the little towns..." (341). Isaac also seems to be losing his authority before an audience. The young men indulge him, but his voice washes against their inattention: "But the old man was speaking, even into the laughter, in that peaceful and still untroubled voice..." (347). And Ike is resigned to the spiritless state of his language, even abandoning a moment when his words begin to find their former vein: "'The woods and fields [man] ravages and the game he devastates will be the consequence and signature of his crime and guilt, and his punishment.—Bed time,' he said. His voice and inflection did not change at all" (329). Isaac has already put his "signature" to a different use of the wilderness, and there will be no restatement. In the last scene of the story, when Isaac is confronted again by the vision of incest, miscegenation, and an endangered legacy, his language stages an insurrection against his better sense, "until he knew that his voice was running away with him and he had neither intended it nor could stop it" (363).

The language of the hunt also subsides into impertinence. Will

Legate makes a smutty parable out of Roth's affair with his black mistress by referring to her as a doe " 'that walks on two legs—when she's standing up, that is. Pretty lightcolored, too' " (337). Ike doesn't understand the joke and later attracts laughter when he innocently refers to Legate's does; he puts the allegorical status of the wilderness out of his mind, silencing both Legate's fable and his own analogy between World War II and hunting: " '. . . all I am worrying about right now is that ten miles of river we still have got to run before we can make camp' " (339). Isaac can no longer use the wilderness to incite his imagination or provoke his speech. When, in the story's last sentence, he sadly draws the resemblance between killing the forest's does and Roth's dismissal of his child's black mother, we are given a kind of souvenir of Ike's once extraordinary language.

Isaac also fails at the last to see that another "desperate emulation" of old Carothers might further the "amelioration" begun by his own revisionary imitation of his grandfather. Roth, like old Carothers, rejects his black mistress, refusing to say "my son" to their child. Overcome by the repetition of incest, miscegenation, and repudiation after five generations, Isaac despairs that memory will accomplish anything and concurs with Roth's decision to forget. An alien voice of impersonal racism speaks through Isaac and advises the woman to marry "a man in your own race" so that she will "forget it ever happened, that he ever existed" (363). Yet Isaac's gestures subvert his harsh voice as he touches the young woman and realizes that his pursuit of James Beauchamp has finally succeeded. He murmurs "Tennie's Jim" as he reflects that the "strong old blood ran after its long lost journey back to home" (362). Ike's confusion is just a step away from resolving into the understanding that Roth's marriage to the last black McCaslin would reverse old Carothers in the very act of imitating his crimes. The barriers of incest and miscegenation have become strictly technical as the result of the widening generations, and if Roth were to marry his mistress and acknowledge his son, old Carothers' obscenities would finally be cleansed. The infant represents the erasure of the distinction between the black and white, male and female, acknowledged and unacknowledged heirs of old Carothers. In this case, the quickest way to forget old Carothers would be to remember by repeating him. But Isaac cannot quite make the gesture; he bequeaths his hunting horn, managing only to beckon the child into the family as he sentences him to anonymity.

Even if Isaac were to see the potential closure of the McCaslin house in Roth's marriage, he would be helpless to do anything but advocate it. For Roth has already decided to restate old Carothers' views of white male privilege. His mistress and child bear an offer of amelioration and restitution, but Roth instructs Ike to "'say I said No'" when he warns that there "'will be a message here some time this morning, looking for me'" (355). Roth contaminates Isaac's voice by making it a conduit for his repudiation and the filth of his money (which repeats no to the message of love). Isaac can no longer speak his own words, and his last bequest pathetically underlines his helplessness. The horn represents a past that the infant will never know; it will sound meaninglessly. Like Hubert's "Thing," the horn would require a legacy of stories and memories to make it say anything, but Ike's speech has subsided into private reminiscence. Isaac's gesture salutes the certainty of forgetting even as it hoped to signal the importance of remembering.

Listening to Isaac's crude advice, Roth's mistress wonders that he could have "forgotten so much" (363). But the disparity between Ike's youth and age arises because the past is perpetually under the revision of memory; the past never exists whole and hard-edged.[24] At the end of his life, Isaac elevates the importance of memory, but what he recalls proves significantly different from earlier accounts. Even in the interval of silence, Ike's memory has rewritten the past; to remember is simultaneously to forget, as Quentin discovered. Isaac pretends to himself that he may join the hunters, but he realizes that he accompanies them each chiefly so that he can meditate in the wilderness on what once was: "Not to hunt, but for this" (349), he muses as he looks back over his youth. One touching example of how memory disfigures the past is the picture of Ike's wife that emerges. Her base greed and willingness to trade on her own body fade as Ike recalls that "he had had a wife and lived with her and lost her... because she loved him. But women hope for so much" (352). As he romanticizes his wife's threat, so Ike imagines a

24. Cf. Jean-Paul Sartre, "On *The Sound and the Fury*: Time in the Work of Faulkner," in *Literary Essays*, trans. Annette Michelson (New York, 1957), p. 82; essays translated from Jean-Paul Sartre, *Situations I* and *III* (Paris: Gallimard, 1955).

fabulous version of the wilderness that has disappeared. The following passage demonstrates the active writing of memory; Isaac imagines a future that is actually an idealized past. In such a dimensionless utopia, the wilderness and its settlement, the hunter and his quarry, corruption and incorruption dwell in dreamy harmony. Like a supplement, this fantasy differs and defers—differing from anything Isaac has ever known in a wilderness that was always already disappearing, and deferring the recovery of a putative origin. The future becomes nostalgia's past:

> He seemed to see the two of them—himself and the wilderness—as coevals . . . the two spans running out together, not toward oblivion, nothingness, but into a dimension free of both time and space where once more the untreed land warped and wrung to mathematical squares of rank cotton for the frantic old-world people to turn into shells to shoot at one another, would find ample room for both—the names, the faces of the old men he had known and loved and for a little while outlived, moving again among the shades of tall unaxed trees and sightless brakes where the wild strong immortal game ran forever before the tireless belling immortal hounds, falling and rising phoenix-like to the soundless guns. [354]

Isaac's voice finally melts into the "constant and grieving rain," but the expression of loss continues.

viii

As the story of execution, mourning, and the rites of burial, "Go Down, Moses" aptly lends its title to the whole novel. One of the story's last images juxtaposes the "catafalque" of Samuel Worsham Beauchamp and his four mourners, who stand in "formal component complement" to it (382). The severe tableau of mourned and mourners epitomizes one of the central situations of *Go Down, Moses,* and the concern of this last variation is to inter grief itself. Samuel is buried by two companies of mourners; each demonstrates a significant detachment from his death as they observe the forms of lamentation. The novel closes amid a sense that the agony of loss throughout the novel has finally been mastered by its ritualistic expression. All that remains is a repercussive sequence of gestures—gestures that have already ossified and which allow the reader to turn away as Gavin Stevens does. "Go Down, Moses" allows the grief of the novel to subside into inarticulate privacy once more: " 'It's all right,' Miss Worsham said. 'It's our grief' " (381), and she closes the door on Stevens.

Mollie and Lucas Beauchamp's grandson summarizes all of the lost and lamented figures of the novel. Nearly the last victim of his traitorous McCaslin brothers and Chicago's Pharoahs (in Mollie's imagery), Samuel seeks to eradicate the heritage that has disenfranchised him. He flaunts his urban modernity—the clothes "had cost too much and were draped too much, with too many pleats" (369)—in an effort to costume his past. He whitens his voice ("which was anything under the sun but a southern voice or even a negro voice") and his hair ("the negroid hair had been treated"), as if the slave might impersonate the master. Joking about his fractured family ("Parents." "Sure. Two. I dont remember them" [370]), Samuel voices the grievance of all of the fatherless heirs in *Go Down, Moses.* Butch's pose, as he "half lay on the steel cot in the steel cubicle just outside which an armed guard had stood for twenty hours now" (369), echoes Isaac's at the conclusion of "Delta Autumn," when he falls prone to the seemingly endless consequences of old Carothers' crimes. Gavin Stevens refers to the project of getting Beauchamp's corpse back to Jefferson as bringing "a dead nigger home," a phrase that resonates with Isaac's recognition that the dead blood of Tennie's Jim has finally made its way "after its long lost journey back to home" (362). Imprisoned, Butch reminds us of Sam Fathers' sense of being caged and of Rider, whose hysterical howling in his cell prefigures the moment of Butch's arrest, when he was "cursing through his broken mouth, his teeth fixed into something like furious laughter through the blood" (372). Beauchamp's broken mouth manages to say nothing to the blood that has disenfranchised him. The victim of his race's and land's exploitation and exhaustion, Samuel is the last quarry of the novel's hunts, "the slain wolf" (382).[25] Like Old Ben, he is even made to seem a presence whose loss has already begun; when Stevens learns that Butch will certainly be executed that night, he decides to tell Mollie "this afternoon that he is dead then" (377).

25. Olga Vickery notices that this image suggests the pattern of the hunt (*The Novels of William Faulkner* [Baton Rouge, 1959], p. 125).

Two parties of mourners contrive to display Butch's corpse on the novel's "catafalque" of grief, to convert death once again into a performed execution. Samuel dies because he is said to have committed a murder, but he is the victim of crimes, too; when Gavin characterizes him as the "bad son of a bad father" (375), he unwittingly points all the way back to old Carothers, who first forces his black sons to say "No family" when, like Butch, they are asked to name their origin. The story suggests that by adding a proper burial to Butch's execution, both his relatives and also the white townspeople at least go through the motions of expressing their own responsibility, remorse, and grief. Their participation in the execution does not make Samuel a scapegoat, however, because their performance betrays disturbing silences and suppressions. The story stages a massive charade that is at once both heartfelt and perfunctory, eloquent and incomprehensible.[26]

Butch's grandmother, Mollie Beauchamp, and her brother's household observe the forms of a family's grief over a lost son. Miss Worsham, Mollie, Hamp, and his wife conduct the last rites not only of Butch, but also of all the McCaslin blacks: they chant their lamentation in a "decaying house" (374). But the rituals themselves suffer decay; after the desperate searches in the early stories for suitable expressions for loss, and after the magnificent statement of dispossession that Ike's career makes, the last story deliberately threatens redundancy. Mollie, whose frailty and decrepitude repeatedly surprise Stevens, deafly recites her own version of the Negro spiritual: "'Roth Edmonds sold my Benjamin... Sold him to Pharoah and now he dead'" (380). But her lyrics conceal old Carothers' primary offense (as the younger Stevens' confusion emphasizes), and her scriptural analogy seems to intend Joseph, not Benjamin, who was sold by his brothers to Egypt. (Benjamin is the youngest brother, held for ransom during another episode of Joseph's Egyptian career.) Mollie's rite of grief serves more as an erasure than an inscription; it presses the novel toward conclusion and silence. The only moving voice of the Worshams' lamentation is inarticulate: Hamp's wife sings a "true constant soprano which

26. I disagree with Early's view that the comic effects of "Go Down, Moses" "undercut the seriousness of the book as a whole" (*Making of "Go Down, Moses,"* p. 104).

ran without words beneath the strophe and antistrophe of the brother and sister" (381). Mollie believes that part of getting Butch home "right" requires public notice in the newspaper, but what the obituary says is of no matter. Mollie can't read, so " 'Miss Belle will show me what to look and I can look at hit' " (383).

Mollie's desires help to accomplish several of Faulkner's usual closing gambits. The forms that create meaning are often disfigured or made obsolete as the novel prepares to abandon its narrative. In *Go Down, Moses* the forms in which loss has been articulated are hollowed out at the close: conversation becomes repetitive chant; biblical history dwindles into monotonous allusion; the procession of statements and gestures that follow loss become Mollie's simple parade through town. The structures in which grief has been spoken are being surrendered by the novel amid the sense that "it's all over and done and finished" (383). These are Gavin Stevens' words, and their resolution to put the matter to rest helps to explain his role in the story.

Stevens is another of the alien proprietors to whom Faulkner occasionally entrusts the conclusions of his stories. Like the furniture salesman in *Light in August* or the deputy sheriff in "Pantaloon," Stevens loses his story's meaning in the very act of trying to find it. He enlists the aid of the editor in soliciting and contributing money to pay for Butch's return, but his exercise succeeds only in a most rudimentary way: getting Butch into Jefferson ground. Stevens closes his eyes to the several gaps at which the community's or the McCaslin family's guilt may be glimpsed. He recognizes for the first time that Mollie and Hamp are sister and brother, but does not reflect on this sample of genealogical violence; nor does he explore the irony that Roth Edmonds and Butch Beauchamp share old Carothers' ancestry. Stevens joins Mollie's conspiracy of illiteracy by voluntarily and involuntarily silencing the expression of loss. He extorts silence from the editor, and as he gathers money around the square he declares, " 'Never mind about a paper to sign: just give me a dollar' " (379). Even the county attorney's "serious vocation" comments on his function as a disposer of the story's sense: Stevens' chief occupation is "a twenty-two-year-old unfinished translation of the Old Testament back into classic Greek," a paradigm of the inward, backward turn of translations in the last story. Butch is buried by a kind of "communal anonymous brotherhood," but it is one whose unfamiliarity and detachment quiet the novel's grief. That Mollie's name is spelled differently than in "The Fire and the Hearth" may also signal that the narrator is making visible the inaudible oddness with which her name is pronounced by one like Stevens who knows nothing of her legacy of loss; a stranger, less intimate hand conducts the story to its close. The two companies of mourners separate at the town line, the Worshams continuing to the burial plot, Stevens and the editor returning to Jefferson. They divide at a sign marked "Corporate Limit," which proclaims the boundary of shared mourning.

Index

Index

Index

*The Play of
Faulkner's Language*

Designed by Richard E. Rosenbaum.
Composed by The Composing Room of Michigan, Inc.
in 10 point Sabon V.I.P., 2 points leaded,
with display lines in Sabon.
Printed offset by Thomson/Shore, Inc. on
Warren's Number 66, 50 pound basis.
Bound by John H. Dekker & Sons, Inc.
in Holliston book cloth.